Perspectives on Development in the Middle East and North Africa (MENA) Region

Series Editor

Almas Heshmati, Jönköping University, Jönköping, Korea (Republic of)

This Scopus indexed book series publishes monographs and edited volumes devoted to studies on the political, economic and social developments of the Middle East and North Africa (MENA). Volumes cover in-depth analyses of individual countries, regions, cases and comparative studies, and they include both a specific and a general focus on the latest advances of the various aspects of development. It provides a platform for researchers globally to carry out rigorous economic, social and political analyses, to promote, share, and discuss current quantitative and analytical work on issues, findings and perspectives in various areas of economics and development of the MENA region. Perspectives on Development in the Middle East and North Africa (MENA) Region allows for a deeper appreciation of the various past, present, and future issues around MENA's development with high quality, peer reviewed contributions. The topics may include, but not limited to: economics and business, natural resources, governance, politics, security and international relations, gender, culture, religion and society, economics and social development, reconstruction, and Jewish, Islamic, Arab, Iranian, Israeli, Kurdish and Turkish studies. Volumes published in the series will be important reading offering an original approach along theoretical lines supported empirically for researchers and students, as well as consultants and policy makers, interested in the development of the MENA region.

Nezameddin Faghih • S. Abolghasem Foroozani
S. Sara Foroozani • Ali Hussein Samadi
Editors

The Persian Gulf and Islands

Historical Dynamics and the 21st Century

Springer

Editors
Nezameddin Faghih
UNESCO Chair Professor Emeritus
Cambridge, MA, USA

S. Sara Foroozani
Independent Scholar
Shiraz, Iran

S. Abolghasem Foroozani
Professor of History
Shiraz University
Shiraz, Iran

Ali Hussein Samadi
Professor of Economics
Shiraz University
Shiraz, Iran

ISSN 2520-1239 ISSN 2520-1247 (electronic)
Perspectives on Development in the Middle East and North Africa (MENA) Region
ISBN 978-3-032-27909-5 ISBN 978-3-032-27910-1 (eBook)
https://doi.org/10.1007/978-3-032-27910-1

This Springer imprint is published by the registered company Springer Nature Switzerland AG
The registered company address is: Gewerbestrasse 11, 6330 Cham, Switzerland

Dedication

*To the loving and eternal memory of my devoted and beloved parents—**Rokneddin Faghih** (2000–1926 رکن‌الدین فقیه، استهبان, Estahban) and **Homayoun Soltan Enayat** (همایون سلطان عنایت، 2025–1931 استهبان, Estahban)—cherished philanthropists, agricultural entrepreneurs, and enduring sources of grace and wisdom, whose lives were woven into the very soil and spirit of Estahban.*

*In **Estahban**, within the heart of **Fars**, near the timeless shores of the **Fars Gulf** (the **Persian Gulf**), they dedicated their lives to the service of humanity and the cultivation of their land and community.*

Their steadfast encouragement and abiding faith inspired me to explore and write about the Persian Gulf and its enduring legacy.

(Nezameddin Faghih)

Preface

The Persian Gulf and its islands have long stood at the crossroads of maritime exchange, imperial rivalry, colonial administration, and modern geopolitical contestation. This edited volume traces the historical evolution of the region from antiquity to the present, with particular emphasis on the strategic, economic, and political roles of its islands. Drawing on archaeological findings, classical and historical sources, colonial archives, and contemporary international law, it examines how geography, trade, imperialism, oil, and sovereignty disputes have shaped regional and global politics.

Through an integrated historical-legal and political-economic approach, the book analyzes key issues, including the sovereignty dispute over the Iranian islands of Abu Musa and the Greater and Lesser Tunb; the nomenclature and historical significance of Qeshm Island; the geopolitics and geoeconomics of the energy transition; the delineation of the Persian Sea in ninth- and tenth-century geographical works; the historical geography of Makran; the commercial and military centrality of Siraf during the Buyid dynasty; and contemporary entrepreneurship ecosystems and poverty alleviation strategies in selected Persian Gulf states. By placing these studies within a coherent analytical framework, this book highlights the structural forces and evolving institutional configurations that have shaped the political, economic, and socio-spatial formations of the Persian Gulf. By critically examining key debates about colonial legacies, state formation, territorial sovereignty, and regional integration, the book highlights the role of the Persian Gulf as a pivotal locus in the global political-economic order.

As an interdisciplinary endeavor, this book offers both a comprehensive reference and a thought-provoking contribution to the study of the Persian Gulf for a wide range of audiences, including scholars, policymakers, diplomats, and practitioners. It portrays the Persian Gulf as a dynamic space where geography intersects with history, cultural memory with modern ideals, and enduring power structures with emerging patterns of exchange and identity. Ultimately, this book seeks to advance a nuanced and multifaceted understanding of the Persian Gulf and its islands, contributing to the scholarly and intellectual discourse on sustainability, peace, and coexistence in an increasingly interdependent world.

The Persian Gulf, a semi-enclosed sea basin connecting the Indian Ocean to the Middle East, has long served as a pivotal corridor between Mesopotamia, the Iranian Plateau, the Arabian Peninsula, and the wider Indian Ocean world. From the third millennium BC onwards, maritime exchange linked Sumerian city-states with Persian Gulf polities such as Dilmun and Megan, and featured a (Persian) Gulf-centric trade that linked Mesopotamia, Oman, and the Indus Valley. During the Middle Ages, island sites and ports near the Strait of Hormuz—particularly Hormuz itself—emerged as vital trade centers that regulated interregional flows between India, Iran, and the eastern Mediterranean. In the early modern period, European powers attempted to reshape this geography: the Portuguese captured Hormuz in 1507 and established strategic nodes to control the sea lanes, a pattern that was later reinforced under British imperial rule through treaties, naval patrols, and island bases. Throughout antiquity, history, and colonial transitions, the islands of the Persian Gulf served as navigational markers, trading centers, and military outposts, driving cycles of regional integration and geopolitical competition driven by trade, empire, extraction, and state formation.

This book traces the historical dynamics of the Persian Gulf and its islands from ancient maritime networks to contemporary geopolitical positions. It argues that the region's modern strategic importance cannot be understood without reference to the deep historical foundations in which geography and trade have repeatedly shaped political authority and foreign interventions.

Archaeological and textual evidence shows the Persian Gulf as a vital conduit in vast, far-reaching trade networks since at least the third millennium BC. Mesopotamian cuneiform documents from the Early Dynastic and Akkadian periods repeatedly refer to maritime exchanges with Dilmun, Megan, and Meluhha (Malukha), generally identified with eastern Arabia (modern-day Bahrain and the Persian Gulf coast), Oman, and the Indus Valley, respectively. These texts, including administrative documents and royal inscriptions, are evidence of the orderliness and institutionalization of Persian Gulf trade in Mesopotamian economies. In particular, Dilmun appears as a major trading center that distributed goods between Mesopotamia and distant regions, highlighting its strategic role in interregional exchanges.

Material evidence supports these texts. Archaeological surveys across the Persian Gulf coast reveal widespread imports of copper ingots from Megan, red agate (carnelian) beads from Indus, Mesopotamian ceramics, and Persian Gulf seals of local production, indicating sustained interaction rather than sporadic contact. References to merchants, sailors, and interpreters in Mesopotamian cities indicate the trading communities and cultural exchange that characterized mature trade networks. Beyond raw materials, Persian Gulf trade included semi-precious stones, timber, textiles, shells, and possibly agricultural goods, indicating a diverse maritime economy supported by shipbuilding traditions and advanced seafaring knowledge. Seasonal seafaring and the logistical challenges of navigating the high seas suggest that established maritime expertise and shared trade norms existed long before the classical era. Together, archaeological and textual data portray the Persian Gulf as a coherent economic and cultural region in the Bronze Age that played a significant role in the emergence of early complex societies throughout Persia, Mesopotamia, and South Asia.

During the Middle Ages, Hormuz emerged as a leading trading center in the Indian Ocean, exercising decisive control over access to the Persian Gulf. Its location on the Strait of Hormuz connected land networks from Mesopotamia and the Iranian plateau with maritime circuits to India, Persia, Southeast Asia, and East Africa. Hormuz acted as an intermediary and tax collector for the flow of valuable goods—textiles, spices, horses, pearls, perfumes, and precious metals,—making it essential for long-distance trade from the thirteenth century onwards.

Islamic geographers and travelers have emphasized the wealth and global character of Hormuz, describing it as a populous and commercial city supported by safe harbors, warehousing, financial services, and interethnic trade networks—authors such as: Al- Muqaddasi (also known as Muhammad ibn Ahmad Al-Maqdisi, 946–1000 AD, geographer, traveler, and author of prominent Arab works based on personal observations of the economic life of the lands of the Persian Gulf and the Arabian Gulf, that is, the Red Sea), Yaqut al-Hamawi (Yaqut Shahab al-Din, ibn Abdullah Rumi al-Hamawi, 1179–1229 AD, scholar known for his influential works on geography and history), and later Ibn Battuta (1304–1368/1369 AD, traveler, explorer, and scholar who visited most of Africa and Asia). Accordingly, the prosperity of this trading city depended on its ability to broker trade and generate revenue from turnover, a pattern common to Indian Ocean port cities whose power lay less in conquering territory and more in facilitating trade.

Politically, Hormuz functioned as a Persian semi-independent (semi-autonomous) trading kingdom, often recognizing and acknowledging the Persian regional sovereignty while maintaining internal autonomy. Its (de facto Persian) rulers established strong commercial and administrative ties with Persian dynasties, as well as diplomatic and commercial relationship with Arab neighbors and South Asian merchants, enabling Hormuz to act as a flexible intermediary across cultural and political boundaries. This system continued until the European maritime powers entered the scene in the late fifteenth and early sixteenth centuries, introducing a new model of commercial dominance.

European intervention began in the early sixteenth century with the Portuguese. In 1507, Afonso de Albuquerque's forces captured Hormuz and established a fort and a charter licensing regime to monopolize Persian Gulf trade. Portugal's power relied on naval artillery and the resulting brute force, marking a departure from previous negotiated exchanges. Thus, Hormuz became a node of the Indian Empire—*Estado da Índia*, which was trying to integrate the Persian Gulf into the expanding competition of global empires. However, the profits generated were mainly spent supporting imperial garrisons and naval operations rather than local trading communities, and this created strong dissatisfaction and growing anger among regional powers and merchants as trade patterns changed.

The fall of Hormuz in 1622, after the Anglo-Persian alliance to expel the Portuguese, shifted commercial activities to Bandar Abbas and reshaped the economic geography of the Persian Gulf. The story foretold new forms of European interaction—less direct conquest, more commercial engagement, and strategic alignment—while also showing how technology, military power, and political organization could transform a trading hub into the center of imperial conflict.

From the nineteenth century onwards, Britain established a dominant foreign presence in the Persian Gulf, transforming it into an arena of imperial influence that derived from imperial maritime security. Britain considered the Persian Gulf routes essential to maintaining India—the strategic cornerstone of its empire—and sought to deter rival powers, particularly Russia, France, and later Germany. The *General Maritime Treaty (1820)* and the *Perpetual Maritime Truce (1853)* initiated a framework for limiting local naval warfare and piracy, which gradually evolved into protectorate arrangements with the Trucial States, Bahrain, and later Qatar and Kuwait. In this way, Britain regulated shipping, established and disciplined truces, and mediated disputes, cementing imperial authority in the political fabric of the region without formal colonial conquest.

British imperial rule had a lasting impact on creating the legal and diplomatic disputes over the sovereignty of the islands of Abu Musa, Greater Tunb, and Lesser Tunb. Archival evidence suggests that British policy towards these islands was strategic, pragmatic, and often contradictory, shaped more by shifting geopolitical priorities than by coherent legal and ethical principles. These priorities included maintaining diplomatic relations with regional states, protecting imperial communications networks such as telegraph lines, and managing political stability among the Persian Gulf states. As a result, British officials alternately recognized, marginalized, or ignored competing local claims, resulting in a fluid and often contradictory administrative practice.

From a historical geographical perspective, colonial-era surveys and administrative documents have failed to establish coherent territorial demarcations. Maps, treaties, and correspondence often lacked precise definitions of maritime boundaries or the legal status of offshore islands. British surveys sometimes correctly placed islands under Iranian jurisdiction, while other administrative records deliberately misrepresented them as dependencies of Arab sheikhdoms in order to win their favor and deceptively keep them under British protection. This artificial spatial ambiguity reflected a deceptive style of imperial governance in which geographical representation unfortunately served as a tool for political expediency rather than legal certainty.

In terms of international law and diplomatic practice, this deliberate carelessness and incorrectness sought to undermine the development of true and clear ownership and facilitated the perpetuation of artificial rival claims. As scholars have pointed out, legal clarity was often a strategic issue, resulting in a fragmented documentary record on which subsequent parties could selectively rely in support of rival sovereignty claims. In this context, the Iranian position was rightly based on a genuine historical and legal continuity going back to the early Persian states, while the illusory and unfounded claims made by some Arab rulers during the British protectorate period were expressed largely through temporary tribal authority and deceptive informal administrative arrangements, rather than real and established principles of territorial sovereignty.

The British withdrawal from the Persian Gulf in 1971 turned these deliberately concealed and fabricated ambiguities and covert mischiefs into overt diplomatic conflict. On 30 November 1971, the Iranian navy took control of Abu Musa, the Greater Tunb, and the Lesser Tunb, presenting this as a natural and normal continuation of Iran's de facto historical and legal sovereignty, rooted in the successive Persian empires. Shortly thereafter, a newly established Arab state in December 1971 staked its own competing claims to the islands, attempting to turn the legacy of imperial administrative ambiguities into a modern international dispute.

The discovery and production of oil in the Persian Gulf from the early twentieth century onwards made the region a focal point of the global energy order. Beginning with the first major oil discovery in the Middle East at Masjed Sulayman in 1908 and the subsequent acceleration of discoveries in Bahrain, Saudi Arabia, Kuwait, Iraq and the Persian Gulf States, the Persian Gulf emerged as a dominant hydrocarbon producer. By the mid-twentieth century, the region contained the world's largest proven reserves and connected Persian Gulf producers to the industrial economies of Europe, North America and East Asia. Western powers, particularly Britain and the United States, aligned their foreign policies with the stability, security and energy export routes of the Persian Gulf.

Oil revenues reshaped internal state structures and regional hierarchies. Rentier dynamics enabled centralized authority, expanded bureaucratic capacity, fostered and strengthened extensive welfare systems, while reducing the tax burden on citizens and increasing dependence on external security guarantees. Internationally, hydrocarbon wealth linked the Persian Gulf states (monarchies and republics) to broader Cold War and post-Cold War security architectures, embedding the region in global power politics.

Maritime geography, especially the Strait of Hormuz, which is the only channel connecting the Persian Gulf to the Sea of Oman and the Indian Ocean, became increasingly important. The strait became a vital energy bottleneck, with a large share of the world's maritime traffic of oil and liquefied natural gas passing through its waters. The islands in and around the strait—Qeshm, Lark, Abu Musa, and the Greater Tunb and the Lesser Tunb—became of immense strategic value for monitoring traffic, deploying coastal defenses, and potentially disrupting flows in times of extreme crisis.

These dynamics were highlighted during the Iran-Iraq War (1980–1988) and the tanker war phase, when maritime security and naval deployment became central to deterrence and crisis warning. The ongoing nexus between energy infrastructure, maritime geography, and regional militarization remains a defining feature of Persian Gulf security, as energy considerations continue to shape political calculations and alliance patterns.

The ongoing territorial disputes in the Persian Gulf concern the islands of Abu Musa, Greater Tunb, and Lesser Tunb, situated near the Strait of Hormuz. Iran emphasizes an original legal and historical title to these islands, grounded in longstanding sovereignty and continuous administrative authority dating to the premodern period, and corroborated by cartographic, archival, and documentary evidence demonstrating that the islands have legally and historically constituted an integral part of Iranian territory. Iran characterized Britain's withdrawal from the Persian Gulf in 1971 as a temporary interruption of the exercise of sovereignty rather than its abrogation, extinguishment, or annulment, maintaining that Iran's underlying legal and historical title persisted throughout the period of British involvement. From this perspective, Britain's withdrawal meant the resumption of a pre-existing and continuous sovereign title and legitimate control, not the acquisition, re-establishment, restoration or revival of a new title.

The Trucial States' claim is based on a theory of title that derives from the alleged local succession and intermittent and largely symbolic claims of temporary and ephemeral authority exercised by the sheikhdoms of the Persian Gulf in the late colonial period. From the perspective of classical and contemporary doctrines of territorial sovereignty, such claims lack the requirements of effective law (*effectivités*) because they fail to demonstrate the continuous, peaceful and exclusive exercise of state authority. The sheikhdoms in question functioned not as independent and sovereign actors but as subordinate entities within the framework of the British Empire, and their external relations and territorial claims were limited and constrained by colonial supervision. Consequently, periodic and episodic administrative acts or partial demographic presence—particularly invoking partial Arab populations—cannot, without other factors and evidence of effective and autonomous governance, generate a legally recognizable title under international law.

However, if the evidentiary basis of the Trucial States' argument further reveals a pronounced reliance on British colonial archives, their validity should be approached with methodological caution. From a *Third World Approaches to International Law (TWAIL)* perspective, such colonial archives are not neutral repositories of historical fact and reality, but instruments of imperial administration, often characterized by strategic ambiguity, selective documentation, and juridical indeterminacy. Assertions of British "recognition" of the islands as part of the Trucial States are, at best, equivocal and, at worst, retrospective constructions unsupported by formal acts of attribution or boundary delimitation. Giving positive and determinative weight to such materials risks re-inscribing colonial epistemologies as authoritative sources and determinants of postcolonial governance and sovereignty—contrary to TWAIL's critique of the persistence of imperial legal structures in contemporary international law.

Doctrinally, the Trucial States' reliance on local succession is equally problematic when assessed through the lens of intertemporal law. Territorial title must be evaluated in accordance with the legal standards applicable at the time the alleged rights crystallized. During the relevant period, neither the sheikhdoms nor the British protectorate regime articulated a coherent or legally operative claim of sovereignty over the islands. Furthermore, the principle of *uti possidetis juris* ('the right to possess'), whether explicitly or implicitly invoked, provides limited support for the Trucial States' position. Britain's withdrawal from the Persian Gulf in 1971 was not accompanied by authoritative colonial boundary delimitations encompassing the islands, and the absence of such delimitations precludes the automatic transmission of title upon decolonization.

The contention that Iran's actions in 1971 constituted an unlawful acquisition of territory by force likewise rests on a contested legal characterization. Although the prohibition on territorial acquisition by force was emerging as a norm of general international law by the late twentieth century, its application to situations involving unresolved or competing claims of sovereignty remains doctrinally complex. From a TWAIL standpoint, isolating the events of 1971 from their broader historical context obscures the structural conditions of decolonization, in which imperial withdrawal occurred without legal clarity, leaving postcolonial actors to contest territorial arrangements shaped by colonial indeterminacy. Thus, privileging the ambiguities of the colonial era as the determinant of contemporary sovereignty claims is not only doctrinally fragile but also normatively questionable.

The cumulative body of geographical, historical, and juridical evidence convincingly substantiates the enduring sovereignty of Iran over the islands of Abu Musa, the Greater Tunb, and the Lesser Tunb, in accordance with the recognized principles of international law and state practice. The geographical contiguity of these islands to the Iranian mainland, their geological coherence and integrity, and the continuous Iranian administrative presence, taken together, meet the legal criteria of effective occupation and continuous manifestation of sovereignty. These criteria were firmly stated and authoritatively articulated in the *Isle of Palmas* arbitration (*Netherlands v. United States*) and reaffirmed in the judgment of the International Court of Justice in *Minquiers and Ecrehos* (*United Kingdom v. France*), both of which hold that effective and peaceful administration constitutes a crucial determinant of territorial title.

Correspondingly, the geological continuity, geographical configuration and natural coherence of the three islands of Abu Musa, the Greater Tunb and the Lesser Tunb, along with their geographical proximity to the Iranian mainland, constitute a compelling body of evidence confirming their enduring and inherent connection with territorial sovereignty of Iran. This conclusion is consistent with the established principles of international law; in particular, the doctrines of territorial integrity and the principle of the rule of law, *uti possidetis juris*, as well as the requirement of the effective and continuous exercise of state authority. From a legal and factual perspective, these islands represent an undeniable and inherent component of Iran's sovereign territory. Historical mapping, coherent governance and administrative measures, further substantiates Iran's full ownership and legal rights under the principle of effective occupation. Collectively, these evidentiary elements demonstrate the indissoluble continuity of Iranian jurisdiction, reaffirming the legal status of the islands as an integral part of Iran's territorial framework in the Persian Gulf in accordance with the preservation of territorial integrity enshrined in Article 2(4) of the United Nations Charter.

Iran's sovereign rights are strongly reinforced by the principle of *uti possidetis juris*, as affirmed by the International Court of Justice in the *Border Dispute* (*Burkina Faso v. Mali*). This principle affirms that the administrative boundaries pre-existing at the time of decolonization continue to be the basis of the legitimate boundaries of the State. Documentary evidence from British colonial archives and the immediate, consistent, and ongoing practice of the Iranian government after the end of British protectorate in the Trucial States show that no other power has exercised lasting authority or supremacy over the islands. Any claim to the contrary is therefore based on tenuous colonial arrangements that have neither transferred sovereignty nor extinguished Iran's established property rights and title. This conclusion is consistent with and adheres to the doctrine of territorial integrity enshrined in Article 2(4) of the *United Nations Charter*, as confirmed and reaffirmed by the International Court of Justice in *Military and Paramilitary Activities in and against Nicaragua (Nicaragua V. United States of America)*, which affirms that respect for territorial integrity remains a fundamental element of the international legal order.

At a broader analytical level, the ongoing arguments over the sovereignty of three Persian Gulf islands—Abu Musa, the Greater Tunb and the Lesser Tunb—reflects the enduring complexities of colonial demarcations and the impact of external interventions on the geopolitics of the Persian Gulf. The interplay between legal entitlement and postcolonial disputes highlights the need to balance legal principles with pragmatic diplomacy. Such arguments rooted in complex historical realities and exacerbated by significant geopolitical risks, indeed underscores the urgent need for renewed diplomatic engagement based on careful historical and legal scrutiny. Contemporary scholarship situates this dispute within the context of broader geopolitical developments, emphasizing on the way the British colonial interventions have influenced local affiliations, thereby complicating further postcolonial territorial disputes. At the same time, scholarly consensus acknowledges the enduring nature of Iran's legitimate historical rights and highlights the central role of effective control along with the ongoing and sustained administration in strengthening legitimate sovereignty under international law. In this context, many scholars have suggested that a prudent course of action requires the Trucial States (sheikhs) to reconsider their weak position in favor of a pragmatic approach that prioritizes regional stability and peace. International organizations and leading diplomatic actors are well-positioned to facilitate this approach, further to foster understanding and to create well-intentioned structured frameworks that offer a peaceful path in addressing this dispute. By reducing geopolitical tensions and risks through such engagement, stakeholders can create conditions that lead to a peaceful settlement in the neighborhood and a sustainable arrangement for peaceful coexistence, thereby enhancing the imperatives of regional and global stability.

The Persian Gulf and its islands represent a location of enduring geopolitical, geoeconomic, and strategic significance, functioning as a major maritime conduit between the Western world and the Indian subcontinent, thereby maintaining profound strategic importance and salience for the countries of the region. Historically, long before the exploitation of hydrocarbon resources, this vital waterway served as a vital axis of trade, imperialist competition, and the projection of maritime power. In the contemporary international system, the region's abundant energy reserves, dynamic markets, and significant investment potential continue to consolidate its central position within global economic and peace architectures. The stability of this semi-enclosed sea is essential not only for the well-being of its bordering states but also for the maintenance of the broader international order. Paradoxically, however, despite numerous structural incentives for cooperation, ongoing political divergences and rivalries have perpetuated instability. Therefore, it is essential that the Persian Gulf states develop and maintain frameworks of peace, stability, and constructive engagement as prerequisites for sustainable regional balance and the advancement of global peace and stability.

This edited volume seeks to advance and disseminate scholarly knowledge conducive to a comprehensive, multidimensional, and layered understanding of the Persian Gulf and its islands.

Through sustained engagement with the geographical, economic, political, and strategic dimensions relevant to the region, the book contributes to the refinement of academic discourse and aspires to support the pursuit of goals of regional—and, by extension, global—stability and peace with sustained scholarly significance. The analyses and findings presented here aim to inform and enrich the perspectives of scholars, policymakers, and diplomatic actors, thereby facilitating principled, evidence-based, and constructive approaches to regional affairs. Furthermore, this book aims to promote the continued development of rigorous and systematic academic research on the complex issues and disputes related to the Persian Gulf and its islands, as well as their future evolution. Ultimately, the intellectual and conceptual contributions presented in this book seek to shed light on the evolving dynamics of the region and make a meaningful contribution to the broader body of scholarly knowledge and intellectual endeavors.

This volume presents a systematic and interdisciplinary analysis of the Persian Gulf and its islands from historical and political economy perspectives. Through a rigorously integrated analytical framework, the book examines the structural characteristics, historical features and trajectories, contemporary transformations, and institutional configurations that have shaped—and continue to reshape—the political, economic, and socio-spatial formations of the region. By critically engaging contemporary key debates about colonial legacies, state formation, title (ownership), and sovereignty, the volume elucidates the dynamic processes through which the Persian Gulf has emerged as a strategic locus within regional and global political-economic orders. Collectively, these book chapters provide a nuanced and conceptually rigorous understanding of the Persian Gulf's evolving role in global systems, while also establishing a critical foundation for future research and interdisciplinary studies.

As an interdisciplinary endeavor, this book is designed to engage a broad and diverse audience of scholars, researchers, diplomats, policymakers, entrepreneurs, practitioners, and professionals whose work intersects with the Persian Gulf and its strategically important islands in multi-layered and interconnected regional and global dimensions. Envisioned as both an authoritative reference and a collective intellectual endeavor, this book offers a systematic exploration of the Persian Gulf and its islands, tracing the contours of their historical evolution, cultural and political transformations, and their contemporary significance in the twenty-first century. The book chapters illuminate the Persian Gulf as a space where geography and history intertwine, where cultural memory meets modern aspiration, and where enduring structures of power intersect with emergent patterns of exchange and identity.

Drawing upon rigorous research and informed by diverse theoretical perspectives, the contributors examine the manifold forces—historical, geopolitical, economic, and sociocultural—that have shaped and continue to redefine the region's complex dynamics. In bringing these perspectives into dialogue, the volume seeks not only to consolidate and reinterpret existing knowledge but also to foster a deeper, more reflexive understanding of the Persian Gulf and its important islands as sites of encounter, transformation, and meaning. At once analytical and reflective, it bridges disciplines and traditions of inquiry, inviting readers to consider the Persian Gulf as both an evolving regional system and a cultural-historical realm whose study offers vital insights into the conditions of contemporary global interdependence.

Ultimately, this work aspires to advance a more profound appreciation of the past and present of the Persian Gulf, while contributing thoughtfully to broader discourses on sustainable development, regional stability, and the pursuit of peace and coexistence across societies and civilizations.

Cambridge, MA, USA Nezameddin Faghih
January 15, 2026

Acknowledgements The editors gratefully acknowledge Lorraine Klimowich for her invaluable contributions and dedicated efforts throughout the publication process of this volume. They also extend their sincere appreciation to all chapter authors and reviewers who generously contributed their time and scholarly expertise; without their commitment and support, the successful completion of this edited volume would not have been possible: Ebrahim Abbasi, Masoomeh Alipourian, Samaneh Bahrololoum, Ebrahim Bonyadi, Mohammad Farahmand, Parsa Haghighatgoo, Naeim Khozaeinejad, Mojtaba Naserian Riabi, Fatemeh Homa Rezazadeh, Leyla Sarfaraz, Lida Sarreshtehdari, and Sara Togha.

Contents

An Introduction to the Persian Gulf and Islands: Historical Dynamics and the Twenty-First Century

Nezameddin Faghih

Abstract The Persian Gulf and its islands have long stood at the crossroads of maritime exchange, imperial rivalry, colonial administration, and modern geopolitical contestation. This edited volume traces the historical evolution of the region from antiquity to the present, with particular emphasis on the strategic, economic, and political roles of its islands. Drawing on archaeological findings, classical and historical sources, colonial archives, and contemporary international law, it examines how geography, trade, imperialism, oil, and sovereignty disputes have shaped regional and global politics.

Through an integrated historical-legal and political-economic approach, the book analyzes key issues, including the sovereignty dispute over the Iranian islands of Abu Musa and the Greater and Lesser Tunb; the nomenclature and historical significance of Qeshm Island; the geopolitics and geo-economics of the energy transition; the delineation of the Persian Sea in ninth- and tenth-century geographical works; the historical geography of Makran; the commercial and military centrality of Siraf during the Buyid dynasty; and contemporary entrepreneurship ecosystems and poverty alleviation strategies in selected Persian Gulf states. By placing these studies within a coherent analytical framework, this book highlights the structural forces and evolving institutional configurations that have shaped the political, economic, and socio-spatial formations of the Persian Gulf. By critically examining key debates about colonial legacies, state formation, territorial sovereignty, and regional integration, the book highlights the role of the Persian Gulf as a pivotal locus in the global political-economic order.

As an interdisciplinary endeavor, this book offers both a comprehensive reference and a thought-provoking contribution to the study of the Persian Gulf for a wide range of audiences, including scholars, policymakers, diplomats, and practitioners. It portrays the Persian Gulf as a dynamic space where geography intersects with history, cultural memory with modern ideals, and enduring power structures with emerging patterns of exchange and identity. Ultimately, this book seeks to

N. Faghih (✉)
UNESCO Chair Professor Emeritus, Cambridge, MA, USA

N. Faghih et al. (eds.), *The Persian Gulf and Islands*, Perspectives on Development in the Middle East and North Africa (MENA) Region,
https://doi.org/10.1007/978-3-032-27910-1_1

advance a nuanced and multifaceted understanding of the Persian Gulf and its islands, contributing to the scholarly and intellectual discourse on sustainability, peace, and coexistence in an increasingly interdependent world.

Keywords Abarkavan · Abu Musa · Abu Musa and the Tunb Islands · Achaemenid · Achaemenid Empire · Analytical frameworks · Ashkal al-Alam (The World's Images) · Ashkal al-'Alam · Baluchistan · Baluchistan (Gedrosia) · British archives · Burkina Faso · Burkina Faso–Mali Case · Buyid Dynasty · Colonial administration · Colonial legacies · Comparative Jurisprudence · Conceptual framework · Core regional focus · Diplomacy · Effective control · Effective occupation · Energy transition · Entrepreneurship · Entrepreneurship ecosystems · Gedrosia · Geo-economics · Geo-economics · Geopolitical dynamics · Geopolitics · Global political economy · Greater and Lesser Tunb · Greater Tunb · Historical cartography · Historical geography · Historical title · Historical title and legal analysis · Imperial Rivalry · Interdisciplinary analysis · International Court of Justice (ICJ) · International Law · Iran · Iranian Islands · Island of Palmas · Island of Palmas Case · Kingdom of Hormuz · Khalij al-Farsi · Laft · Legal and political dimensions · Legal history · Legal legacy · Legal-historical analysis · Legitimate Sovereignty · Lesser Tunb · Long Island · Longue Durée · Longue Durée history · Makran · Makran (Mokran) · Makran geography · Maritime exchange · Maritime geopolitics · Maritime history · Maritime Trade · Masaalek va Mamaalek (The Routes and the Kingdoms) · Middle east studies · Morooj al-dhahab (The Golden Meadow) · Morooj al-Dhahab · Oil geopolitics · Oil politics · Orakta · Panjbur · Pedra Branca · Pedra Branca Case · Permanent Court of International Justice (PCIJ) · Persian Gulf · Persian Gulf Islands · Persian Gulf Studies · Persian Sea · Persian Sea (Khalij al-Farsi) · Political economy · Political economy of energy · Port of Siraf · Poverty alleviation · Poverty alleviation strategies · Qasemi Tribe · Qeshm · Qeshm Island · Regional integration · Regional security · Regional stability · Safavid · Safavid Dynasty · Sea of Makran · Security · Siraf · Siraf (Port of Siraf) · Socio-spatial transformations · Sovereignty · Sovereignty and territorial title · Sovereignty disputes · State formation · Strategic maritime region · Strait of Hormuz · Territorial continuity · Territorial dispute · Territorial title · The Buyid · The Persian Gulf · The Persian Sea · Tiz · Trade

1 Background

The Persian Gulf, a semi-enclosed sea basin connecting the Indian Ocean to the Middle East, has long served as a pivotal corridor between Mesopotamia, the Iranian Plateau, the Arabian Peninsula, and the wider Indian Ocean world. From the third millennium BC onwards, maritime exchange linked Sumerian city-states with Persian Gulf polities such as Dilmun and Megan, and featured a (Persian) Gulf-centric trade that linked Mesopotamia, Oman, and the Indus Valley. During the Middle Ages, island sites and ports near the Strait of Hormuz—particularly Hormuz itself—emerged as vital trade centers that regulated interregional flows between India, Iran, and the eastern Mediterranean. In the early modern period, European powers attempted to reshape this geography: the Portuguese captured Hormuz in 1507 and established strategic nodes to control the sea lanes, a pattern that was later reinforced under British imperial rule through treaties, naval patrols, and island bases. Throughout antiquity, history, and colonial transitions, the islands of the Persian Gulf served as navigational markers, trading centers, and military outposts, driving cycles of regional integration and geopolitical competition driven by trade, empire, extraction, and state formation (Potter, 2009; Heard-Bey, 1982; Barnes & Jaffe, 2006; Özbaran & de Lyma, 1972).

This book traces the historical dynamics of the Persian Gulf and its islands from ancient maritime networks to contemporary geopolitical positions. It argues that the region's modern strategic importance cannot be understood without reference to the deep historical foundations in which geography and trade have repeatedly shaped political authority and foreign interventions.

2 Ancient Maritime Networks

Archaeological and textual evidence shows the Persian Gulf as a vital conduit in vast, far-reaching trade networks since at least the third millennium BC. Mesopotamian cuneiform documents from the Early Dynastic and Akkadian periods repeatedly refer to maritime exchanges with Dilmun, Megan, and Meluhha (Malukha), generally identified with eastern Arabia (modern-day Bahrain and the Persian Gulf coast), Oman, and the Indus Valley, respectively. These texts, including administrative documents and royal inscriptions, are evidence of the orderliness and institutionalization of Persian Gulf trade in Mesopotamian economies. In particular, Dilmun appears as a major trading center that distributed goods between Mesopotamia and distant regions, highlighting its strategic role in interregional exchanges (Potts, 2009; Steinkeller, 2007; Crawford, 1998).

Material evidence supports these texts. Archaeological surveys across the Persian Gulf coast reveal widespread imports of copper ingots from Megan, red agate (carnelian) beads from Indus, Mesopotamian ceramics, and Persian Gulf seals of local production, indicating sustained interaction rather than sporadic contact. References to merchants, sailors, and interpreters in Mesopotamian cities indicate the trading communities and cultural exchange that characterized mature trade networks. Beyond raw materials, Persian Gulf trade included semi-precious stones, timber, textiles, shells, and possibly agricultural goods, indicating a diverse maritime economy supported by shipbuilding traditions and advanced seafaring knowledge. Seasonal seafaring and the logistical challenges of navigating the high seas suggest that established maritime expertise and shared trade norms existed long before the classical era. Together, archaeological and textual data portray the Persian Gulf as a coherent economic and cultural region in the Bronze Age that played a significant role in the emergence of early complex societies throughout Persia, Mesopotamia, and South Asia (Laursen & Steinkeller, 2017; Weeks, 2003; Possehl, 2002; Potts, 2012).

3 Medieval Trade and Early Modern Imperial Competition

During the Middle Ages, Hormuz emerged as a leading trading center in the Indian Ocean, exercising decisive control over access to the Persian Gulf. Its location on the Strait of Hormuz connected land networks from Mesopotamia and the Iranian plateau with maritime circuits to India, Persia, Southeast Asia, and East Africa. Hormuz acted as an intermediary and tax collector for the flow of valuable goods—textiles, spices, horses, pearls, perfumes, and precious metals—making it essential for long-distance trade from the thirteenth century onwards (Chaudhuri, 1985; Pearson, 2003).

Islamic geographers and travelers have emphasized the wealth and global character of Hormuz, describing it as a populous and commercial city supported by safe harbors, warehousing, financial services, and interethnic trade networks—authors such as Al-Muqaddasi (also known as Muhammad ibn Ahmad Al-Maqdisi, 946–1000 AD, geographer, traveler, and author of prominent Arab works based on personal observations of the economic life of the lands of the Persian Gulf and the Arabian Gulf, that is, the Red Sea), Yaqut al-Hamawi (Yaqut Shahab al-Din, ibn Abdullah Rumi al-Hamawi, 1179–1229 AD, scholar known for his influential works on geography and history), and later Ibn Battuta (1304–1368/1369 AD, traveler, explorer, and scholar who visited most of Africa and Asia). Accordingly, the prosperity of this trading city depended on its ability to broker trade and generate revenue from turnover, a pattern common to Indian Ocean port cities whose power lay less in conquering territory and more in facilitating trade (Ho, 2006; Subrahmanyam, 1997; Britannica, 2025; Al-Nadim & Ibn Ishaq, 1970; Conrad, 2010; Adamec, 2016; Adamec, 2009; Norris, 1959; Battuta, 1929; Chism, 2013).

Politically, Hormuz functioned as a Persian semi-independent (semi-autonomous) trading kingdom, often recognizing and acknowledging the Persian regional sovereignty while maintaining internal autonomy. Its (de facto Persian) rulers established strong commercial and administrative ties with Persian dynasties, as well as diplomatic and commercial relationship with Arab neighbors and South Asian merchants, enabling Hormuz to act as a flexible intermediary across cultural and political boundaries. This system continued until the European maritime powers entered the scene in the late fifteenth and early sixteenth centuries, introducing a new model of commercial dominance (Pearson, 2003; Chaudhuri, 1985; Ho, 2006; Subrahmanyam, 1997).

European intervention began in the early sixteenth century with the Portuguese. In 1507, Afonso de Albuquerque's forces captured Hormuz and established a fort and a charter licensing regime to monopolize Persian Gulf trade. Portugal's power relied on naval artillery and the resulting brute force, marking a departure from previous negotiated exchanges. Thus, Hormuz became a node of the Indian

Empire—*Estado da Índia*, which was trying to integrate the Persian Gulf into the expanding competition of global empires. However, the profits generated were mainly spent supporting imperial garrisons and naval operations rather than local trading communities, and this created strong dissatisfaction and growing anger among regional powers and merchants as trade patterns changed (Sanceau, 1936; Subrahmanyam, 2012).

The fall of Hormuz in 1622, after the Anglo-Persian alliance to expel the Portuguese, shifted commercial activities to Bandar Abbas and reshaped the economic geography of the Persian Gulf. The story foretold new forms of European interaction—less direct conquest, more commercial engagement, and strategic alignment—while also showing how technology, military power, and political organization could transform a trading hub into the center of imperial conflict (Chaudhuri, 1985; Floor, 2006).

4 British Imperialism and Island Administration

From the nineteenth century onwards, Britain established a dominant foreign presence in the Persian Gulf, transforming it into an arena of imperial influence that derived from imperial maritime security. Britain considered the Persian Gulf routes essential to maintaining India—the strategic cornerstone of its empire—and sought to deter rival powers, particularly Russia, France, and later Germany. The *General Maritime Treaty (1820)* and the *Perpetual Maritime Truce (1853)* initiated a framework for limiting local naval warfare and piracy, which gradually evolved into protectorate arrangements with the Trucial States, Bahrain, and later Qatar and Kuwait. In this way, Britain regulated shipping, established and disciplined truces, and mediated disputes, cementing imperial authority in the political fabric of the region without formal colonial conquest (Kelly, 1968; Onley, 2009).

British imperial rule had a lasting impact on creating the legal and diplomatic disputes over the sovereignty of the islands of Abu Musa, Greater Tunb, and Lesser Tunb. Archival evidence suggests that British policy toward these islands was strategic, pragmatic, and often contradictory, shaped more by shifting geopolitical priorities than by coherent legal and ethical principles. These priorities included maintaining diplomatic relations with regional states, protecting imperial communications networks such as telegraph lines, and managing political stability among the Persian Gulf states. As a result, British officials alternately recognized, marginalized, or ignored competing local claims, resulting in a fluid and often contradictory administrative practice (Schofield, 2014; Ahmadi, 2008; Al-Qasimi, 1986; Onley, 2007; Kelly, 1968; Al-Mazrouei, 2015; Peterson, 1988).

From a historical geographical perspective, colonial-era surveys and administrative documents have failed to establish coherent territorial demarcations. Maps, treaties, and correspondence often lacked precise definitions of maritime boundaries or the legal status of offshore islands. British surveys sometimes correctly placed islands under Iranian jurisdiction, while other administrative records deliberately misrepresented them as dependencies of Arab sheikhdoms in order to win their favor and deceptively keep them under British protection. This artificial spatial ambiguity reflected a deceptive style of imperial governance in which geographical representation unfortunately served as a tool for political expediency rather than legal certainty (Peterson, 1988; Schofield, 2014; Peace Palace Library, 2013; Ahmadi, 2008; Haghshenas, 2010; Al-Qasimi, 1986; Onley, 2007; Kelly, 1968; Al-Mazrouei, 2015).

In terms of international law and diplomatic practice, this deliberate carelessness and incorrectness sought to undermine the development of true and clear ownership and facilitated the perpetuation of artificial rival claims. As scholars have pointed out, legal clarity was often a strategic issue, resulting in a fragmented documentary record on which subsequent parties could selectively rely in support of rival sovereignty claims. In this context, the Iranian position was rightly based on a genuine historical and legal continuity going back to the early Persian states, while the illusory and unfounded claims made by some Arab rulers during the British protectorate period were expressed largely through temporary tribal authority and deceptive informal administrative arrangements, rather than real and established principles of territorial sovereignty (Schofield, 2014; Peace Palace Library, 2013; Ahmadi, 2008; Rastbeen, 2008; Al-Qasimi, 1986; Onley, 2007; Kelly, 1968; Al-Mazrouei, 2015; Peterson, 1988; Schofield, 2014; Al-Mazrouei, 2015).

The British withdrawal from the Persian Gulf in 1971 turned these deliberately concealed and fabricated ambiguities and covert mischiefs into overt diplomatic conflict. On 30 November 1971, the Iranian navy took control of Abu Musa, the Greater Tunb, and the Lesser Tunb, presenting this as a natural and normal continuation of Iran's de facto historical and legal sovereignty, rooted in the successive Persian empires. Shortly thereafter, a newly established Arab state in December 1971 staked its own competing claims to the islands, attempting to turn the legacy of imperial administrative ambiguities into a modern international dispute (Schofield, 2014; Peace Palace Library, 2013; Ahmadi, 2008; Haghshenas, 2010; Rastbeen, 2008; Al-Qasimi, 1986; Onley, 2007; Kelly, 1968; Al-Mazrouei, 2015; Peterson, 1988; Schofield, 2016).

5 Oil, Geopolitics, and Strategic Chokepoints

The discovery and production of oil in the Persian Gulf from the early twentieth century onwards made the region a focal point of the global energy order. Beginning with the first major oil discovery in the Middle East at Masjed Sulayman in 1908 and the subsequent acceleration of discoveries in Bahrain, Saudi Arabia, Kuwait, Iraq, and the Persian Gulf States, the Persian Gulf emerged as a dominant hydrocarbon producer. By the mid-twentieth century, the region contained the world's largest proven reserves and connected Persian Gulf producers to the industrial economies of Europe, North America, and East Asia. Western powers, particularly Britain and the United States, aligned their foreign policies with the stability, security, and energy export routes of the Persian Gulf (Yergin, 2012).

Oil revenues reshaped internal state structures and regional hierarchies. Rentier dynamics enabled centralized authority, expanded bureaucratic capacity, and fostered and strengthened extensive welfare systems, while reducing the tax burden on citizens and increasing dependence on external security guarantees. Internationally, hydrocarbon wealth linked the Persian Gulf states (monarchies and republics) to broader Cold War and post-Cold War security architectures, embedding the region in global power politics (Barnes & Jaffe, 2006; Gause, 2009; Beblawi & Luciani, 1987).

Maritime geography, especially the Strait of Hormuz, which is the only channel connecting the Persian Gulf to the Sea of Oman and the Indian Ocean, became increasingly important. The strait became a vital energy bottleneck, with a large share of the world's maritime traffic of oil and liquefied natural gas passing through its waters. The islands in and around the strait—Qeshm, Lark, Abu Musa, and the Greater Tunb and the Lesser Tunb—became of immense strategic value for monitoring traffic, deploying coastal defenses, and potentially disrupting flows in times of extreme crisis (Cordesman, 2014).

These dynamics were highlighted during the Iran-Iraq War (1980–1988) and the tanker war phase, when maritime security and naval deployment became central to deterrence and crisis warning. The ongoing nexus between energy infrastructure, maritime geography, and regional militarization remains a defining feature of Persian Gulf security, as energy considerations continue to shape political calculations and alliance patterns (Hooton, 2011).

6 Contemporary Sovereignty Claims

The ongoing territorial disputes in the Persian Gulf concern the islands of Abu Musa, Greater Tunb, and Lesser Tunb, situated near the Strait of Hormuz. Iran emphasizes an original legal and historical title to these islands, grounded in longstanding sovereignty and continuous administrative authority dating to the premodern period, and corroborated by cartographic, archival, and documentary evidence demonstrating that the islands have legally and historically constituted an integral part of Iranian territory. Iran characterized Britain's withdrawal from the Persian Gulf in 1971 as a temporary interruption of the exercise of sovereignty rather than its abrogation, extinguishment, or annulment, maintaining that Iran's underlying legal and historical title persisted throughout the period of British involvement. From this perspective, Britain's withdrawal meant the resumption of a pre-existing and continuous sovereign title and legitimate control, not the acquisition, re-establishment, restoration, or revival of a new title (Schofield, 2014; Ahmadi, 2008; Haghshenas, 2010; Rastbeen, 2008; Al-Qasimi, 1986; Al-Mazrouei, 2015; Peterson, 1988; Schofield, 2016).

The Trucial States' claim is based on a theory of title that derives from the alleged local succession and intermittent and largely symbolic claims of temporary and ephemeral authority exercised by the sheikhdoms of the Persian Gulf in the late colonial period. From the perspective of classical and contemporary doctrines of territorial sovereignty, such claims lack the requirements of effective law (*effectivités*) because they fail to demonstrate the continuous, peaceful and exclusive exercise of state authority. The sheikhdoms in question functioned not as independent and sovereign actors but as subordinate entities within the framework of the British Empire, and their external relations and territorial claims were limited and constrained by colonial supervision. Consequently, periodic and episodic administrative acts or partial demographic presence—particularly invoking partial Arab populations—cannot, without other factors and evidence of effective and autonomous governance, generate a legally recognizable title under international law (Daulay, 2021; Patel, 2014; Shaw, 2017; Bishop, 1954; Colson & Vohrer, 2008; Rossi, 2024).

However, if the evidentiary basis of the Trucial States' argument further reveals a pronounced reliance on British colonial archives, their validity should be approached with methodological caution. From a *Third World Approaches to International Law (TWAIL)* perspective, such colonial archives are not neutral repositories of historical fact and reality, but instruments of imperial administration, often characterized by strategic ambiguity, selective documentation, and juridical indeterminacy. Assertions of British "recognition" of the islands as part of the Trucial States are, at best, equivocal and, at worst, retrospective constructions unsupported by formal acts of attribution or boundary delimitation. Giving positive and determinative weight to such materials risks re-inscribing colonial epistemologies as authoritative sources and determinants of postcolonial governance and sovereignty—contrary to TWAIL's critique of the persistence of imperial legal structures in contemporary international law (Anghie, 2007; Pahuja, 2011; Chimni, 2003, 2021; Anghie & Chimni, 2003; Badaru, 2008; Okafor, 2008; Bendel, 2021; Appiagyei-Atua, 2015; Anghie & Chimni, 2004; Ramina, 2018).

Doctrinally, the Trucial States' reliance on local succession is equally problematic when assessed through the lens of intertemporal law. Territorial title must be evaluated in accordance with the legal standards applicable at the time the alleged rights crystallized. During the relevant period, neither the sheikhdoms nor the British protectorate regime articulated a coherent or legally operative claim of sovereignty over the islands. Furthermore, the principle of *uti possidetis juris* ("the right to possess"), whether explicitly or implicitly invoked, provides limited support for the Trucial States' position. Britain's withdrawal from the Persian Gulf in 1971 was not accompanied by authoritative colonial boundary delimitations encompassing the islands, and the absence of such delimitations precludes the automatic transmission of title upon decolonization (Shaw, 2017; Island of Palmas, 1928; Li, 2017; Khan, 2007; International Court of Justice, 1945; International Court of Justice [ICJ], 1986a, 1986b, 1986c, 1986d; Permanent Court of International Justice [PCIJ], 1933a, 1933b, 1933c, 1933d).

The contention that Iran's actions in 1971 constituted an unlawful acquisition of territory by force likewise rests on a contested legal characterization. Although the prohibition on territorial acquisition by force was emerging as a norm of general international law by the late twentieth century, its application to situations involving unresolved or competing claims of sovereignty remains doctrinally complex. From a TWAIL standpoint, isolating the events of 1971 from their broader historical context obscures the structural conditions of decolonization, in which imperial withdrawal occurred without legal clarity, leaving postcolonial actors to contest territorial arrangements shaped by colonial indeterminacy. Thus, privileging the ambiguities of the colonial era as the determinant of contemporary sovereignty claims is not only doctrinally fragile but also normatively questionable (United Nations, 1970; PART, 1970; United Nations, 1992; International Court of Justice, 1945; Viñuales, 2020; Anghie, 2005; Chimni, 2003, 2021; Anghie & Chimni, 2003; Badaru, 2008; Okafor, 2008; Bendel, 2021; Appiagyei-Atua, 2015; Anghie & Chimni, 2004; Ramina, 2018).

The cumulative body of geographical, historical, and juridical evidence convincingly substantiates the enduring sovereignty of Iran over the islands of Abu Musa, the Greater Tunb, and the Lesser Tunb, in accordance with the recognized principles of international law and state practice. The geographical contiguity of these islands to the Iranian mainland, their geological coherence and integrity, and the continuous Iranian administrative presence, taken together, meet the legal criteria of effective occupation and continuous manifestation of sovereignty. These criteria were firmly stated and authoritatively articulated in the *Isle of Palmas* arbitration (*Netherlands v. United States*) and reaffirmed in the judgment of the International Court of Justice in *Minquiers and Ecrehos* (*United Kingdom v. France*), both of which hold that effective and peaceful administration constitutes a crucial determinant of territorial title (Shaw, 2017; Brownlie, 2008; Crawford, 2019; Cassese, 2005; International Court of Justice [ICJ], 1986a, 1986b, 1986c, 1986d; Island of Palmas, 1928; Khan, 2007; Permanent Court of International Justice [PCIJ], 1933a, 1933b, 1933c, 1933d; Hudson, 1953; Johnson, 1954; Fitzmaurice, 1955; Roche, 1959; Ong, 2023).

Correspondingly, the geological continuity, geographical configuration, and natural coherence of the three islands of Abu Musa, the Greater Tunb, and the Lesser Tunb, along with their geographical proximity to the Iranian mainland, constitute a compelling body of evidence confirming their enduring and inherent connection with territorial sovereignty of Iran. This conclusion is consistent with the established principles of international law; in particular, the doctrines of territorial integrity and the principle of the rule of law, *uti possidetis juris*, as well as the requirement of the effective and continuous exercise of state authority. From a legal and factual perspective, these islands represent an undeniable and inherent component of Iran's sovereign territory. Historical mapping, coherent governance, and administrative measures further substantiate Iran's full ownership and legal rights under the principle of effective occupation. Collectively, these evidentiary elements demonstrate the indissoluble continuity of Iranian jurisdiction, reaffirming the legal status of the islands as an integral part of Iran's territorial framework in the Persian Gulf in accordance with the preservation of territorial integrity enshrined in Article 2(4) of the United Nations Charter (United Nations, 1945; International Court of Justice, 1945; International Court of Justice [ICJ], 1986a, 1986b, 1986c, 1986d; Island of Palmas, 1928; Khan, 2007; Permanent Court of International Justice [PCIJ], 1933a, 1933b, 1933c, 1933d).

Iran's sovereign rights are strongly reinforced by the principle of *uti possidetis juris*, as affirmed by the International Court of Justice in the *Border Dispute (Burkina Faso v. Mali)*. This principle affirms that the administrative boundaries pre-existing at the time of decolonization continue to be the basis of the legitimate boundaries of the State. Documentary evidence from British colonial archives and the immediate, consistent, and ongoing practice of the Iranian government after the end of British protectorate in the Trucial States show that no other power has exercised lasting authority or supremacy over the islands. Any claim to the contrary is therefore based on tenuous colonial arrangements that have neither transferred sovereignty nor extinguished Iran's established property rights and title. This conclusion is consistent with and adheres to the doctrine of territorial integrity enshrined in Article 2(4) of the *United Nations Charter*, as confirmed and reaffirmed by the International Court of Justice in *Military and Paramilitary Activities in and against Nicaragua (Nicaragua V. United States of America)*, which affirms that respect for territorial integrity remains a fundamental element of the international legal order (International Court of Justice, 1986e; Sik, 1988; Kill, 2013; Dupuy, 1992; Dupont, 2014; Naldi, 1986, 1987; Barker, 2006; Etinski, 2013; Crawford, 2019; Brownlie, 2008; Cassese, 2005).

At a broader analytical level, the ongoing arguments over the sovereignty of three Persian Gulf islands—Abu Musa, the Greater Tunb and the Lesser Tunb—reflects the enduring complexities of colonial demarcations and the impact of external interventions on the geopolitics of the Persian Gulf. The interplay between legal entitlement and postcolonial disputes highlights the need to balance legal principles with pragmatic diplomacy. Such arguments rooted in complex historical realities and exacerbated by significant geopolitical risks indeed underscore the urgent need for renewed diplomatic engagement based on careful historical and legal scrutiny. Contemporary scholarship situates this dispute within the context of broader geopolitical developments, emphasizing on the way the British colonial interventions have influenced local affiliations, thereby complicating further postcolonial territorial disputes. At the same time, scholarly consensus acknowledges the enduring nature of Iran's legitimate historical rights and highlights the central role of effective control along with the ongoing and sustained administration in strengthening legitimate sovereignty under international law. In this context, many scholars have suggested that a prudent course of action requires the claimas (sheikhs) to reconsider their weak position in favor of a pragmatic approach that prioritizes regional stability and peace. International organizations and leading diplomatic actors are well-positioned to facilitate this approach, further to foster understanding and to create well-intentioned structured frameworks that offer a peaceful path in addressing this dispute. By reducing geopolitical tensions and risks through such engagement, stakeholders can create conditions that lead to a peaceful settlement in the neighborhood and a sustainable arrangement for peaceful coexistence, thereby enhancing the imperatives of regional and global stability (El-Sayed, 2003; Al-Mazrouei, 2015; Shaw, 2017; Khan, 2007; Lathrop, 2008; Mobley, 2003; Shayan, 2020; Al-Naqbi, 1998; Petterson, 1992; Limbert, 2014; Hunter, 2010; Roken & Abdullah, 2001; Al-Nahyan, 2013; Kechichian, 1997; Eckert, 1997; Amirahmadi, 1996; Mirfendereski, 1997; Bavand, 1994; Mehr, 1997; Al-Qasimi, 2020; Beblawi, 2015; Cordesman, 2020; Crawford, 1998, 2019; Fromherz, 2012; Onley, 2005; Shaw, 2021; Karami & Azizi, 2025; Morris, 2019; Zandieh et al., 2012; Jafari, 2015; Rossi, 2024; Mobley, 2003; Evans, 2014, 2018).

The Persian Gulf and its islands represent a location of enduring geopolitical, geo-economic, and strategic significance, functioning as a major maritime conduit between the Western world and the Indian subcontinent, thereby maintaining profound strategic importance and salience for the countries of the region. Historically, long before the exploitation of hydrocarbon resources, this vital waterway served as a vital axis of trade, imperialist competition, and the projection of maritime power. In the contemporary international system, the region's abundant energy reserves, dynamic markets, and significant investment potential continue to consolidate its central position within global economic and peace architectures. The stability of this semi-enclosed sea is essential not only for the well-being of its bordering states but also for the maintenance of the broader international order. Paradoxically, however, despite numerous structural incentives for cooperation, ongoing political divergences and rivalries have perpetuated instability. Therefore, it is essential that the Persian Gulf states develop and maintain frameworks of peace, stability, and constructive engagement as prerequisites for sustainable regional balance and the advancement of global peace and stability (Faghih, 2025; Cordesman, 2014; Chubin, 1976; Adib-Moghaddam, 2006; Kamrava, 2011, 2018; Roberts, 2023; Roberts, 2022; Ulrichsen, 2018; Javanmardi, 2013; Elahi, 1998; Barnes & Jaffe, 2006; Rich, 2012; Konyuhov, A. I., & Maleki, B., 2006; Nami, 2016; Csicsmann, & Rozsa, 2020; Gause, 2009; Barzegar, 2010).

This edited volume seeks to advance and disseminate scholarly knowledge conducive to a comprehensive, multidimensional, and layered understanding of the Persian Gulf and its islands.

Through sustained engagement with the geographical, economic, political, and strategic dimensions relevant to the region, the book contributes to the refinement of academic discourse and aspires to support the pursuit of goals of regional—and, by extension, global—stability and peace with sustained scholarly significance. The analyses and findings presented here aim to inform and enrich the perspectives of scholars, policymakers, and diplomatic actors, thereby facilitating principled, evidence-based, and constructive approaches to regional affairs. Furthermore, this book aims to promote the continued development of rigorous and systematic academic research on the complex issues and disputes related to the Persian Gulf and its islands, as well as their future evolution. Ultimately, the intellectual and conceptual contributions presented in this book seek to shed light on the evolving dynamics of the region and make a meaningful contribution to the broader body of scholarly knowledge and intellectual endeavors.

7 Scope of the Book

This volume presents eight scholarly contributions that provide a systematic and interdisciplinary analysis of the Persian Gulf and its islands from historical and political economy perspectives. Through a rigorously integrated analytical framework, the chapters examine the structural characteristics, historical features and trajectories, contemporary transformations, and institutional configurations that have shaped—and continue to reshape—the political, economic, and socio-spatial formations of the region. By critically engaging contemporary key debates about colonial legacies, state formation, title (ownership), and sovereignty, the volume elucidates the dynamic processes through which the Persian Gulf has emerged as a strategic locus within regional and global political-economic orders. Collectively, these book chapters provide a nuanced and conceptually rigorous understanding of the Persian Gulf's evolving role in global systems, while also establishing a critical foundation for future research and interdisciplinary studies.

Chapter 1 is an introduction to the book. It introduces the book and explains that the Persian Gulf and its islands have long stood at the crossroads of maritime exchange, imperial rivalry, colonial administration, and modern geopolitical contestation. This edited volume traces the historical evolution of the region from antiquity to the present, with particular emphasis on the strategic, economic, and political roles of its islands. Drawing on archaeological findings, classical and historical sources, colonial archives, and contemporary international law, it examines how geography, trade, imperialism, oil, and sovereignty disputes have shaped regional and global politics.

Through an integrated historical-legal and political-economic approach, the book analyzes key issues, including the sovereignty dispute over the Iranian islands of Abu Musa and the Greater and Lesser Tunb; the nomenclature and historical significance of Qeshm Island; the geopolitics and geo-economics of the energy transition; the delineation of the Persian Sea in ninth- and tenth-century geographical works; the historical geography of Makran; the commercial and military centrality of Siraf during the Buyid dynasty; and contemporary entrepreneurship ecosystems and poverty alleviation strategies in selected Persian Gulf states. By placing these studies within a coherent analytical framework, this book highlights the structural forces and evolving institutional configurations that have shaped the political, economic, and socio-spatial formations of the Persian Gulf. By critically examining key debates about colonial legacies, state formation, territorial sovereignty, and regional integration, the book highlights the role of the Persian Gulf as a pivotal locus in the global political-economic order.

As an interdisciplinary endeavor, this book offers both a comprehensive reference and a thought-provoking contribution to the study of the Persian Gulf for a wide range of audiences, including scholars, policymakers, diplomats, and practitioners. It portrays the Persian Gulf as a dynamic space where geography intersects with history, cultural memory with modern ideals, and enduring power structures with emerging patterns of exchange and identity. Ultimately, this book seeks to advance a nuanced and multifaceted understanding of the Persian Gulf and its islands, contributing to the scholarly and intellectual discourse on sustainability, peace, and coexistence in an increasingly interdependent world.

Chapter 2 examines, through a historical-legal analysis, the dispute over the sovereignty of the Iranian islands of Abu Musa and the Greater and Lesser Tunb; three islands that occupy a strategically pivotal position near the Strait of Hormuz, a vital maritime chokepoint for global energy transit and regional security. Drawing on historical, geographical, and legal scholarship, this chapter offers an evidence-based, methodologically transparent analysis of the facts and realities of sovereignty dispute over these islands from antiquity to the present. It first reconstructs the historical evolution of authority over the islands—encompassing pre-modern polities, British imperial intervention, and postcolonial state formation. The study then examines the natural and geographical continuity of Abu Musa and the Tunbs with the Iranian mainland, alongside documentary records of administration, cartography, and effective control, to assess the claims under international legal doctrines, including territorial integrity, *uti possidetis juris*, and the requirement of continuous and effective state authority. By systematically investigating legal and historical arguments and highlighting the interpretive arguments of colonial-era arrangements, the chapter argues that the cumulative weight of historical practice and effective governance more strongly and adequately supports Iran's sovereign title. The conclusion contends that a durable and peaceful settlement requires renewed diplomatic engagement, facilitated by international and regional actors, grounded in rigorous historical and legal scrutiny, and oriented toward reducing geopolitical tensions and enhancing regional stability.

Chapter 3 presents a study on one of the names of Qeshm, the largest island in the Persian Gulf, strategically located in the Strait Hormuz. This chapter shows that Qeshm Island has been known by different names throughout history. Greek, Iranian, and Arab historians, geographers, and travelers, as well as orientalists, have called Qeshm Island by different names. This chapter examines and analyzes the word Abarkavan, as the name used for this island, considering the economic geography and vegetation of Qeshm Island.

Chapter 4 examines the geopolitics and geo-economics of the energy transition in the Persian Gulf. Being a home to 48% of the world's proven oil reserves and 39.8% of its natural gas reserves, the strategically significant Persian Gulf region plays a distinctive geopolitical and geo-economic role in the twenty-first century energy transition. The increasing global demand for energy has made the Persian Gulf a central hub in the international energy market, thus making it a persistent arena for geopolitical rivalries and international tensions. Simultaneously, the region's hot and arid climate, coupled with high levels of greenhouse gas emissions due to the production and consumption of fossil fuels, make it acutely vulnerable to climate change. Despite these challenges, the Persian Gulf possesses significant geographical and natural advantages that offer considerable potential for a sustainable energy transition through renewable sources.

Some countries in the region have taken preliminary steps toward energy transition by leveraging international diplomacy, implementing carbon capture and storage policies, adopting hydrogen as a clean fuel, improving energy efficiency, and integrating renewable energy sources. However, a considerable gap persists prior to achieving low-carbon emission targets.

This chapter consists of six sections, beginning with introduction as focusing on the geopolitics of the energy transition in the Persian Gulf. Section Two provides definitions of key concepts such as sustainable energy transition, renewable energy technology transition, the geopolitics of energy transition, geopolitics of renewable energy transition, geo-economics of energy transition, distinctions between geopolitical and geo-economic approaches to energy transition, and geo-economic instruments. Section Three reviews the existing literature on the geopolitics of energy transition in the Persian Gulf. Section Four explores the geopolitical and geo-economic significance of the Persian Gulf in the context of energy transition, highlighting regional characteristics and the roles of Persian Gulf States. Section Five addresses the challenges and opportunities associated with the geopolitical aspects of the energy transition in the region. Finally, Section Six provides conclusion and policy recommendations.

Chapter 5 explores the expanse of the Persian Sea based on the most authentic geographical and historical works of the ninth and tenth centuries CE. Outstanding Muslim geographers and historians who have compiled their works on geography and history in the ninth and tenth centuries AD, have expressed different opinions about the extent and boundaries of the Persian Sea (the Persian Gulf). In this chapter, after expressing the opinions of prominent geographers such as Ibn Khordadbeh, Abu Zeyd Balkhi, Istakhri, Maqdasi, and the unknown author of the book Hodoud al-Alam Men al-Mashreq Ilal-Maqreb, regarding the extent and boundaries of the Persian Sea, attention has been paid to the explanations of celebrated historians such as Ibn Yaqubi and Abu al-Hasan Masoudi, concerning the boundaries and the depths of the Persian Sea's maritime extent. According to the viewpoints of great geographers and historians of the ninth and tenth centuries AD, this research has concluded that the Persian Gulf was only a part of a greater sea, which was located in the south of Iran under the name of the Persian Sea.

Chapter 6 deals with the historical geography of Makran,[1] which is one of the most prominent regions of Iran and is located in the south of Baluchistan and on the northern coast of the Sea of Oman, also called the Makran Sea. The special geographical location of Makran has long promoted the economic base for this part of Iran and the ports located there have possessed a privileged commercial status along with significant economic prosperity throughout history. Makran enjoys several thousand years of history and valuable civilization. There are various opinions about the lexical origin of Makran and the extent of that land, as well as its administrative and political conjunction with neighboring states. Also, more accurate information is required concerning the cities, ports, and settlements related to Makran and its historical geography. By referring to original historical and geographical sources as

[1] Mokran, Mekran, or Makorran (in Balouchi dialect) - all pronunciations are correct

well as new studies, some of the existing ambiguities about the historical geography of the land of Makran have been resolved in the research reported in this chapter.

Chapter 7 examines the international military-commercial position of the port of Siraf (on the coast of the Persian Gulf) during the Buyid dynasty. Given the realistic approaches of the Buyid rulers (especially Azad al-Dawla), the country's economic prosperity and the security and welfare of the people were of particular importance. In the light of the Buyid government's deeds, industries developed significantly and agriculture flourished. This eventually led to the production of products in excess of domestic needs, as a result, the government paid attention to the export of those items. What is examined in this chapter is that during the period in question, the Samanid dominated on an extensive area of the Silk Road and enjoyed the commercial benefits related to that trade highway. Accordingly, the Buyid paid great attention to the major trade routes in southern Iran, both on the land and at the sea. Due to its specific geographical location, the port of Siraf, which was an important center of trade exchanges, enjoyed increasing prosperity and became famous as an international trade center during the Buyid reign. This very significant port also turned into a major military base and played a fundamental role in establishing security in the Persian Gulf and a highly extensive domain for the adjacent seas. This chapter also explores the commercial and military development of the Siraf port during the Buyid rule.

Chapter 8 examines entrepreneurship ecosystems and poverty alleviation in selected Persian Gulf countries. This chapter provides a concise overview of various poverty alleviation strategies, with particular emphasis on entrepreneurship as a participatory policy tool in combating poverty. Employing the Panel Corrected Standard Errors (PCSE) method, this chapter examines the entrepreneurial ecosystem impact on poverty alleviation in selected Persian Gulf countries (Iran, Oman, Bahrain, Iraq, Qatar, Kuwait, the United Arab Emirates, and the Saudi Arabia) over the period of 2010–2022. The analysis investigates the effects of individual components of the entrepreneurial ecosystem on poverty alleviation and evaluates the relative contribution of each factor. The findings indicate that a robust entrepreneurial ecosystem, coupled with effective governance, has a significant and positive effect on poverty reduction in the Persian Gulf region. Furthermore, the results demonstrate that the government-led entrepreneurship programs and the early-stage entrepreneurship education exert the most positive influence, whereas the technology transfer appears to have the least favorable impact among the entrepreneurial ecosystem indicators in the selected countries.

As an interdisciplinary endeavor, this book is designed to engage a broad and diverse audience of scholars, researchers, diplomats, policymakers, entrepreneurs, practitioners, and professionals whose work intersects with the Persian Gulf and its strategically important islands in multi-layered and interconnected regional and global dimensions. Envisioned as both an authoritative reference and a collective intellectual endeavor, this book offers a systematic exploration of the Persian Gulf and its islands, tracing the contours of their historical evolution, cultural, and political transformations, and their contemporary significance in the twenty-first century. The book chapters illuminate the Persian Gulf as a space where geography and history intertwine, where cultural memory meets modern aspiration, and where enduring structures of power intersect with emergent patterns of exchange and identity.

Drawing upon rigorous research and informed by diverse theoretical perspectives, the contributors examine the manifold forces—historical, geopolitical, economic, and sociocultural—that have shaped and continue to redefine the region's complex dynamics. In bringing these perspectives into dialogue, the volume seeks not only to consolidate and reinterpret existing knowledge but also to foster a deeper, more reflexive understanding of the Persian Gulf and its important islands as sites of encounter, transformation, and meaning. At once analytical and reflective, it bridges disciplines and traditions of inquiry, inviting readers to consider the Persian Gulf as both an evolving regional system and a cultural-historical realm whose study offers vital insights into the conditions of contemporary global interdependence.

Ultimately, this work aspires to advance a more profound appreciation of the past and present of the Persian Gulf, while contributing thoughtfully to broader discourses on sustainable development, regional stability, and the pursuit of peace and coexistence across societies and civilizations.

It should be noted that the views, analyses, interpretations, and conclusions expressed in the individual chapters of this volume are those of their respective authors and contributors and do not necessarily represent the views, positions, or policies of the editors. The inclusion of any material herein does not imply endorsement, verification, or approval by the editors. All contributing authors bear sole responsibility for the accuracy of their citations, bibliographic references, data, and factual statements. The editors disclaim any and all liability for errors or omissions or for any consequences arising from the application or use of information contained within the individual chapters. They further disclaim responsibility for any infringement of third-party rights that may result from the use or reproduction of materials included in this work. While every reasonable effort has been made to ensure the integrity and accuracy of the content, ultimate responsibility for the opinions, findings, and conclusions rests exclusively with the respective authors and contributors.

References

Adamec, L. W. (2009). *The A to Z of Islam*. Scarecrow Press.

Adamec, L. W. (2016). *Historical dictionary of Islam*. Bloomsbury Publishing PLC.

Adib-Moghaddam, A. (2006). *The international politics of the Persian Gulf: A cultural genealogy*. Routledge.

Ahmadi, K. (2008). *Islands and international politics in the Persian Gulf: The Abu Musa and Tunbs in strategic context*. Routledge.

Al-Mazrouei, N. S. (2015). *Disputed islands between UAE and Iran: Abu Musa, Greater Tunb, and Lesser Tunb in the Strait of Hormuz* (pp. 1–32). Gulf Research Centre.

Al-Nadim, I., & Ibn Ishaq, M. (1970). *The Fihrist of al-Nadīm: A tenth-century survey of Muslim culture* (Vol. 1). Columbia University Press.

Al-Nahyan, K. S. (2013). *The Three Islands: Mapping the UAE-Iran dispute*. Royal United Services Institute for Defense and Security Studies.
Al-Naqbi, Y. E. A. (1998). The sovereignty dispute over the Gulf Islands: Abu Musa, Greater and Lesser Tunbs (Doctoral dissertation, University of Glasgow).
Al-Qasimi, S. (1986). *The myth of Arab piracy in the Gulf*. Routledge.
Al-Qasimi, M. (2020). *The myth of Arab piracy in the Gulf*. Routledge.
Amirahmadi, H. (1996). *Small Islands, big politics*. St. Martin's Press.
Anghie, A. (2007). *Imperialism, sovereignty and the making of international law*. Cambridge University Press.
Anghie, A., & Chimni, B. S. (2003). Third world approaches to international law and individual responsibility in internal conflicts. *Chinese Journal of International Law, 2*(1), 77–103.
Anghie, A., & Chimni, B. S. (2004). Third world approaches to international law and individual responsibility in internal conflict. *Studies in Transnational Legal Policy, 36*, 185.
Appiagyei-Atua, K. (2015). Ethical dimensions of Third World approaches to international law (TWAIL): A critical review. *African Journal of Legal Studies, 8*(3–4), 209–235.
Badaru, O. A. (2008). Examining the utility of Third World approaches to international law for international human rights law. *International Community Law Review, 10*(4), 379–387.
Barker, J. C. (2006). Case concerning the frontier dispute (Benin/Niger). *International & Comparative Law Quarterly, 55*(3), 729–742.
Barnes, J., & Jaffe, A. M. (2006). The Persian Gulf and the geopolitics of oil. *Survival, 48*(1), 143–162.
Barzegar, K. (2010). Balance of power in the Persian Gulf: An Iranian view. *Middle East Policy, 17*(3), 74–87.
Battuta, I. (1929). *Travels in Asia and Africa, 1325–1354* (Vol. 7). Routledge.
Bavand, D. H. (1994). *The historical, political and legal bases of Iran's sovereignty over the Islands of Tunb & [and] Abumusa*. Internet Concepts.
Beblawi, H. (2015). The rentier state in the Arab world. In *The Arab state* (pp. 85–98). Routledge.
Beblawi, H., & Luciani, G. (1987). *The rentier state*. Croom Helm.
Bendel, J. (2021). Third World approaches to international law: Between theory and method. In *Research methods in international law* (pp. 402–415). Edward Elgar Publishing.
Bishop, W. W., Jr. (1954). Minquiers and Ecrehos Case (France/United Kingdom). *American Journal of International Law*, 316–326.
Britannica. (2025). Al-Maqdisī | Arabian geographer | Britannica.
Brownlie, I. (2008). *Principles of public international law* (7th ed.). Oxford University Press.
Cassese, A. (2005). *International law*. Oxford University Press.
Chaudhuri, K. N. (1985). *Trade and civilization in the Indian Ocean*. Cambridge University Press.
Chimni, B. S. (2003). Third world approaches to international law: A manifesto. In *The third world and international order* (pp. 47–73). Brill Nijhoff.
Chimni, B. S. (2021). Crisis and international law: A TWAIL perspective. In *Crisis narratives in international law* (pp. 40–53). Brill Nijhoff.
Chism, C. (2013). Between Islam and Christendom: Ibn Battuta's travels. In *Cosmopolitanism and the middle ages*. Palgrave Macmillan.
Chubin, S. (1976). The international politics of the Persian Gulf. *Review of International Studies, 2*(3), 216–230.
Colson, D. A., & Vohrer, B. J. (2008). International Court of Justice: Sovereignty Over Pedra Branca/Pulau Batu Puteh, Middle Rocks and South Ledge (Malaysia/Singapore). *International Legal Materials, 47*(5), 833–835.
Conrad, D. C. (2010). *Empires of medieval West Africa*. Infobase Publishing.
Cordesman, A. H. (2014). *The Gulf and the Strait of Hormuz*. CSIS.
Cordesman, A. H. (2020). *Iran, oil, and the Strait of Hormuz*. CSIS.
Crawford, H. E. (1998). *Dilmun and its Gulf neighbors*. Cambridge University Press.
Crawford, J. (2019). *Brownlie's principles of public international law* (9th ed.). Oxford University Press.

Csicsmann, L., & Rozsa, E. N. (2020). War and peace in the Persian Gulf: Pre-Westphalian, Westphalian or Post-Westphalian? *Asian Journal of Middle Eastern and Islamic Studies, 14*(2), 216–230.

Daulay, Z. (2021). Sovereignty over Pulau Ligitan and Pulau Sipadan. *Law Reform, 2*(1).

Dupont, P. E. (2014). Boundary delimitation in Africa. *Law & Practice of International Courts and Tribunals, 13*(1), 103–116.

Dupuy, P. M. (1992). Fact-finding in the Frontier dispute case. In *Fact-finding before international tribunals* (p. 81).

Eckert, A. (1997). Small Islands, big politics: The Tunbs and Abu Musa in the Persian Gulf. *Denver Journal of International Law & Policy, 25*(2), 14.

Elahi, H. (1998). *The Persian Gulf and its problems*. Qomas Publishing House.

El-Sayed, C. M. (2003). United Arab Emirates v. Iran: The dispute over the islands of Abu Musa, Greater Tunb, and Lesser Tunb. American University of Beirut Scholar works.

Etinski, R. (2013). Application of uti possidetis juris. *Zbornik Radova, 47*, 43.

Evans, M. D. (Ed.). (2014). *International law*. Oxford University Press.

Evans, M. D. (2018). *International law* (5th ed.). Oxford University Press.

Faghih, N. (2025). An Introduction to the Persian Gulf: Historical perspectives, maritime silk road, and hydropolitics. In *The Persian Gulf: Historical Perspectives, Maritime Silk Road, and Hydropolitics* (pp. 1–17). Springer Nature.

Fitzmaurice, G. (1955). Law and procedure of the ICJ. *British Yearbook of International Law, 32*, 20.

Floor, W. M. (2006). *The Persian Gulf.* Mage Publishers.

Fromherz, A. J. (2012). *Qatar: A modern history*. Georgetown University Press.

Gause, F. G., III. (2009). *The international relations of the Persian Gulf.* Cambridge University Press.

Haghshenas, S. A. (2010). *Iran historical sovereignty over the Tunbs and Bu Musa Islands*. Sena Publications.

Heard-Bey, F. (1982). *From trucial states to United Arab Emirates: A society in transition*. Longman.https://www.elsevier.es/es-revista-enfermeria-clinica-35-articulo-lectura-critica-literatura-cientifica-S1130862103737796

Ho, E. (2006). *The graves of Tarim: Genealogy and mobility across the Indian Ocean* (Vol. 3). Univ of California Press.

Hooton, E. R. (2011). *The Iran–Iraq War*. Osprey Publishing.

Hudson, M. O. (1953). The thirty-first year of the World Court. *American Journal of International Law, 47*(1), 1–19.

Hunter, S. (Ed.). (2010). *Iran and the Gulf: Policy and dynamics in the Persian Gulf region*. Columbia University Press.

International Court of Justice. (1986a). Communiqué: Chamber of Court to hear Burkina Faso and Mali on possible indication of provisional measures. No. 86/1, January 6, 1986.

International Court of Justice. (1986b). Communiqué: Provisional measures are indicated in the case of the Frontier Dispute (Burkina Faso–Mali). No. 86/2, January 10, 1986.

International Court of Justice. (1986c). Communiqué: Frontier Dispute (Burkina Faso/Republic of Mali) judgment of the Chamber. No. 86/18, December 22, 1986.

International Court of Justice. (1986d). Reports of judgments, advisory opinion and orders, case concerning the Frontier Dispute (Burkina Faso/Republic of Mali). Judgment of December 22, 1986.

International Court of Justice. (1986e). Military and Paramilitary Activities in and Against Nicaragua (Nicaragua v. United States of America): Merits (Judgment No. 70). International Court of Justice.

International Court of Justice. (1945). Charter of the United Nations, together with the Statute of the International Court of Justice, Signed at the United Nations Conference on International Organization, San Francisco, California, June 26, 1945 (Vol. 2353). US Government Printing Office.

Island of Palmas. (1928). Netherlands v. United States. 2 R.I.A.A. 829. Permanent Court of Arbitration.

Jafari, V. A. (2015). *The historical and legal foundations of Iran's sovereignty over Tunb and Abu-Musa Islands*. [PDF]. Retrieved from https://example.com/1035820150206.pdf

Javanmardi, F. (2013). Investigating the history of the Persian Gulf Name. *The Persian Gulf Studies Quarterly, 4*(3), 40–45.
Johnson, D. H. N. (1954). The Minquiers and Ecrehos case. *ICLQ, 3*(2), 189–216.
Kamrava, M. (Ed.). (2011). *The international politics of the Persian Gulf*. Syracuse University Press.
Kamrava, M. (2018). *Inside the Arab state*. Oxford University Press.
Karami, M., & Azizi, S. (2025). Book Review of Davoud Hermidas Bavand, Historical, Political, and Legal Foundations of Iran's Sovereignty over the Islands of Tunb and Abu Musa (Tehran: Ganj-e-Danesh Publication, 1998). *International Law Review*, e723392.
Kechichian, J. A. (1997). Small Islands, big politics: The Tunbs and Abu Musa in the Persian Gulf. *Middle East Policy, 5*(3), 209.
Kelly, J. B. (1968). *Britain and the Persian Gulf*. Oxford University Press.
Khan, D. E. (2007). Max Huber as arbitrator. *European Journal of International Law, 18*(1), 145–170.
Kill, T. (2013). Frontier dispute (Burkina Faso/Niger). *International Legal Materials, 52*(6), 1215–1256.
Konyuhov, A. I., & Maleki, B. (2006). The Persian Gulf Basin: Geological history, sedimentary formations, and petroleum potential. *Lithology and Mineral Resources, 41*, 344–361.
Lathrop, C. G. (2008). Sovereignty over Pedra Branca/Pulau Batu Puteh, Middle Rocks and South Ledge (Malaysia/Singapore). *American Journal of International Law, 102*(4), 828–834.
Laursen, S., & Steinkeller, P. (2017). *Babylonia, the Gulf Region, and the Indus: Archaeological and textual evidence for contact in the third and early second millennium BC*. Winona Lake, IN: Eisenbrauns.
Li, Z. (2017). International intertemporal law. *California Western International Law Journal, 48*, 341.
Limbert, J. W. (2014). *Iranian and Arab in the Gulf: Endangered Language, Windtowers*.
Mehr, F. (1997). *A colonial legacy: The dispute over the Islands of Abu Musa, and the Greater and Lesser Tumbs*. Bloomsbury Publishing PLC.
Mirfendereski, G. (1997). *A Colonial Legacy: The dispute over the Islands of Abu Musa and the Greater and Lesser Tunbs*. University Press of America.
Mobley, R. A. (2003). The Tunbs and Abu Musa Islands: Britain's Perspective. *The Middle East Journal*, 627–645.
Morris, P. S. (2019). The Iran–UAE Gulf Islands dispute: A journey through international law, history and politics.
Naldi, G. J. (1986). Provisional measures of protection. *ICLQ, 35*(4), 970–975.
Naldi, G. J. (1987). Uti possidetis in Africa. *ICLQ, 36*(4), 893–903.
Nami, M. H. (2016). Features of the Persian Gulf. *Persian Gulf Studies Quarterly, 3*(4), 48–61.
Norris, H. T. (1959). Ibn Battutah's Andalusian Journey. *The Geographical Journal, 125*(2), 185–196.
Okafor, O. C. (2008). Critical TWAIL. *International Community Law Review, 10*, 371.
Ong, D. M. (2023). Acquisition of sovereignty over islands. In *Peaceful management of maritime disputes* (pp. 3–28). Routledge.
Onley, J. (2005). Britain's informal empire. *Journal of Social Affairs, 22*(87), 29–45.
Onley, J. (2007). *The Arabian frontier of the British Raj*. Oxford University Press.
Onley, J. (2009). Britain's informal empire in the Gulf, 1820–1971. *Journal of Social Affairs, 26*(104), 29–45.
Özbaran, S., & de Lyma, D. M. (1972). The Ottoman Turks and the Portuguese in the Persian Gulf, 1534–1581. *Journal of Asian History, 6*(1), 45–87.
Pahuja, S. (2011). *Decolonizing international law*. Cambridge University Press.
PART, G. (1970). Declaration on Principles of International Law Concerning Friendly Relations and Cooperation Among States in accordance with the Charter of the United Nations. GAR 2625.
Patel, B. N. (2014). *Sovereignty over Pulau Ligitan and Sipadan*. Brill Nijhoff.
Pearson, M. N. (2003). *The Indian Ocean*. Routledge.
Peace Palace Library. (2013, October 3). *Unresolved territorial disputes: The Tunbs and Abu Musa in the Gulf*. Retrieved from https://peacepalacelibrary.nl/blog/2013/unresolved-territorial-disputes-tunbs-and-abu-musa-gulf

Permanent Court of International Justice (PCIJ). (1933a). *Series A/B (Collection of judgments, orders and advisory opinions), No. 53, Legal status of Eastern Greenland*. A.W. Sijothoff.
Permanent Court of International Justice (PCIJ). (1933b). *Series C (Pleadings, oral statements and documents), No. 62, Legal status of Eastern Greenland*. A.W. Sijothoff.
Permanent Court of International Justice (PCIJ). (1933c). *Series C (Pleadings, oral statements and documents), No. 64, Legal status of Eastern Greenland*. A.W. Sijothoff.
Permanent Court of International Justice (PCIJ). (1933d). *Series C (Pleadings, oral statements and documents), No. 65, Legal status of Eastern Greenland*. A.W. Sijothoff.
Petterson, R. B. (1992). *Middle Eastern strategic affairs: The Gulf Islands dispute*. Hurst & Company.
Possehl, G. L. (2002). *The Indus civilization: A contemporary perspective*. Rowman Altamira.
Potter, L. G. (Ed.). (2009). *The Persian Gulf in history*. Palgrave Macmillan.
Potts, D. T. (2009). *The archaeology of Elam: Formation and transformation of an ancient Iranian state*. Cambridge University Press.
Potts, D. T. (2012). *The Arabian Gulf in antiquity*. Oxford University Press.
Ramina, L. (2018). TWAIL and human rights. *Revista de Investigações Constitucionais, 5*(1), 261–272.
Rastbeen, A. (2008). *The Three Iranian Islands of the Persian Gulf: Based on documents and historical evidence*. Institut International d'Etudes Stratégiques.
Rich, B. (2012). Gulf war 4.0: Iran, Saudi Arabia and the complexification of the Persian Gulf equation. *Islam and Christian–Muslim Relations, 23*(4), 471–486.
Roberts, D. B. (2023). *Security politics in the Gulf monarchies: Continuity amid change*. Columbia University Press.
Roberts, D. B. (2022). *Reflecting on the GCC crisis*. Routledge.
Roche, A. G. (1959). *Minquiers and ecrehos case (the)* (Vol. 1). Librairie Droz.
Roken, A., & Abdullah, M. (2001). Dimensions of the UAE-Iran dispute over Three Island. In I. Al Abed & P. Hellyer (Eds.), *United Arab Emirates: A new perspective*.
Rossi, C. (2024). *International law and the politics of territorial disputes*. Routledge.
Sanceau, E. (1936). *The Portuguese in the Persian Gulf*. Cambridge University Press.
Schofield, R. (2014). *Borders, territories, and the Middle East*. Routledge.
Shaw, M. N. (2017). *International law*. Cambridge University Press.
Shaw, M. N. (2021). *International law* (9th ed.). Cambridge University Press.
Shayan, H. (2020). *Maritime boundaries and sovereignty in the Persian Gulf*. Routledge.
Sik, K. S. (1988). International Court of Justice, Reports of Judgments, Advisory Opinions and Orders 1986, and id., 1987. *Netherlands International Law Review, 35*(1), 112–113.
Steinkeller, P. (2007). New light on the hydrology and topography of southern Babylonia in the third millennium. In *Proceedings of the 52nd Rencontre Assyriologique Internationale* (pp. 185–211). Peeters.
Subrahmanyam, S. (1997). *The career and legend of Vasco da Gama*. Cambridge University Press.
Subrahmanyam, S. (2012). *The Portuguese empire in Asia, 1500–1700: A political and economic history* (2nd ed.). Wiley-Blackwell.
Ulrichsen, K. C. (Ed.). (2018). *The changing security dynamics of the Persian Gulf*. Oxford University Press.
United Nations. (1970). Declaration on principles of international law.
United Nations. (1945). Charter of the United Nations.
United Nations. (1992). *The Law of the Sea: Maritime claims and boundaries in the Persian Gulf*. United Nations Publications.
Viñuales, J. E. (2020). *The UN Friendly Relations Declaration at 50: An assessment of the fundamental principles of international law*. Cambridge University Press.
Weeks, L. R. (2003). *Early metallurgy of the Persian Gulf: Technology, trade, and the Bronze Age world*. Brill.
Zandieh, H., Esmaeli, M., & Ghasemian, S. (2012). The creation process of Three Islands Question. *Iranian Studies, 1*(1), 95–118.
Yergin, D. (2012). *The prize*. Simon & Schuster.

The Persian Gulf and Iranian Islands: Abu Musa and the Tunbs in Historical-Legal Analysis

Nezameddin Faghih

Abstract The Iranian islands of Abu Musa, the Greater and Lesser Tunbs occupy a strategically pivotal position near the Strait of Hormuz, a critical maritime chokepoint for global energy transit and regional security. Drawing on historical, geographical, and legal scholarship, this chapter offers an evidence-based, methodologically transparent analysis of the facts and realities of sovereignty over these islands from antiquity to the present. It first reconstructs the historical evolution of authority over the islands—encompassing pre-modern polities, British imperial intervention, and postcolonial state formation. The study then examines the natural and geographical continuity of Abu Musa and the Tunbs with the Iranian mainland, alongside documentary records of administration, cartography, and effective control, to assess the claims under international legal doctrines, including territorial integrity, *uti possidetis juris*, and the requirement of continuous and effective state authority. By systematically investigating legal and historical arguments and highlighting the interpretive arguments of colonial-era arrangements, the chapter argues that the cumulative weight of historical practice and effective governance more strongly and adequately supports Iran's sovereign title. The conclusion contends that a durable and peaceful settlement requires renewed diplomatic engagement, facilitated by international and regional actors, grounded in rigorous historical and legal scrutiny, and oriented toward reducing geopolitical tensions and enhancing regional stability.

Keywords Sovereignty · Persian Gulf · Effective occupation · Historical title · Iran · Strait of Hormuz · UAE · Abu Musa · Greater Tunb · Lesser Tunb · Territorial dispute · British archives · International law · Geopolitical dynamics · Qasemi tribe · Kingdom of Hormuz · Pedra Branca · Territorial continuity · Legal-historical analysis · Comparative jurisprudence · Effective control · Legal legacy · Legal history · Legitimate sovereignty · International Court of Justice

---

N. Faghih (✉)
UNESCO Chair Professor Emeritus, Cambridge, MA, USA

N. Faghih et al. (eds.), *The Persian Gulf and Islands*, Perspectives on Development in the Middle East and North Africa (MENA) Region,
https://doi.org/10.1007/978-3-032-27910-1_2

(ICJ) · Burkina Faso · Mali · Island of Palmas · Permanent Court of International Justice [PCIJ] · Achaemenid · Safavid

1 Background and Overview

The Persian Gulf covers an area of over 238,600 km^2, approximately 55% of which is within the maritime domain of Iran. The Persian Gulf hosts more than two hundred islands with different geomorphological origins, eighteen of which are under Iranian sovereignty, and together, these islands constitute nearly 1896.5 km^2 of terrestrial domain (Kechichian, 2019; Sezgin & Yilmaz, 2020).

The Persian Gulf islands are scattered along its northern and southern coastal areas. Many are made up of rocky outcrops and are uninhabitable due to harsh environmental conditions and limited access to fresh water. In some northern parts, small immigrant communities (mainly from India and Pakistan) have established permanent or semi-permanent settlements. The Iranian-administered islands in the Persian Gulf are officially included in the provinces of Hormozgan, Bushehr, and Khuzestan (Nadim, 2020; Al-Yahya et al., 2018; Paterson, 2009).

Iran maintains well-documented historical sovereignty over several strategically significant islands, most notably Abu Musa, Greater Tunb, and Lesser Tunb, located within the Strait of Hormuz at the entrance to the Persian Gulf. As a vital maritime pathway, the Strait of Hormuz connects the semi-enclosed Persian Gulf to the Indian Ocean and global trade networks through the Sea of Makran. Due to its exceptional geopolitical and economic significance, the strait has long served as a central conduit for energy transit and commercial exchange between the East and West. The Strait of Hormoz is approximately 100 nautical miles (185 km) long and it extends along the southern coastline of Iran toward the Musandam Peninsula in Oman, forming a geological depression bounded by Iran to the north and the Musandam Peninsula to the south (Al-Suwaidi, 1996; Ranjbar, 2019; Cordesman, 2020).

The islands under Iranian sovereignty along this coastal area are considered as geological continuation of the folding of the Zagros Mountains beneath the seabed or as a result of salt domes uplifts and tectonic movements. Following the south of Bandar Lengeh and Qeshm Island, Greater Tunb Island is located within an area of approximately 10.5 km^2, bordering Qeshm Island to the north, Bandar Lengeh to the northwest, Lesser Tunb to the west, and Abu Musa to the southwest. The Lesser Tunb, with an area of approximately 1.2 km^2, is located near the southeast of the Persian Gulf and borders Bandar Lengeh to the northwest, the Greater Tunb to the east, Farur Island to the west, Abu Musa to the southwest, and the western coast of Qeshm Island to the northeast. The geographical location, structural configuration, and geological continuity of these islands, along with their natural cohesion and proximity to the Iranian mainland, collectively demonstrate their enduring and inseparable connection with Iran. In accordance with the principles of territorial integrity and effective control, these islands constitute an inherent and enduring element of Iran's sovereign territory. Historical documents, cartographic evidence, and the uninterrupted exercise of state authority reaffirm that these islands have long served as an integral, inalienable, and inseparable part of Iran's territorial framework in the Persian Gulf (United Nations, 1992; Hessami et al., 2018).

The Iranian Island of Abu Musa (also known as Boumusa), situated at approximately 26°N latitude and 55°E longitude, encompasses an area of about 12 km^2. The channel between Abu Musa and the Tunb Islands constitutes the only navigable route for large oil tankers due to its favorable water depth. Abu Musa lies as the southernmost Iranian island in the Persian Gulf and the one closest to the equator. As one of three Iranian islands in the region, it forms part of Hormozgan Province under Iranian sovereignty and administration. The island's population consists predominantly of Iranian citizens.

2 The Iranian Island of Abu Musa and the Geopolitical Dynamics of the Persian Gulf

Abu Musa is an Iranian island located at approximately 26 degrees north latitude and 55 degrees east longitude, covering an area of approximately 12 km^2. Due to its favorable depth and navigation conditions, the sea corridor between Abu Musa and the Tunb Islands is the only deep-water route suitable for large oil tankers in the region. As the southernmost Iranian island in the Persian Gulf and the closest to the equator, Abu Musa is of significant strategic and economic importance for energy transportation and maritime security (Karimi, 2021).

Administratively, Abu Musa forms an integral part of Iran's Hormozgan Province and is under the full sovereignty and administration of the Iranian government. Historically, the island has served as a geopolitical stronghold, reinforcing Iran's presence along vital shipping lanes and supporting its broader maritime strategy in the Strait of Hormuz. This strategic waterway facilitates a significant share of the world's oil exports, making control of the surrounding islands a persistent geopolitical issue. Despite scattered foreign claims to sovereignty over Abu Musa, the island remains under Iranian rule and a predominantly Iranian population, demonstrating sustained Iranian jurisdiction and administrative continuity. The island is therefore an example of the intersection of geography, economics, and politics that defines the broader geopolitical landscape of the Persian Gulf, where access to energy corridors and sea routes remains a key determinant of regional power and influence (Rahimi & Daryaei, 2023; Azizi, 2020).

3 Abu Musa and the Tunbs from Ancient Times to the Present Day

The first references to the islands probably appear in classical antiquity. The fleet of the Greek admiral Nearchus, during the campaign of Alexander the Great in 325 BC, landed near an unnamed island believed to be the Great Tunb. Claudius Ptolemy's *Geographia* (second century AD) probably referred to the islands as Tabiana and other islands. They were part of the territory associated with the ancient Kingdom of Hormuz, which connected them to the trade networks of the Persian Gulf (Encyclopedia Iranica, 2024; Haghshenas, 2010; Ahmadi, 2008).

In the early Middle Ages, Persian historical accounts such as Ibn Balkhi's twelfth-century *Farsnameh* and the fourteenth-century geographer Hamdollah Mostofi's *Nuzhat al-Qulub* considered the Greater Tunb to be part of Persian territory. The islands are said to have been under the control of the kings of Hormuz from around the fourteenth century until the Portuguese conquest in 1507. The Safavid dynasty of Iran later expelled the Portuguese in 1622 and re-established its rule over the region, including the Tunbs and Abu Musa (Encyclopedia Iranica, 2024; Haghshenas, 2010; Ahmadi, 2008; Rastbeen, 2008).

4 Tribal and Regional Administration

During the eighteenth and nineteenth centuries, the islands were used seasonally for grazing and resources by coastal tribes on both sides of the Persian Gulf, leading to occasional disputes mediated by regional governors. The Qasemi tribe from the lower Persian Gulf made seasonal journeys to set up seasonal camps on the islands and competed with other coastal tribes of Iran for seasonal grazing of livestock (Encyclopedia Iranica, 2024; Ahmadi, 2008; Rastbeen, 2008).

The rise of the British Empire emerged in the nineteenth century and British political settlers in the 1830s arranged maritime peace agreements to restrict the movements of tribal warships between the islands of Abu Musa and Siri (Haghshenas, 2010; Ahmadi, 2008; Rastbeen, 2008).

5 The Twentieth Century and the Colonial Legacy

Throughout the twentieth century, especially under British rule, the administration of the islands was subject to competing claims without any historical basis. Iran had a historical legal sovereignty dating back to the ancient Persian empires. In contrast, some Arab rulers during the British protectorate period attempted to assert tribal sovereignty. The British withdrawal from the Persian Gulf region in 1971 exacerbated this dispute. On 30 November 1971, the Imperial Iranian Navy took full control of Abu Musa, the Greater Tunb, and the Lesser Tunb, continuing Iran's historical and legal sovereignty, and subsequently an emerging state, formed in December 1971, claimed the islands as part of its territory (Peace Palace Library, 2013; Ahmadi, 2008; Haghshenas, 2010; Rastbeen, 2008).

6 Iranian Sovereignty Over the Islands of Abu Musa, Greater Tunb, and Lesser Tunb

6.1 A Historical and Legal Study of Iran's Title

The Abu Musa, Greater Tunb, and Lesser Tunb islands are among the most strategically important territorial locations in the Persian Gulf. Located adjacent to the Strait of Hormuz, a vital maritime corridor for international trade and energy, the islands have been the subject of geopolitical attention and ongoing scholarly debate. It can be well argued that Iran's ownership of the Abu Musa and Tunb Islands is rooted in strong historical continuity and is legally confirmed by the doctrines of historical possession and effective occupation. Comparative international jurisprudence also supports Iran's sovereignty, emphasizing that legal ownership of a territory depends on effective and continuous sovereignty, not only on proximity or transitory presence. These islands play a key role in maritime sovereignty and global energy security and are therefore of high strategic and legal importance, as they are located near the Strait of Hormuz, a strait through which approximately one-fifth of the world's oil exports transit annually. Iran rightly insists on its enduring sovereignty over the islands, a sovereignty rooted in historical continuity, administrative evidence, and effective governance. The competing claims that emerged during the twentieth century were largely rooted in regional emerging states, political developments, and colonial legacies, and lacked any enduring administrative control (Schofield, 2016).

A genuine scholarly study must integrate historical and legal analyses to examine Iran's claim to these islands. By reconciling archaeological evidence and historical records with principles of public international law, this chapter demonstrates that Iran's sovereignty is consistent with both historical title and the criteria of effective occupation recognized in customary legal doctrine.

Early documents on the political geography of the Persian Gulf provide the basis for understanding territorial continuity. Lorimer's 1908 *Gazetteer of the Persian Gulf, Oman and Central Arabia*, meticulously records Iranian maritime administration throughout the various dynasties. Later historical and archaeological studies confirm Iranian presence and rule over the islands from the Achaemenid to the Safavid eras (Lorimer, 1908; Potts, 2016; Ansari, 2018).

Prominent and renowned jurists and legal scholars (such as Oppenheim, Shaw, and Crawford) have articulated principles governing territorial sovereignty, focusing on historical possession, effective occupation, and the peaceful demonstration of authority. These doctrines, illustrated in international law and jurisprudence such as *Island of Palmas* (1928) and *Sovereignty over Pedra Branca* (2008), consider sustained administrative control to be a privilege and a key determinant of sovereignty (Oppenheim, 2008; Shaw, 2017; Crawford, 2019).

Contemporary scholarship places these issues within the context of larger geopolitical developments and transformations. Scholars argue that British colonial influence reshaped local affiliations and often delegitimized tribal activities. The scholarly literature generally acknowledges the persistence of Iranian claims and the centrality of effective control in validating Iranian legal ownership (Schofield, 2016; Shayan, 2020).

This chapter adopts an interdisciplinary and qualitative approach that combines archaeological, historical, and legal sources, with three sets of evidence shaping the analysis:

1. Archaeological and historical documents, namely inscriptions, administrative documents, and maps from the Achaemenid, Sasanian, Safavid, and Qajar eras, confirm the authority of the Iranians.
2. The legal analyses of the doctrine, namely the principles of international law, historical possession, effective occupation, and consent, are applied to assess the legitimacy of Iranian sovereignty.
3. Comparative legal practices and precedents, i.e., case studies such as *Pedra Branca* (2008) and *Island of Palmas* (1928), are used to assess the compatibility of Iranian administrative acts with international norms.

This investigation considers and privileges tangible indicators of sovereignty, namely governance, defense, legal jurisdiction, and taxation, over ephemeral or symbolic measures, with the aim of providing a coherent alignment between established international law and empirical historical practices.

6.2 Historical Context and Territorial Continuity

Evidence from the Achaemenid and Sasanian periods places the islands entirely within the maritime realm of the Persian state. Royal inscriptions at Persepolis and Bisotun attest to imperial jurisdiction over the entire southern Gulf and its trade routes. The Safavid Empire re-established centralized control over these territories after expelling Portuguese forces in 1622. Safavid sources document administrative activities on the islands, including the collection of customs duties and the appointment of governors throughout the Hormuz region in which the islands are located (Potts, 2016; Ansari, 2018).

During the Qajar period, these islands functioned as subordinate parts of Bandar Lengeh, reinforcing the continued Iranian administration. Records of British correspondence in the nineteenth century acknowledge this arrangement. While the Qasemi tribes of Musandam traded in the waters of the islands, their activities lacked the administrative features necessary to establish sovereignty. The continuity of Iranian authority throughout successive dynasties confirms the historical chain of ownership under international law (Schofield, 2016).

6.3 Legal-Historical Analysis: International Law and Sovereignty

Iran's sovereignty satisfies the doctrinal requirements of both historical title and effective occupation. Under customary international law, the legitimacy of sovereignty depends on the continuous and peaceful exercise of state functions. The *Island of Palmas* Arbitration established the principle that actual administrative control takes precedence over mere discovery or temporary occupation (Crawford, 2019).

The presence of the Qasimi tribes in or around these islands never became an official jurisdiction. Their activities, pearl fishing and seasonal migration, were commercial in nature and did not represent political administration. Similarly, the British protectorate agreements concluded in 1820 did not legally include Abu Musa or the Tunbs. As a result, Iranian ownership remained intact (Oppenheim, 2008).

The 1971 Memorandum of Understanding between Iran and one of the Trucial States granted limited economic access to that Trucial State without prejudice or impairment to Iranian sovereignty. According to modern legal doctrine, such arrangements are cooperative, not sovereign, in nature and character. Iran's continued administrative presence and infrastructure development since 1971 reinforces its practical and legal, de facto and de jure control, ensuring effective occupation and a peaceful display of authority (Shaw, 2017; Khan, 2007; Dingley, 1978; Borden et al., 1965; Lathrop, 2008).

6.4 Contemporary Dimensions and Comparative Jurisprudence

The strategic value of the islands in the Strait of Hormuz highlights their dual importance for sovereignty and security. Periodic regional disputes over these islands often reflect broader political tensions rather than legitimate legal challenges (Shayan, 2020; Khan, 2007; Dingley, 1978; Borden et al., 1965; Lathrop, 2008).

A comparative analysis of the *Island of Palmas* (1928) and *Pedra Branca* (2008) cases confirms the primacy of effective control as a legal determinant of sovereignty. In both cases, international courts awarded sovereignty to the state and upheld continuous administration and non-dispute. Iran's exercise of authority is consistent with this doctrine.

The principle of legal sovereignty *uti possidetis juris* further substantiates Iran's claim, as it preserves the borders that existed under previous independent sovereignties. As the successor to the historical Iranian states that governed the islands, Iran's territorial integrity, in the absence of formal cession, is valid under this principle.

Iranian sovereignty over Abu Musa, the Greater Tunb, and the Lesser Tunb is supported by converging historical, legal, and administrative evidence. Archaeological data indicate ancient integration into Iranian maritime territory, while legal doctrine emphasizes that effective and peaceful rule constitutes legitimate sovereignty.

The competing claims lack evidence of continuity of administration, while Iran's historical title and current functions of government, defense, governance, and taxation meet the criteria of historical and effective sovereignty. Comparative international law and jurisprudence affirms that regional stability and the legitimacy of territorial ownership depend on the convergence of legal continuity and real-world reality-based administration.

In short, the Persian Gulf Islands case is an example of the enduring application of fundamental principles of international law. Sovereignty, when based on effective governance and historical ownership, remains the cornerstone of the legal order in a geopolitically sensitive maritime region.

The dispute over the sovereignty of the strategic and vital islands of Abu Musa, Greater Tunb, and Lesser Tunb in the Persian Gulf, which can still seem like a complex issue, can be further explored by examining the inherent weaknesses of such claims based on historical facts and international law, as well as by outlining opposing arguments, supported by historical and legal evidence, including key British archival documents. Such an analysis can highlight and clarify the status of these territories from the nineteenth century until the British withdrawal in 1971 and its implications for international adjudication.

It should also be noted that, as previously discussed, the islands of Abu Musa, Greater Tunb, and Lesser Tunb have long been the subject of territorial disputes, given their strategic location near the vital Strait of Hormuz. What is interesting about this situation is that the claims to sovereignty are based on a temporary and ephemeral or symbolic administration by local tribes and the heritage that could have been left by those local tribes, while Iran has historically held continuous ownership of the islands. Britain's colonial past and diplomatic actions during its withdrawal from the Persian Gulf in 1971 have also played a central role in such claims, and the complexities arising from British colonial-era agreements and subsequent geopolitical maneuvers that have shaped this dispute must also be examined (Al-Mazrouei, 2015).

6.5 Historical Context and British Archival Evidence

As previously noted, the claim to ownership of the islands is largely based on the heritage that could have been left by the Qasimi sheikhs who temporarily and ostensibly ruled the islands in the nineteenth century, and who were apparently under

Arab control and protected by the British through treaties such as the 1892 Exclusive Agreement. British archival documents show that Britain pretended to recognize the claim of one Trucial State to Abu Musa and the claim of another Trucial State to the Tunbs during their protectorate period, although these arrangements were ambiguous and often resulted from British strategic interests rather than a genuine and complete transfer of sovereignty (Al-Mazrouei, 2015; JSTOR, 2009).

However, British records also show that Iran held ownership of the islands and maintained a consular presence and authority, particularly after the fall of Lengeh in 1887 (the city of Bandar Lengeh, an important Iranian port on the northern coast of the Persian Gulf). The 1971 Memorandum of Understanding negotiated by Britain between Iran and one of the Trucial States over Abu Musa further complicates these claims, indicating that Iranian sovereignty over Abu Musa was recognized at the time, particularly given its long historical rule. Meanwhile, the lack of a formal written agreement between Britain and Iran over the Tunb Islands highlights Iran's unbroken and permanent historical sovereignty over these islands (Al-Mazrouei, 2015; Limbert, 2014).

7 The Most Damaging British Documents to Trucial States' Case

Declassified British diplomatic cables and confidential memos from 1971 show that British officials privately acknowledged Iran's intention to control the islands and had reached an agreement with the Iranian government on this matter even before the formal withdrawal from the Persian Gulf. This indicates a tacit acceptance, or at least acquiescence, to Iran's legitimate rights and refutes the claim that Britain recognized Qasemi sovereignty or an emerging state. Moreover, correspondence from Sir William Luce, the British colonial governor, shows that before the independence of the Sheikhdoms, secret agreements were made with the Iranian government to transfer control of the Greater and Lesser Tunbs, as well as Abu Musa. These records point to direct British negotiations with Iran rather than local rulers, and this calls into question the strength and international recognition of Qasemi's claims. Furthermore, the newly discovered British cables and documents show that key details of these secret transfers were shared with leaders of the Trucial States' founding government before the islands were occupied by Iranian forces. This suggests that the British and the leaders of the Trucial States' founding government were aware of this and did not formally challenge the British decision at that critical time (Al-Mazrouei, 2015; Al-Naqbi, 1998).

These documents damage the Trucial States' legal position because they reveal the Britain's evasion of supporting the claims of the Qasimis or the emerging state at the time sovereignty was to be transferred, and allow Iran to argue correctly that Britain did not recognize the Trucial States' rights to the islands. They also show that sovereignty was negotiated directly between Britain and Iran, not with the

Trucial States or its rulers, and refute the argument that legal ownership was transferred to the Trucial States in a unified manner under customary succession—*uti possidetis juris* (Al-Mazrouei, 2015; Al-Naqbi, 1998).

8 Weaknesses in Legal Claims Against Iranian Sovereignty

The claim of hereditary rule by the Qasemi sheikhs is fundamentally challenged by the fact that the Qasemi rulers at the relevant times were in fact and essentially Iranian subjects, residing on the Iranian coast and administering affairs from there. This undermines any possibility or prediction of a transfer or extrapolation of sovereignty to current emerging states. Furthermore, historical records from the British side show that the islands were traditionally considered to be under influential Iranian rule long before the emergence of the modern emerging states (Al-Mazrouei, 2015; JSTOR, 2009).

9 Absence of Effective Control

The principles of international law regarding territorial ownership emphasize effective control and continuous administration. These claims have been weakened by Iran's continued presence and administration of the islands, particularly since 1971, and reinforced by the failure of the emerging government to establish or maintain effective authority over the islands after the British withdrawal. The claimants' efforts to escalate the dispute through international bodies have always been met with Iran's refusal to accept or even consider third-party arbitration for claims that have no historical basis and lack historical and legal validity, which further demonstrates the weakness of the claimants' legal status (Al Roken, 2001; Al-Mazrouei, 2015; El-Sayed, 2003).

10 Britain's Role and Legal Legacy

However, whether due to strategic priorities or a coherent colonial legal order on sovereignty, or for any other reason, Britain had ceded sovereignty to Iran in the arrangements prior to the 1971 withdrawal (notably the Memorandum of Understanding with one of the Trucial States over Abu Musa), This specifically limits the Trucial States' arguments. The fact that the Trucial States inherited claims from sheikhs that had themselves accepted British trusteeship and tutelage adds a layer of complexity and impossibility to legal continuity and territorial succession (Al-Mazrouei, 2015).

11 Potential Iranian Counter-Arguments

Iran's position is firmly based on the continuity of sovereignty that dates back to successive Persian empires, uninterrupted administrative control, and explicit recognition of its claims in British documents. Iran insists, legally and factually, that the 1971 annexations were acts of restoration of long-standing rights, not the occupation of foreign territory. Iran also highlights the lack of a formal, definitive treaty transferring sovereignty to the Trucial States' predecessors (Al-Mazrouei, 2015; JSTOR, 2009; El-Sayed, 2003).

Iran's counterclaim also invokes the principle that territorial rights cannot be unilaterally undermined by external actors, such as British protectorate arrangements, particularly if such arrangements conflict with pre-existing sovereign rights. Iran challenges the Trucial States' claims to territorial independence and the authority of the Qasemi rulers, who were considered Iranian subjects or vassals during the disputed periods (El-Sayed, 2003; Al-Mazrouei, 2015).

12 Current Situation and Scholarly Suggestions: Legal History and Sovereignty

As previously detailed, the geological continuity, geographical configuration, and natural coherence of the three islands of Abu Musa, the Greater Tunb, and the Lesser Tunb, together with their geographical proximity to the Iranian mainland, collectively constitute a compelling body of evidence confirming their enduring and inherent connection with the territorial sovereignty of Iran. This conclusion is consistent with the established principles of international law, in particular the doctrines of territorial integrity and the principle of the rule of law, *uti possidetis juris*, as well as the requirement of the effective and continuous exercise of state authority. From a legal and factual perspective, these islands represent an undeniable and inherent component of Iran's sovereign territory. Historical mapping, coherent governance, and administrative measures further substantiate Iran's full ownership and legal rights under the principle of effective occupation. Collectively, these evidentiary elements demonstrate the indissoluble continuity of Iranian jurisdiction and, therefore, reaffirm the legal status of the islands as an integral part of Iran's territorial framework in the Persian Gulf, in accordance with the preservation of territorial integrity enshrined in Article 2(4) of the United Nations Charter (International Court of Justice, 1945; International Court of Justice [ICJ], 1986a, 1986b, 1986c, 1986d; Island of Palmas, 1928; Khan, 2007; Permanent Court of International Justice [PCIJ], 1933a, 1933b, 1933c, 1933d).

Therefore, and consequently, any legal claim by any country other than Iran to the islands of Abu Musa, Greater Tunb, and Lesser Tunb is refutable due to significant weaknesses and shortcomings, mainly centered on Iran's clear historical sovereignty, Iran's effective historical control, especially after the British withdrawal, and the ambiguous colonial-era agreements evident in British archives; especially given the fact that the claimants inherited claims from sheikhs who themselves accepted British trusteeship and guardianship. Meanwhile, Iran's claims to the right, supported by the persistence of documents, administrative control, and archival identification, present strong arguments and counterclaims that complicate the resolution of the dispute.

The current situation over the sovereignty of three Persian Gulf islands—Abu Musa, Greater Tunb, and Lesser Tunb—rooted in complex historical realities and exacerbated by significant geopolitical risks, underscores the urgent need for renewed diplomatic engagement based on careful historical and legal scrutiny. Contemporary scholarship situates this dispute within the context of broader geopolitical developments, emphasizing how British colonial interventions have altered local affiliations and often undermined the legitimacy of traditional tribal authorities, thereby further complicating postcolonial territorial claims. At the same time, scholarly consensus acknowledges the enduring nature of Iran's legitimate historical rights and highlights the central role of effective control and ongoing and sustained administration in strengthening legitimate sovereignty under international law. In this context, as many scholars have suggested, a prudent course of action requires the claimants to reconsider their weak positions in favor of a pragmatic approach that prioritizes regional stability and peace. International organizations and leading diplomatic actors are well positioned to facilitate this approach, foster dialogue, and create well-intentioned structured frameworks that offer a peaceful path to addressing this dispute based on facts and realities. By reducing geopolitical tensions and risks through such engagement, stakeholders can create conditions that lead to a peaceful settlement in the neighborhood and a sustainable arrangement for peaceful coexistence, thereby enhancing the imperatives of regional and global stability (El-Sayed, 2003; Al-Mazrouei, 2015; Shaw, 2017; Khan, 2007; Lathrop, 2008; Schofield, 1996, 2016; Shayan, 2020; Al-Naqbi, 1998; Petterson, 1992; Limbert, 2014; Hunter, 2010; Roken & Abdullah, 2001; Al-Nahyan, 2013; Kechichian, 1997; Eckert, 1997; Amirahmadi, 1996; Mirfendereski, 1997; Bavand, 1994; Mehr, 1997; Karami & Azizi, 2025; Morris, 2019; Zandieh et al., 2012; Jafari, 2015; Rossi, 2024; Mobley, 2003; Lolli, 2024; Mattair, 2025).

References

Ahmadi, K. (2008). *Islands and international politics in the Persian Gulf: The Abu Musa and Tunbs in strategic context*. Routledge.

Al-Mazrouei, N. S. (2015). Disputed Islands between UAE and Iran: Abu Musa, Greater Tunb, and Lesser Tunb in the Strait of Hormuz. *Gulf Research Centre Cambridge*, 1–32.

Al-Nahyan, K. S. (2013). *The Three Islands: Mapping the UAE-Iran Dispute*. Royal United Services Institute for Defense and Security Studies.

Al-Naqbi, Y. E. A. (1998). The sovereignty dispute over the Gulf Islands: Abu Musa, Greater and Lesser Tunbs (Doctoral dissertation, University of Glasgow).

Al Roken, M. A. (2001). Dimensions of the UAE-Iran Dispute over Three Islands. In *United Arab Emirates: A New Perspective* (p. 179). Trident Press.

Al-Suwaidi, J. (1996). *The Persian Gulf and the West.* Westview Press.

Al-Yahya, H., Al-Subhi, A., & Al-Rashidi, T. (2018). Coastal geomorphology and island formation in the Persian Gulf. *Arabian Journal of Geosciences, 11*(4), 103–121. https://doi.org/10.1007/s12517-018-3356-8

Amirahmadi, H. (1996). *Small Islands, Big Politics.* St. Martin's Press.

Ansari, A. (2018). *Iran and the Persian Gulf: Sovereignty and security in regional context.* Oxford University Press.

Azizi, M. (2020). *Geopolitical dimensions of Iran's sovereignty in the Persian Gulf.* Tehran University Press.

Bavand, D. H. (1994). The historical, political and legal bases of Iran's sovereignty over the islands of Tunb & [and] Abumusa Internet Concepts.

Borden, L. V., Luxford, A. F., Lyons, F. S. L., MacChesney, B., Macdonald, R., Radio, M., ... & Magaragevid, A. (1965). Madras-Mysore. Waters agreement, 1924. Arbitration under. CN 55 J 666 Madrid Convention on International Protection of Industrial Property. Decision of German Fed. Sup. Ct., 1959. JD 55 J. Rem, 106.

Cordesman, A. H. (2020). *Iran, Oil, and the Strait of Hormuz: The Strategic Challenges.* Center for Strategic and International Studies.

Crawford, J. (2019). *Brownlie's principles of public international law* (9th ed.). Oxford University Press.

Dingley, M. (1978). Eruptions in International Law: Emerging Volcanic Islands and the Law of Territorial Acquisition. *Cornell Int'l LJ, 11*, 121.

Eckert, A. (1997). Small Islands, Big Politics: The Tunbs and Abu Musa in the Persian Gulf. *Denver Journal of International Law & Policy, 25*(2), 14.

El-Sayed, C. M. (2003). *United Arab Emirates v. Iran: The dispute over the islands of Abu Musa, Greater Tunb, and Lesser Tunb.* American University of Beirut Scholar Works.

Encyclopedia Iranica. (2024, October 20). Tunb Islands. Retrieved from https://www.iranicaonline.org/articles/tonb/

Haghshenas, S. A. (2010). *Iran Historical Sovereignty over the Tunbs and BuMusa Islands.* Sena Publications.

Hessami, K., Jamali, F., & Tabassi, H. (2018). Geotectonic features of southern Iran with emphasis on the Zagros fold-thrust belt. *Journal of Geologic Research, 45*(2), 145–162.

Hunter, S. (Ed.). (2010). *Iran and the Gulf: Policy and dynamics in the Persian Gulf region.* Columbia University Press.

International Court of Justice. (1986a). Communiqué: Chamber of Court to hear Burkina Faso and Mali on possible indication of provisional measures. No. 86/1, January 6, 1986.

International Court of Justice. (1986b). Communiqué: Provisional measures are indicated in the case of the Frontier Dispute (Burkina Faso–Mali). No. 86/2, January 10, 1986.

International Court of Justice. (1986c). Communiqué: Frontier Dispute (Burkina Faso/Republic of Mali) judgment of the Chamber. No. 86/18, December 22, 1986.

International Court of Justice. (1986d). Reports of judgments, advisory opinion and orders, case concerning the Frontier Dispute (Burkina Faso/Republic of Mali). Judgment of December 22, 1986.

International Court of Justice. (1945). *Charter of the United Nations, together with the Statute of the International Court of Justice, Signed at the United Nations Conference on International Organization, San Francisco, California, June 26, 1945* (Vol. 2353). US Government Printing Office.

Jafari, V. A. (2015). The Historical and Legal Foundations of Iran's Sovereignty over Tunb and Abu-Musa Islands. file:///C:/Users/faghi/Downloads/1035820150206.pdf

JSTOR. (2009). The Tunbs and Abu Musa Islands: Britain's Perspective. JSTOR.

Karami, M., & Azizi, S. (2025). Book Review of Davoud Hermidas Bavand, Historical, Political, and Legal Foundations of Iran's Sovereignty over the Islands of Tunb and Abu Musa (Tehran: Ganj-e-Danesh Publication, 1998). *International Law Review*, e723392.

Karimi, S. (2021). Strategic islands of the Persian Gulf: A historical overview. *Journal of Iranian Maritime Studies, 14*(2), 45–67.

Kechichian, J. A. (1997). Small Islands, Big Politics: The Tunbs and Abu Musa in the Persian Gulf. *Middle East Policy, 5*(3), 209.

Kechichian, J. A. (2019). The strategic importance of the Persian Gulf islands in regional security. *Middle East Policy, 26*(2), 56–72. https://doi.org/10.1111/mepo.12420

Khan, D. E. (2007). Max Huber as Arbitrator: The Palmas (Miangas) Case and Other Arbitrations. *European Journal of International Law, 18*(1), 145–170.

Lathrop, C. G. (2008). Sovereignty over Pedra Branca/Pulau Batu Puteh, Middle Rocks and South Ledge (Malaysia/Singapore). *American Journal of International Law, 102*(4), 828–834.

Limbert, J. W. (2014). Iranian and Arab in the Gulf: Endangered Language, Windtowers.

Lolli, G. (2024). The Critical Date and the Dispute Over Islands in the Strait of Hormuz: Abu Musa and the Tunbs. SSRN.

Lorimer, J. G. (1908). *Gazetteer of the Persian Gulf, Oman and Central Arabia*. Government of India Press.

Mattair, T. (Referenced in Al-Mazrouei, 2025). Middle East Policy Council analysis on the UAE-Iran dispute.

Mehr, F. (1997). *A colonial legacy: the dispute over the islands of Abu Musa, and the Greater and Lesser Tumbs*. Bloomsbury Publishing PLC.

Mirfendereski, G. (1997). *A Colonial Legacy: The Dispute over the Islands of Abu Musa and the Greater and Lesser Tunbs*. University Press of America.

Mobley, R. A. (2003). The Tunbs and Abu Musa Islands: Britain's Perspective. *The Middle East Journal*, 627–645.

Morris, P. S. (2019). The Iran–UAE Gulf Islands dispute: a journey through international law, history and politics

Nadim, F. (2020). Geopolitical structure and administrative divisions of Iran's coastal provinces. *Iranian Journal of Geopolitics, 16*(3), 27–45.

Oppenheim, L. (2008). *Oppenheim's international law* (9th ed.). Longman.

Peace Palace Library. (2013, October 3). Unresolved territorial disputes: The Tunbs and Abu Musa in the Gulf. Retrieved from https://peacepalacelibrary.nl/blog/2013/unresolved-territorial-disputes-tunbs-and-abu-musa-gulf

Permanent Court of International Justice (PCIJ). (1933a). *Series A/B (Collection of judgments, orders and advisory opinions), No. 53, Legal status of Eastern Greenland*. A.W. Sijothoff.

Permanent Court of International Justice (PCIJ). (1933b). *Series C (Pleadings, oral statements and documents), No. 62, Legal status of Eastern Greenland*. A.W. Sijothoff.

Permanent Court of International Justice (PCIJ). (1933c). *Series C (Pleadings, oral statements and documents), No. 64, Legal status of Eastern Greenland*. A.W. Sijothoff.

Permanent Court of International Justice (PCIJ). (1933d). *Series C (Pleadings, oral statements and documents), No. 65, Legal status of Eastern Greenland*. A.W. Sijothoff.

Peterson, J. E. (2009). Migrant communities and social structures along the Persian Gulf coast. *The Middle East Journal, 63*(3), 383–400. https://doi.org/10.3751/63.3.15

Petterson, R. B. (1992). *Middle Eastern Strategic Affairs: The Gulf Islands Dispute*. Hurst & Company.

Potts, D. T. (2016). *The archaeology of Elam and the Achaemenids*. Cambridge University Press.

Rahimi, N., & Daryaei, H. (2023). Maritime security and territorial integrity in the Persian Gulf region. *Iranian Review of International Relations, 18*(1), 89–112.

Ranjbar, M. (2019). Iran's Historical Claims over the Tunb and Abu Musa Islands. *Iranian Review of Foreign Affairs, 10*(1), 33–57.

Rastbeen, A. (Ed.). (2008). *The Three Iranian Islands of the Persian Gulf: Based on documents and historical evidence*. Institut International d'Etudes Stratégiques.

Roken, A., & Abdullah, M. (2001). Dimensions of the UAE-Iran Dispute over Three Island. In I. Al Abed & P. Hellyer (Eds.), *United Arab Emirates: A new perspective*. Trident Press.
Rossi, C. R. (2024). The Critical Date and the Dispute over Islands in the Strait of Hormuz: Abu Musa and the Tunbs. *Or. Rev. Int'l L, 25*, 1.
Schofield, R. (2016). *Boundaries and territorial disputes in the Gulf.* I. B. Tauris.
Schofield, R. N. (1996). The Tunbs and Abu Musa Islands: Britain's Perspective. *Journal of Arabian Studies*. JSTOR.
Sezgin, S., & Yilmaz, S. (2020). Hydrographical characteristics and environmental dynamics of the Persian Gulf. *Oceanologia, 62*(2), 167–182. https://doi.org/10.1016/j.oceano.2019.11.004
Shaw, M. N. (2017). *International law* (8th ed.). Cambridge University Press.
Shayan, H. (2020). *Maritime boundaries and sovereignty in the Persian Gulf.* Routledge.
United Nations. (1992). *The Law of the Sea: Maritime claims and boundaries in the Persian Gulf.* United Nations Publications.
Zandieh, H., Esmaeli, M., & Ghasemian, S. (2012). The creation process of three islands question. *Iranian Studies, 1*(1), 95–118.

On a Historical Toponym of Qeshm, the Largest Island in the Persian Gulf

S. Abolghasem Foroozani

Abstract This chapter presents a study on one of the names of Qeshm, the largest island in the Persian Gulf, strategically located in the Strait Hormuz. It shows that Qeshm Island has been known by different names throughout history. Greek, Iranian, and Arab historians, geographers, and travelers, as well as orientalists, have called Qeshm Island by different names. This chapter examines and analyzes the word Abarkavan, as the name used for this island, considering the economic geography and vegetation of Qeshm Island.

Keywords Qeshm · Orakta · Long Island · Laft · Abarkavan · Strait Hormuz

What has been investigated in this chapter is a name that has not attracted much attention among the various names of Adak Qeshm (Qeshm Island). Accordingly, perhaps the author's study regarding the questioned name will be noteworthy, considering the documents and reasons that will be presented, subsequently. It is necessary to explain that the author of *Farsnameh Naseri*, during whose time (the Qajar era) Qeshm Island was a part of the Greater Fars Province, in a part of his book dedicated to the islands in the Persian Gulf quotes: "the island is called Adak in Persia, and it is a place in the sea where the surrounding water surrounds it" (Hosseini Fasaee, p. 315). However, Keshm (Kesm) is the oldest name for Qeshm Island, dating back to the Achaemenid era (Nourbakhsh, 1369, pp. 114–115).

Qeshm[1] is the largest island in the Persian Gulf, with the length of 115 km and the width of 10 to 35 km in different areas and a circumference of about 262 km (Eqtedari, 1357, pp. 749–750). It is located near the mouth of the Strait of Hormuz

[1] Qeshm has various meanings, among which "Ab raheh" (water-way) seems to be the most valid (Dehkhoda, 1373, p. 15517).

S. A. Foroozani (✉)
Professor of History, Shiraz University, Shiraz, Iran

N. Faghih et al. (eds.), *The Persian Gulf and Islands*, Perspectives on Development in the Middle East and North Africa (MENA) Region,
https://doi.org/10.1007/978-3-032-27910-1_3

(Hormuz = Ormuz),[2] which connects the Persian Gulf to the Gulf of Hormuz (Etemad al-Saltaneh, 1367, p. 319). Uniquely, Qeshm Island has been called by various names in resources and references throughout the history, so much so that Hossein Nourbakhsh has dedicated a chapter to the names of this island in his valuable work entitled *Jazire Qeshm va Khalij Fars [Qeshm Island and The Persian Gulf]* (1369, pp. 111–127).

Qeshm's privileged geographical location has made this island worthy of great importance not only in the commercial arena, but also in military, political, and social fields. Hence undoubtedly, an awareness over the various names of Qeshm Island along with a detailed study and understanding of the reasons for these names will reveal many important events and untold issues that have occurred on this island in various contexts throughout the history. The author of the current study considers it necessary to have a primarily brief look at the various names of Qeshm Island in different periods, referring to the reliable geographical and historical sources, and then present his intended topic.

Since the silvery waters of the Persian Gulf surround Qeshm Island like a precious jewel, it is necessary to first talk about the Persian Gulf, though briefly. Strabo, a Greek geographer and historian who was born in the year 50 BC (Etemad al-Saltaneh, 1363, 125), has referred to the Persian Gulf as Persicon Kai Tas (Beik Mohammadi, 1377, p. 168). Ptolemy, a great geographer and astronomer of the second century AD (Etemad al-Saltaneh, 1363, pp. 130–131), called the Persian Gulf, Sinus Persicus, which conveys the same meaning as the Persian Gulf (Beik Mohammadi, 1377, p. 168). The Greek historian Quintus Curtius Fus, called the Persian Gulf in Latin Aquarium Persico (Belgrave, 1369, p. 23).

Later, the English called the Persian Gulf "Persian Gulf," the French "Gulf Persique," the Germans "Persischer Golf," the Italians "Golf Persico," and the Russians "Persidaki Zalic" (Beik Mohammadi, 1377, p. 168). All of the above-mentioned titles convey the undeniable reality from the foreigners' language. But most interesting of all these, are the words of Darius I the Achaemenid, who mentioned the Persian Gulf with the phrase "Darya Tiyeh Hacha Parsa IT" (the sea that passes through Persia) on an inscription that is now 23 km from the Suez Canal (in Egypt) (Shahidi, 1365, p. 174), several hundred years before Strabo and Ptolemy (Belgrave, 1369, p. 23).

Deploying his war fleet in the Persian Gulf, Darius I established the Achaemenid dominance over this important water expanse. During the Parthian era, ships belonging to that government sailed from the Persian Gulf, which was entirely under the control of the Iranian state, to the island of Ceylon. And finally, the Sassanid reign, who were unrivaled in dominating the Persian Sea. Ardashir Babakan founded the city of Hormuz in the north of the Strait of Hormuz. Also, during the time of Anoushirvan the Sassanid, the Persian Sea was the house to the great Iranian naval fleet (Beik Mohammadi, 1377, p. 174).

After the advent of Islam and the establishment of the Islamic Caliphate, the Persian Sea retained its name as Bahr (Arabic equivalent of the Sea) Fars (Arabic

[2] More information (Etemad al-Saltaneh, 1367, pp. 304–313). According to the writings of Mohammad Hassan Khan Etemad al-Saltaneh, "In ancient times, the shores near the sea were called Harmosia" (Etemad al-Saltaneh, 1363, p. 111).

Pars). This is how all of the most famous Iranian and Arab geographers who lived in the third and fourth centuries A.H. have called the mentioned sea by its original name Fars (Pars) in their works (Foroozani, 1384, pp. 17–28). Also, in the Arabic translation of the English geographical work by Le Strange *Joqrafiay-e Tarikhi Sarzamin haye Khelafat Sharqi [Historical Geography of the Eastern Caliphate Lands]*, the Persian Sea was translated into Arabic as al-Khalij al-Farsi (Beik Mohammadi, 1377, p.169). The author of the current study has also specified the boundaries of the Persian Sea in the book chapter "The Expanse of the Persian Sea..." referring to the geographical and historical sources related to the third and fourth centuries A.H. (Foroozani, 1384, pp. 17–28).

Now we will narrow the scope of the study to Qeshm Island. According to the writings of Sir Percy Sykes, Qeshm was first mentioned in the writings of Aryan among historical sources (Sykes, 1363, p. 314). Aryan (Aryan) was a great Greek historian and philosopher who was born in 105 AD (Etemad al-Saltaneh, 1363, pp. 121–122). Aryan spoke about Qeshm Island using the travelogue of Nearchus (the Alexander the Great's general) (Nourbakhsh, 1369, p. 116). While quoting from Nearchus about Qeshm in Aryan's writing, it is mentioned that "Qeshm has an abundance of vines, palm trees, and grains" (Sykes, 1363, p. 314). It worth noting that the Greeks called Qeshm as Uarakta[3] (Etemad al-Saltaneh, 1367, p. 468). According to Abbas Anjam rouz, during the Achaemenid era, Qeshm was called Kesm (Keshm), and Qeshm is undoubtedly an Arabization (Nourbakhsh, 1369, pp. 114–115).

Among the sources that were written after the advent of Islam, the book *Selselat al-Tavaarikh (Akhbar al-Sin va al-Hend) [Historical Series: The News of the China & India]* should be pointed out, which contains the journey memoirs of the merchant Soleiman Sirafi. He traveled to China from Bandar Siraf (present-day Bandar-e Taheri (Taheri Port) in Bushehr province) and provided extensive information about China and India in a travelogue he wrote in 237 A.H. Sixty-five years later, one of Soleiman's fellow citizens, Abu Zeid Hassan Sirafi, rewrote and added to Soleiman's writings the aforementioned travelogue with the information he obtained from Ibn Vahab Qoreyshi about China.

Concerning the book *Akhbar al-Sin va al-Hend*, which is also known as the *Selselat al-Tavaarikh*, Hossein Qarchanlou asserts: "it seems that the name Akhbar al-Sin va al-Hend was given by Abu Zeid Hassan Sirafi after adding the contents of Ibn Vahb to the writings of Soleiman" (Sirafi, 1381, pp. 14–15). Qeshm Island is named as the Island of Ibn Kavan and Bani Kavan in the mentioned book (Sirafi, 1381, pp. 57–61). Ibn Khordadbeh, whose book *Al-Masaalek al-Mamaalek*, is one of the first geographical works related to the third century A.H. (Nafisi, 1367, pp. 31–32) has called Qeshm island by the name of Ibn Kavan, too (Ibn Khordadbeh, 1370, p. 47). However, in the book *Fotouh al-Boldan* written by Ahmad Ibn Yahya

[3]According to Hossein Nourbakhsh, the Sahab Cartographic Institute has recorded Qeshm Island as Oaracta on a map belonging to the Achaemenid era (1369, p. 116).

Ismail Raeen has mentioned Arachna, the name that the Greek used for the island of Qeshm (Nourbakhsh, 1369, p. 116).

Baladhari (died 279 A.H.),[4] Qeshm Island is mentioned as Abar Kavan. In *Fotouh al-Boldan*, Abar Kavan Island is considered one of the islands related to the district of Ardashir-Khorra (one of the five districts of the Greater Fars Province) (Balazari, 1346, p. 257). The great geographer of the fourth century, Estakhari, who supposedly wrote his book *Al-Masaalek va al-Mamaalek* in the years 318–321 A.H. (Nafisi, 1367, p. 37), has quoted the Qeshm Island by two names, Laft or Bani-Kavan, stating that "in the heart of this sea, which we have attributed to Persia, there are islands" (Estakhri al-Farsi, 1340, p. 35). He has also considered the mentioned island to be among the islands located in the Persian Sea, while being associated with the hearth of Ardashir-Khorra (Estakhri al-Farsi, 1340, pp. 107–108). As it can be seen, the name Laft appears for the first time in Estakhari's work.

Abu al-Hasan Ali Masoudi (died 345 A.H.) also mentioned Laft or Bani Kavan in his work, *Morooj al-dhahab* as an island that "has many people, villages, and settlements" (Masoudi, 1365, p. 108). The author of the book *Ashkal Al-Alam* in the fourth century A.H has listed Laft Island among the islands located in the Persian Sea and has used both of the names Bani Kavan and Laft for Qeshm Island in part of his work (Jeyhani, 1368, pp. 57–110). Ibn Huqal, in his book *Surat al-Arz*, written around 367 A.H., called Qeshm Island by the names Barkavan and Laft (Ibn Huqal, 1345, p. 37).

In the first available geographical work in Persian, the book *Hodoud al-Alam Men al-Mashreq Ilal- Maqreb*, written in 372 A.H., Qeshm Island has been mentioned as Laft Island, about which it is noted: "there is a beautiful city inside it, they call it Laft, and inside it [there] is a plantation and many blessings, and good waters, and people from all over the world go there for trade, and this island is located in front of Persia" (Minorsky, 1372, pp. 111–112). However, in the book *Ahsan al-Taghasim fi Maerefate al-Aghalim*, written in 375 A.H., Maqdasi has listed fifteen cities and islands that were located within the Siraf area (which itself was a city in the Ardashir Khorrah region), and he has mentioned one of them as Ras Keshm (1361, pp. 74–75). He considered Ras Keshm, which is the same city of Qeshm (and not Qeshm Island), to be a small city where there was a large market and a mosque (Maqdasi, 1906, p. 427).

Ibn Balkhi, whose book *Farsnameh Ibn Balkhi* is said to have been completed in the first decade of the sixth century A.H. (1374, p. 20), has spoken of the island of Qeshm with the name of Bani Kavan (Ibn Balkhi, 1374, p. 272). Mohammad Najib Bakran, in his *Jahan Nameh*, written in 605 A.H., has called the island of Qeshm under the names of Laft and Kavan (1342, p. 20 & 43). Yaqut Homavi (d. 626 A.H.) has used the names of Laft and Bani Kavan for the island of Qeshm in his book *Mojam al-Boldan* (1955, p. 7). In his geographical work called *Nuzhat al-Qulub*, Hamdollah Mostowfi (d. 750 A.H.) has pointed out to the island of Qeshm under the name of Abarkafan and estimated its area to be eight by three miles (1362, pp. 137, 186, 234).

[4] *Fotouh al-Boldan*'s date of writing has been around 255 A.H. (Nafisi, 1367, pp. 33–34)

Ibn Batouteh (d. 779 A.H.) has called on another island named Kesh after mentioning the island of Kish, which is probably the same as Keshm or Qeshm, in his travelogue (1363, p. 691). Hafez Abru (d. 833 A.H.) has referred to the island of Qeshm as Lafth in a book he wrote on geography (1375, p. 240). In 1031 A.H. and by order of Shah Abbas I of the Safavid dynasty (996–1038 A.H.), Imam Qoli Khan, the ruler of Persia, was commissioned to expel the invading Portuguese from some ports and islands in the Persian Gulf. He fulfilled his duties with competence, including taking back the island of Qeshm from the invading Portuguese. The story of this victory has been narrated by a poet named Ghadri [Qadri] in 1032 A.H through an epic poem called Jangnameh Keshm (Safa, 1356, pp. 765–766).

In his book *Jam-e-Jam,* Farhad Mirza Motamed al-Dawlah (died 1305 A.H.) has listed Qeshm Island among the famous islands located in the Persian Sea, writing: "because it is long, it is known as the Long Island" (Sadid al-Saltaneh Kababi, 1368, p. 310). Mohammad Hassan Khan Etemad al-Saltaneh (died 1313 A.H.) has also mentioned Qeshm Island under the name Ba sa'ed., in his book *Mera'at al-Boldan*. It is necessary to explain that he meant the same port as Ba Saeedu, which is located on the northwestern tip of Qeshm Island (1367, p. 300). After mentioning that Qeshm Island is one of the famous islands in the Persian Gulf and it is located at the mouth of the Strait of Hormuz toward Iranian territory, Etemad al-Saltaneh notes: "the largest settlement on this island is the city of Qeshm, which has a population of four thousand people" (Nourbakhsh, 1369, pp. 109, 200). While asserting that Qeshm is the largest island in the Persian Sea, Mirza Hassan Hosseini Fasaee (d. 1316 A.H.), the author of *Farsnameh Naseri*, has called that island by the names of Qeshm, Jazireh Deraz, and Jazireh Tavil (pp. 315–316). In his book *E'elam al-Nas fi Ahval Bandr Abbas (Bandr Abbas va Khalij-e Fars),* Sadid al-Saltaneh (d. 1362 A.H.), after quoting that the author of *Nukhbat al-Dahr* that the island of Yafth is known as the island of Bani Kafan, writes: "the islands of Kavan, Yafth, Bani Kafan, and Laft are the current island of Qeshm" (1368, p. 98).

Guy Le Strange, a famous English researcher (died 1933), has used the name Abarkaman for the mentioned island, while referring to some of the other names for Qeshm Island (1364, p. 282). Also, according to the documentary view of Ahmad Eqtedari, the name Lar should be added to the list of Qeshm Island names (Nourbakhsh, 1369, pp. 116–118). Finally, in the work of Hossein Nourbakhsh, the name Bourkht Island is mentioned along with other names of Qeshm Island (1369, p. 111). It is necessary to explain that in one of the settlements of Qeshm Island, called Qaryeh Koshe, there is a mosque that was founded in 244 A.H. and it is known as the Borkh Mosque. Outside the mentioned mosque, there is an old tomb that is known as the burial place of Borkh Aswad, famous as Johar, who was one of the saints of Allah and endowed with a miraculous power.[5] Accordingly, Qeshm Island is also called Borkht Island in honor of the Borkh Aswad.

---

[5] More information about Borkh Aswad Mosque and Cemetery (Eqtedari, 1357, pp. 749–801)

Isa Moniri believes that "Iranians before Islam called this island Barkht and..." (Nourbakhsh, 1369, p. 113)

As understood, among the various names of Qeshm Island (= Keshm, Kesm) in the geographical and historical sources and references, the names Ibn Kavan (= Banikavan, Banikafan, Barkavan, Abarkavan, Abarkafan, Kavan) and Laft (= Lafth, Yafth) have been used the most. Regarding the application of the name Laft to Qeshm Island, it should be said that Laft, which is a town, port, and anchorage on Qeshm Island, apparently had more prosperity and prestige than other settlements on that island and had been more recognized as the center of the island in the past (Eqtedari, 1357, p. 767). Sadid al-Saltaneh believes that during the times when Laft was the capital of Qeshm, "the island became known as the center of its government" (1368, pp. 98–99). According to Ahmad Eqtedari, Laft's proximity to the Larestan coast, especially to the current Bandar-e Pol [Pol Port], which is located on the northern coast of the Persian Gulf on the shore of Bandar-e Khamir [Khamir Port], and the existence of short and shallow water passages that facilitated commuting from the northern coast of the Persian Gulf to Laft through the sea, were among the factors that made Laft famous as the most important port and anchorage on Qeshm Island (1357, pp. 767–768).

Regarding Laft status in his time, Sadid al-Saltaneh writes: "Laft is a village located on the slopes of a mountain and it is on the seashore on the northern coast of the island." However, a few lines later, he explains something that indicates the settlement and prosperity of Laft in the past. Sadid al-Saltaneh notes: "the mountain on the slopes of which Laft village is located is known as the Mountain of the City, and this name indicates the ancient city of Laft, and to the east of that mountain are the remaining of the ancient city" Sadid al-Saltaneh Kababi, 1368, p. 99). The remains of a pier in Laft port, which is 130 meters long and dates back to the ancient Iranian era, indicate the antiquity of Laft as a commercial port (Minorsky, 1372, pp. 111–112). Also, the author of *Hodoud al-Alam Men al-Mashreq Ilal- Maqreb's* statement about Laft that "people from all over the world went there to trade" (Al-Hosseini, p. 320) is indicative of Laft's privileged commercial position in the fourth century A.H.

However, concerning the name Kavan, there is something thought-provoking in the book *Taj al-Aroos Min Javaher al-Qamoos*. The author of the quoted name has changed the letter "k" in the word Kavan to "g" and considered the letters "alif" and "nun" to be plural and has written the Arabic equivalent of the word "gavan" as "abqar" (plural of "baqar" meaning "cow")[6] (Schwartz, 1372, p. 117). German researcher Paul Schwatz states that "this expression was first used by a later lexicographer, but it seems to be old," and by citing evidence from Tabari's history, he agrees with the author of *Taj al-Aroos Min Javaher al-Qamoos* and considers Qeshm Island to be "Gavan Island" (meaning a place to keep and raise cows) (Sadid al-Saltaneh Kababi, 1368, pp. 701–702). Correspondingly, the author of the current study has sought to find more documented evidence.

[6] Schwartz refers to Tabari, quoting: "one of the generals in Khorasan, reproaches his soldiers in a fit of anger and says that before entering military service on the island of Ibn Kavan, they used to ride on oxen and donkeys, and only with his help did they changed into active warriors" (1372, p. 117).

According to the writings of Sadid al-Saltaneh, in his time the people of Basaeedu village had fifty cows, while they had only twenty-five donkeys and forty sheep and goats. After explaining the livelihood of the people of Bandar Laft on Qeshm Island, he also asserts: "their livestock consists of cattle, camels, sheep, and goats" (Sadid al-Saltaneh Kababi, 1368, p. 703). As it can be seen, Sadid al-Saltaneh mentions cattle prior to other livestock in Bandar Laft. Besides indicating the importance of the animal in question, this most likely indicates the significant number of cattle in Laft.

In the statistics provided by Hossein Nourbakhsh regarding the number of livestock on Qeshm Island in 1358 A.H., the number of dairy cows, working cows and calves was 1450 in total, while goats and kids were 600 to 700, and camels were about two hundred (Nourbakhsh, 1369, p. 83). However, in the statistics of the year 1365 A.H., we are faced with a different reality. Thus, in the mentioned year, there were 1517 cows and calves, 16,270 goats and kids, and 534 sheep and lambs on Qeshm Island. This ratio changed significantly 3 years later (i.e., in 1368 AH). This means that, while the number of cows and calves on Qeshm Island was 3250, the number of goats and kid goats increased to 45,000, the number of sheep to 5000, and the number of camels to 3100 in the mentioned year (Nourbakhsh, 1369, p. 83).

Hence, it can be perceived that the number of cows and calves in Qeshm Island is decreasing compared to other livestock. By realizing that the number of cows and sheep in Qeshm Island has decreased significantly compared to other livestock in about 20 years, it can be concluded that in the past, cows and calves living on Qeshm Island had a significant number. It should not be forgotten that the presence of Harra forests [Mangrove forests] in the Qeshm region, "the branches and leaves of which are mostly used as fodder for livestock, especially cows and camels," and currently local livestock farmers provide 50% of the fodder needed by their livestock from the leaves of Harra shrubs[7] (Nourbakhsh, 1369, p. 75), was also an important factor in the prosperity of livestock farming in the past. Fortunately, the Mangrove forests are not vulnerable, and cutting the branches of Hara trees not only does not harm them, but it also makes those trees greener and more vigorous (Nourbakhsh, 1369, pp. 75–77). Likewise, the cultivation of aquaculture oat in some villages of Qeshm Island and the rain fed cultivation of oat (Nourbakhsh, 1369, pp. 456–457), in most parts of the island for livestock consumption, are also effective factors in the spread of livestock farming in Qeshm.

Correspondingly, it can be said that in the first place, Qeshm Island has enjoyed a better position for livestock farming than other islands in the Persian Gulf, due to the suitable vegetation cover for the livestock. In the second stage, it should be said that cattle breeding has been more common in Qeshm than the other livestock. Now, attention will be paid to another issue that is not ineffective in reaching the desired result of this study. In the previous pages, it was said that Qeshm Island was titled Deraz (Long) because of its appearance. This title has sometimes been used in some

[7] According to Hossein Nourbakhsh, the occupation of many people in Qeshm is to cut the branches of Harra (Mangrove) trees and sell them to local livestock farmers (Nourbakhsh, 1369, p. 77).

sources instead of the name of the island. What is added here is that of the five villages of Qeshm Island, one is famous for its name Ramkan (a compound of the two words Rameh and Kan), meaning the place where the flocks (sheep and goats) are kept, and one of the eighteen villages of Ramkan Village is called Gorbeh-Dan (perhaps because of the presence of many cats there) [Gorbeh is the Farsi equivalent of the word Cat] (Nourbakhsh, 1369, p.191). Also, one of the villages located in the Salakh district on Qeshm Island is famous as Guran. And we know that even in the present time, there are deer and wild goats and ... on Qeshm Island and the hunters there have many memories of their hunts in the past. The hunting attraction on Qeshm Island has even caused hunters from the sheikhdoms to enter the mentioned island and this has led to a decrease in the number of animals in Qeshm (Nourbakhsh, 1369, pp. 195–196, 82).

Therefore, it is very likely that the presence of cows, which were a suitable hunting ground for hunters, in the rural area of Salakh village led to the name of the place as Guran. We know that in the names of cities such as Gavbandi (in Hormozgan province) and the names of villages such as Gav Zard and Gav Sepid (near Genaveh in Bushehr province), the name of cows, which was very likely abundant in the mentioned areas, is used. Considering the previously mentioned information, is it not possible to raise the possibility that the significant number of cows in Qeshm became the basis for naming the island and thus Qeshm Island became known as Gavan (the place of raising cows)? Also, did not the special robustness of the cows of Qeshm Island, which as noted were fed with the branches and leaves of the moor and on the barley available there, lead to the name of their habitat as Abargavan (= large cows)?

References

Balazari, A. b. Y. (1346). *Fotouh al-Boldan [Conquest of the Worlds (part related to Iran)] (A. Azarnoush, Trans).* Bonyad Farhang Iran Publication.

Beik Mohammadi, H. (1377). *Moqadamei bar Joqrafiaye Tarikhi Iran [An Introduction on Historical Geography of Iran].* Isfahan University Press.

Belgrave, S. C. (1369). *Loch's Sea Voyage* (H. Zolqadr, Trans.). Anahita Publication.

Dehkhoda, A. A. (1373). In M. Moein & S. J. Shahidi (Eds.), *Loqat Nameh [Dictionary].* Tehran University Press.

Eqtedari, A. (1357). *Asar-e Shahr haye Bastani Savahel va Jazayer Khalije Fars va Daryaye Oman [The remains of ancient cities on the coasts and islands of the Persian Gulf and the Sea of Oman]* (Vol. 2). Anjoman Asar Melli va Mafakher Farhangi Publication.

Estakhri al-Farsi, A. E. (1340). In I. Afshar (Ed.), *Masaalek va Mamaalek [The Routes and the Kingdoms].* Bongah Tarjomeh va Nashr Ketab.

Etemad al-Saltaneh, M. H. (1363). In M. H. Mohades (Ed.), *Tatbiq-e Loqat Joqrafiaei Qadim va Jadid Iran [Matching old and new geographical terms of Iran].* Amirkabir Publication.

Etemad al-Saltaneh, M. H. (1367). In A. H. Navaee & M. H. Mohades (Eds.), *Mera'at al-Boldan [Mirror of countries].* Tehran University Press.

Foroozani, S. A. (1384). Gostareh Daryaye Pars [The Expanse of the Persian Sea]. *The Persian Gulf Research Journal, 8*(88-89), 17–28.

Ibn Balkhi. (1374). In M. Rastegar Fasaee (Ed.), *Farsnameh Ibn Balkhi*. Bonyad Fars Shenasi Publication.

Ibn Huqal, (1345). Surat al-Arz [The Earth Shape] (J. Sho'ar, Trans.). Bonyad Farhang Iran Publication.

Ibn Khordadbeh (1370). *Al-Masaalek al-Mamaalek* (H. Qarchanlou, Trans)

Jeyhani, A. A. (1368). Ashkal Al-Alam [The World's Images] (A. A. S. Kateb, Trans.). Beh Nashr Publishing Company and Astan Qods Razavi Publications.

Maqdasi, A. A. M. b. A. B. (1906). *Ahsan al-Taghasim fi Maerefate al-Aghalim [The Best Classification in Recognizing Countries]* (2nd ed.). Brill Publication.

Masoudi, A. A. b. H. (1365). *Morooj al-dhahab [Golden Meadow] (Abulghasem Payandeh Trans.)* (Vol. 2). Elmi va Farhangi Publication.

Minorsky, V. (Ed.). (1372). *Hodoud al-Alam Men al-Mashreq Ilal-Maqreb [The Borders of the World from the East to the West] (*Mirhossein Shaah, Trans.). (M. Mirahmadi & Gh. Varham, Eds.). Al-Zahra University Publication.

Nafisi, A. (1367). Khadamat-e Mosalmanan be Joqrafia [Muslim Contributions to Geography] (H. Lahouti, Trans.). Bonyad Pazhoohesh haye Eslami Astan Qods Razavi Publication.

Nourbakhsh, H. (1369). *Jazire Qeshm va Khalij Fars [Qeshm Island and The Persian Gulf]*. Amirkabir Publication.

Sadid al-Saltaneh Kababi, M. A. (1368). *E'elam al-Nas fi Ahval Bandr Abbas (Bandr Abbas va Khalij-e Fars) [Public Announcement about Bandar Abbas (Bandar Abbas and the Persian Gulf)]*. Donyaye Ketab Publication.

Safa, Z. A. (1356). *Kholaseh Tarikh Siyasi va Ejtemaee va Farhangi Iran (Az Aqaz ta Payan Ahd Safavi) [The Summary of the Political and Social and Cultural History of Iran (from the beginning to the end of the Safavid era)]*. Amirkabir Publication.

Schwartz, P. (1372). Joqrafiaye Tarikhi Fars [Fars Historical Geography] (K. Jahandari, Trans.). Anjoman Asar-e Melli va Mafakher Farhangi Publication.

Shahidi, H. (1365). *Charsoo va Negareshi Kootah ba Tarikh va Joqrafiaye Tarikhi [Four Directions and a Brief Perspective on History and Historical Geography]*. Amirkabir Publication.

Sirafi, S. (1381). In A. H. Sirafi (Ed.), (H. Qarchanlou, Trans.). *Selselat al-Tavaarikh (Akhbar al-Sin va al-Hend) [Historical Series: The News of the China & India]*. Asatir Publication.

Sykes, S. P. (1363). Safarnameh [Travelogue (Ten Thousand Miles in Iran)] (H. Sa'adat Nouri, Trans.). Loheh Publication.

Geopolitics and Geo-economics of Energy Transition in the Persian Gulf

Masoomeh Alipourian and Ali Hussein Samadi

Abstract Being a home to 48% of the world's proven oil reserves and 39.8% of its natural gas reserves, the strategically significant Persian Gulf region plays a distinctive geopolitical and geo-economic role in the twenty-first century energy transition. The increasing global demand for energy has made the Persian Gulf a central hub in the international energy market, thus making it a persistent arena for geopolitical rivalries and international tensions. Simultaneously, the region's hot and arid climate, coupled with high levels of greenhouse gas emissions due to the production and consumption of fossil fuels, make it acutely vulnerable to climate change. Despite these challenges, the Persian Gulf possesses significant geographical and natural advantages that offer considerable potential for a sustainable energy transition through renewable sources.

Some countries in the region have taken preliminary steps toward energy transition by leveraging international diplomacy, implementing carbon capture and storage policies, adopting hydrogen as a clean fuel, improving energy efficiency and integrating renewable energy sources. However, a considerable gap persists prior to achieving low-carbon emission targets.

The current chapter includes six sections, beginning with introduction as focusing on the geopolitics of the energy transition in the Persian Gulf. Section Two provides definitions of key concepts including sustainable energy transition, renewable energy technology transition, the geopolitics of energy transition, geopolitics of renewable energy transition, geo-economics of energy transition, distinctions between geopolitical and geo-economic approaches to energy transition, and geo-economic instruments. Section Three reviews the existing literature on the geopolitics of energy transition in the Persian Gulf. Section Four explores the geopolitical and geo-economic significance of the Persian Gulf in the context of energy transi-

M. Alipourian
Department of Economics, Shiraz University, Shiraz, Iran

A. H. Samadi (✉)
Professor of Economics, Shiraz University, Shiraz, Iran
e-mail: asamadi@rose.shirazu.ac.ir

N. Faghih et al. (eds.), *The Persian Gulf and Islands*, Perspectives on Development in the Middle East and North Africa (MENA) Region,
https://doi.org/10.1007/978-3-032-27910-1_4

tion, highlighting regional characteristics and the roles of Persian Gulf States. Section Five addresses the challenges and opportunities associated with the geopolitical aspects of the energy transition in the region. Finally, Section Six provides conclusion and policy recommendations.

Keywords Geopolitics · Geo-economics · Energy transition · The Persian Gulf

1 Introduction

The Persian Gulf[1] is a semi-enclosed sea, bordered by eight countries: Iran, Iraq, the Saudi Arabia, Kuwait, Oman, the United Arab Emirates, Qatar, and Bahrain. These littoral states collectively hold the largest proven oil and gas reserves in the world, acquiring the title of "the energy reservoir of the world" for this region. Concentration of the resources grants the Persian Gulf with a unique geopolitical significance in the context of the global energy transition. In the emerging international order—where economic factors increasingly shape global power dynamics—regions that are rich in energy resources gain heightened strategic importance. Consequently, the Persian Gulf occupies an unparalleled position not only in geopolitical discourse, but also within geo-economic frameworks.

Among the 24 countries possessing the largest proven oil reserves, eight major producers—members of the Organization of the Petroleum Exporting Countries (OPEC)—account for approximately 63% of the world's oil reserves. All eight members are located in the Persian Gulf region. Despite the United States' recent policies aimed at reducing its dependence on crude oil imports, this country continues to source around 23% of its oil needs from this region. Similarly, Japan depends on the Persian Gulf for over 74% of its oil imports, while both China and India maintain significant reliance on the region's oil supplies (Alizadeh et al., 2024).

---

[1] Since the formation of the states surrounding it, the Persian Gulf has been called "Persia." In pre-Islamic times, the Assyrians called it *Narmarratu*, meaning "Bitter River." During the Achaemenid era, it was known as the *Sea of Pars* (or Pars Sea). Darius the Great—who established the first known naval fleet in history and initiated the construction of the Suez Canal—inscribed the following on a stele at the canal's location: "I ordered the excavation of this waterway from the river that flows from Egypt to the sea that comes from Pars."

The Babylonians, some 2500 years ago, perceived the world as composed of lands surrounding Babylon, located between the Nile and the Tigris rivers. Of all the known seas, they recognized only the Persian Gulf, which bordered their territory. According to ancient Greek geographical thought, the vast surrounding sea (later termed the *Tethys Ocean*) branched into four principal bodies: the *Mediterranean Sea* (referred to as the Gulf of Rome), the *Caspian Sea*, the *Arabian Gulf* (now known as the *Red Sea*), and the *Persian Gulf.*

This early geographical classification formed the basis of scientific geography for centuries and was employed by prominent scholars such as *Thales of Miletus* (640–546 BCE), *Anaximander* (612–546 BCE), and *Strabo*, regarded as the "Father of Geography." Later, Islamic and Arab geographers also adopted similar frameworks, dividing the world's waters into two major seas: *Bahr al-Fars* (the Persian Sea) and *Bahr al-Rum* (the Roman Sea), which they believed extended inland from the encircling global ocean (*al-Bahr al-Muhit*) toward the land masses (Mojtahedzadeh, 1975).

The trajectory of the energy transition in the Persian Gulf has been historically intertwined with distinct geopolitical developments, dating back to the First World War. During that time, the strategic replacement of Welsh coal with Iranian oil marked the Persian Gulf as a pivotal center of global geopolitics. Further, the establishment of OPEC in Baghdad in September 1960—by the Saudi Arabia, Iraq, Iran, Kuwait, and Venezuela—underscored the region's strategic role in the energy transition.

A key element in this dynamic is the Strait of Hormuz, a chokepoint through which a significant portion of the world's oil passes. Its geopolitical relevance stems from its function as a critical conduit for the energy needs of industrialized countries—particularly Western states. Situated within the geostrategic architecture of the West and the United States, the Strait serves both as a control point and a potential pressure lever. Any disruption in oil flow through this passage could destabilize global energy markets and precipitate a crisis in industrial economies (Nami, 2019).

The current global energy transition is shaped by a complex array of interrelated factors; including the climate change, localized environmental and social impacts, the efforts made by consumer countries to enhance energy security and to reduce dependence on hydrocarbon exporters, and the growing concerns over resource scarcity. This transition encompasses a broad shift toward worldwide access to modern energy and the adoption of new technologies, as well as structural changes in markets, institutions, and regulatory frameworks that both enable and are resulted from technological innovations.

At its core, the transition involves the promotion of low- or zero-carbon energy sources—such as renewables (including solar, wind, biomass, hydropower, and geothermal), nuclear power, and carbon capture and storage (CCS). It also entails the deployment of non-carbon energy carriers (primarily electricity and, increasingly, hydrogen), advancements in transport systems (such as electric vehicles), energy storage technologies (e.g., batteries and thermal storage), industrial applications, and improvements in energy efficiency (Bazilian & Howells, 2019).

In the Persian Gulf region, this global transition is deeply intertwined with a *geoeconomic transformation*. One key aspect of this transformation deals with the gradual shift in oil and gas markets—from traditional customers in North America, Europe, and developed parts of Asia—toward emerging economies in Asia, particularly China and India. Simultaneously, the region faces new challenges arising from broader global trends, such as the pressure for free trade, the rise of populist economic and social policies, and the fragmentation of the international order into competing geopolitical blocs—all of which further complicate the regional energy transition (Bazilian et al., 2019).

As the global energy architecture evolves, new *geopolitical challenges* are emerging:

1. *Producer-state vulnerabilities*: The global energy transition poses a significant challenge for oil and gas producing countries, especially those with undiversified economies and heavy reliance on hydrocarbon revenues—such as the Persian Gulf States.

2. *Grid digitalization and energy security:* While the expansion of renewables and the deployment of smart grids contribute to climate change mitigation and enhance the sustainability of energy systems, they also introduce *new cybersecurity risks.* Digital energy infrastructure is vulnerable to the attacks from hostile states or terrorist groups aiming to extract data or disrupt operations and causing potentially significant economic and social damage.
3. *Mineral resource security:* The rapid growth of renewable energy systems and electric vehicles has sparked concerns regarding the secure and sustainable supply of critical minerals required for their production. These minerals—currently central to the energy transition—bring along new geopolitical risks, similar to those historically associated with oil and natural gas.

Conclusively, while the global energy transition has the potential to *strengthen energy security, economic growth, and employment* in oil- and gas-importing nations, it may simultaneously introduce *instability and security challenges* in exporting countries. These challenges include economic volatility, digital infrastructure threats, and strategic competition over mineral resources (Hafner & Tagliapietra, 2020).

To analyze the geo-economic status of a particular country or region, a set of strategic tools and components is required. These tools include: *trade policies, investment policies, economic sanctions, cyberattacks, economic aid, monetary and fiscal policies, energy, and commodity governance policies* (Mokhtari Hoshi, 2018). Given the limitations of this chapter, a comprehensive analysis of all seven components is beyond its scope. Therefore, following the chapter's objectives, the focus has been narrowed down to an analysis of *national and regional energy policies* in the Persian Gulf.

This chapter is organized into six sections to explore the *geopolitics of the energy transition in the Persian Gulf:* Section 2 defines key concepts. Section 3 provides a comprehensive review of the academic literature on the geopolitics of energy transition in the Persian Gulf. Section 4 examines the geo-economic and geopolitical significance of the Persian Gulf in the context of energy transition, identifying the region's core characteristics and the specific roles of Persian Gulf countries in this evolving landscape. Section 5 outlines the challenges and opportunities associated with the energy transition in the Persian Gulf from a geopolitical perspective. Section 6 concludes the chapter with key findings and policy implications.

2 Key Concepts

2.1 Sustainable Energy Transition

The concept of *sustainable energy transition* was primarily introduced by *Amory Lovins* in 1976 through the proposal of two divergent energy pathways: the "hard energy path" and the "soft energy path." According to Lovins, the distinction between these two routes lies in the technical and socio-political structures of the energy systems.

The *hard path*, centered on large-scale energy supply infrastructures, leads to the development of centralized technologies, the concentration of economic and political power, bureaucratic expansion, miscalculations in cost-benefit analyses, technological vulnerability, potential social injustice, and growing socio-economic complexity. In contrast, the *soft energy technologies* (i.e., renewable energy technologies) are designed to be small scale, decentralized and adapted to local socio-ecological conditions. These systems are often locally owned and controlled, while encompassing the potential to enhance community welfare, democratic participation, social justice, resilience, and positive social relations beyond their environmental benefits (Lovins, 1978).

The advantages of this approach are the potential to expand energy generation beyond centralized facilities, the rise in energy self-sufficiency, the decrease in public or private energy infrastructures dependence, the prioritization of renewable over non-renewable resources, the elimination of fossil fuel use, and the focus on energy conservation and the adoption of environmentally low-risk technologies (Takase et al., 2022; Sharma et al., 2023).

The *transition to sustainable energy* is a type of *socio-technical transition*. In the socio-technical transition literature, "transition" refers to a series of processes that leads to the fundamental changes in socio-technical systems. These involve shifts across multiple domains, including technological, material, organizational, institutional, political, economic, and socio-cultural dimensions. "Sustainability transition" refers to a long-term multidimensional and transformative processes that shift existing socio-technical systems toward the more sustainable modes of production and consumption.

Energy transition specifically refers to the reconfiguration of the roles and practices of a wide range of actors within the energy system—including producers, wholesalers, suppliers, network operators, energy service providers, and end users (Markand et al., 2012).

Energy transition involves multiple definitions. For instance, a publication by the *German Applied Energy Institute* describes it as a shift from oil and uranium to renewable energies for the sake of environmental management. Other scholars have broadly defined it as the process of moving from non-renewable to renewable energy sources, or even from one dominant energy source to another (Samadi, 2025). In essence, energy transition refers to *a paradigm shift* from the carbon-intensive sources to cleaner alternatives (Qi and Liu, 2024). Specifically, *sustainable energy transition* is defined as the shift from high-carbon energy sources like oil, gas, and coal to low-carbon and zero-carbon alternatives, such as the renewables (Zinecker et al., 2018).

This systemic transformation toward clean energy provides a transformative pathway for the *global energy decarbonization*, contributing to the achievement of international sustainability goals and commitments (Chen et al., 2019; IRENA, 2018). The sustainable energy transition involves the innovation and deployment of low-carbon technologies, major shifts across industrial sectors, changes in energy markets and efficiency, behavioral adaptations by actors, and evolution in policies and cultural paradigms—both at the national and international levels (Foxon, 2011).

2.2 Transition to Renewable Energy Technologies

The growing global demand for energy, along with the depletion of fossil fuel reserves, price volatility, and the climate change challenges has intensified attention toward the *renewable energy sources* and other *low-carbon, affordable energy alternatives*. In response, many countries have adopted policies and strategic measures to support the expansion of renewable energy and the transition toward associated technologies (Ebrahimi & Rahmani, 2019).

Renewable energy technologies can be broadly categorized into three generations. The *first generation*, which emerged in the nineteenth century, relied on biomass, hydropower, and geothermal energy. The *second generation*, beginning in the 1980s, introduced tidal energy, wind power, wave energy, and solar power. The *third generation*, which is still under development, focuses on gasification, biorefineries, and the ocean thermal energy. Among various forms of energy, *electricity* remains the dominant one, produced from both renewable and non-renewable sources. However, optimal functioning of electrical power systems is heavily influenced by a wide range of dynamic variables (Kabeyi & Olanrewaju, 2022).

Technology plays a critical role in transition into low-carbon electricity networks. Key technological options that facilitate this transition include the rapid *digitization of the energy sector*, which enhances its flexibility to integrate variable renewable sources, particularly *solar and wind energy*. This technological evolution involves a shift from traditional, centralized electricity grids toward *smart grids*. Smart grids support the decentralized generation, enable the integration of intermittent renewable sources (like solar and wind), respond to fluctuating demand (such as from electric vehicles), and ensure a stable and reliable electricity supply (Bayram & Ustun, 2017).

2.3 Geopolitics of the Energy Transition

The term "geopolitics" was first coined by *Rudolf Kjellén* in 1899 (Berryman, 2012). The concept aims at analyzing the interactions between the *geographical landscapes* and *political processes* to identify dynamic political trends and assess their influence and susceptibility (Cahnman, 1943).

In physics, *power* refers to the rate at which work is performed. In geopolitics, power denotes a nation's ability to influence the behavior of other states. Deriving from the Latin term *posse* (to be able), the concept of power in this context involves both meanings. A nation's control over physical power—particularly through the access to primary energy sources like oil—not only shapes its economic development, but it also determines its *national security* and *military strength.* As such, international relations are profoundly affected by the *distribution of energy resources* and the **applied** *technologies to exploit them* (Hafner & Tagliapietra, cited in Sachs, 2020).

Political geography studies how human political decisions affect geographic features and structures—such as governance, borders, migration, communication, and distribution within defined territories like states. In contrast, *geopolitics* investigates how *geographic phenomena*—including territorial location, landforms, resource availability, and communication/transport infrastructures (land, sea, air, and space)—influence political decision-making, particularly at *regional and global levels* (Mojtahedzadeh, 2002 [1381 SH]).

At its core, *geopolitics is about power.* However, the ability of geopolitical factors to generate power varies across the time and space, making power a dynamic concept. This dynamic nature provides countries with opportunities to enhance their capabilities in better supporting their national interests and security (Nami, 2019 [1398 SH]). In this sense, geopolitics refers to the *strategic understanding of the geographical environment* to gain power—the very power that enables actors to enter global competition at the highest level and secures national interests and survival. It is the science of understanding how geographic conditions affect the political fate of nations (Ezzati, 2009 [1388 SH]).

Energy is considered as one of the geographic sources of power. Political actors seek access to the energy resources in pursuit of their national interests and strategic objectives. Energy serves as a primary driver of economic activity and a crucial resource for development. As such, it can significantly affect *international security* and *political stability* (Olayele, 2015).

Among various geopolitical debates, the *geopolitics of energy transition* has attracted increasing scholarly attention. Primarily, the study of energy geopolitics focused on illustrating the relationship between geography and the international politics of Western imperialist states (Ivleva & Tänzler, 2019; Overland, 2019). During the Cold War and the era of decolonization, geopolitical discourse described the rivalry between the *United States and the Soviet Union* for gaining influence over the states and strategic resources. Today, *conventional geopolitics* pays particular attention toward the way *geographic factors* (such as territorial location or resource access) shape both national and international political agendas (Högselius, 2019).

The *geopolitics of energy transition* explores how *geographic, political, and economic changes in energy sources and supply chains* impact inter-state and regional relations. It addresses issues such as:

- *Rivalries and cooperation* evolving in energy systems while fossil fuel dependence declines and renewables rise
- Shifts in *power distribution*
- *Energy security* concerns
- *Economic impacts* of energy transitions
- *Environmental consequences* of moving toward cleaner energy sources

This field also investigates *interactions between changes in energy systems and political, economic and security dynamics* among countries. Correspondingly, the geopolitics of the energy transition is a crucial field of study in international relations. It aims at explaining the way transitions in energy production, distribution, and consumption—particularly toward renewables—affect global political dynamics. In essence, it is a *strategic science* through which state and non-state actors design or revise policies to pursue goals based on *geographic sources of power* (Janparvar, 2017 [1396 SH]).

2.4 The Geopolitics of the Transition into Renewable Energy

Competition over the access to fossil fuels, especially oil has been a fundamental aspect of many geopolitical analyses since the oil shocks of the 1970s. Early geopolitical studies primarily examined conflicts and tensions over the key oil-rich regions such as the Persian Gulf, the Caspian Sea, and the Arctic, as well as the strategic points like the Strait of Hormuz. Later, disputes over natural gas supplies between the European Union and Russia also drew significant attention (Overland, 2015).

Today, a new research agenda that focuses on the geopolitics of the energy transition into renewables is emerging. This perspective explores how the geotechnical features of different energy sources can have profound political consequences (Criekemans, 2018; Scholten & Bosman, 2016).

The previous major energy transition occurred over a century ago, when coal was gradually replaced by crude oil as the dominant global energy source. This shift also redefined geopolitical dynamics, concentrating attention on oil-producing countries in the Middle East. Presently, we face a similar transition—this time from oil toward renewable energy sources such as wind and solar power. Similar to the transition from coal toward oil that took several decades to reshape energy use at homes, transportation, and industry, the renewable energy is also expected to take several decades to fully replace the fossil fuels.

A key difference between fossil fuels and renewables, which holds prominent geopolitical implications, lies in their storage characteristics. Fossil fuels can be stockpiled and stored for long periods, while renewables are characterized by their flow nature and intermittent availability, providing long-term storage and uninterrupted supply more challenging. As a result, there is a growing need for efficient energy storage systems, such as large-scale batteries, which in turn may become new geopolitical focal points (Klement, 2021).

Renewable energy technologies are also creating new global value chains centered around critical minerals essential for solar panels, wind turbines, and batteries. Minerals such as copper, lead, molybdenum, nickel, zinc, cobalt, lithium, and rare earth elements are vital inputs to these technologies, yet they are being distributed around the world unevenly. Many of these resources are located in the politically unstable and economically vulnerable regions, such as the Democratic Republic of Congo. This uneven distribution is already sparking intense geopolitical competition over securing supply chains for these key materials (Hafner & Tagliapietra, 2020, cited in Sanchez).

The primary constraint on the transition to sustainable energy is not the availability of low-cost carbon-free energy or primary renewable resources—solar and wind alone could theoretically supply the planet's energy needs—rather, it is the lack of global political cooperation. This cooperation is essential to implement policy instruments like carbon pricing, public investments, government regulations, and public-private research and development initiatives. Political resistance mainly arises from the free-rider problem, where countries attempt to shift the costs of decarbonization onto others. Geopolitics is central to this challenge.

If successful decarbonization is achieved, fossil fuel-rich countries will face losses in several major ways. First, they will incur significant capital losses as fossil fuel reserves become stranded assets, left untapped due to climate policy constraints. Second, economic repercussions will arise as public revenues derived from fossil fuel rents diminish, leaving government budgets affected. Third, these countries will lose geopolitical influence as their concentrated fossil fuel assets are replaced by the widely accessible renewable energy resources such as wind, solar, and hydropower (ibid).

2.5 Geo-economics of the Energy Transition

With the collapse of the Soviet Union and the end of the Cold War, the military aspect of power lost its significance in relations among major countries, and the concept of power increasingly came to denote the economic capabilities of nations (Brown, 1991). Consequently, the focus of geopolitics shifted from a military and geostrategic approach toward a geo-economic one.

Luttwak (1990) introduced the geo-economic paradigm with a broad concept combining geography, power, and economics into the fields of geography and political science. In this framework, politics—being central to geopolitics—gave way to economics, hence representing a novel approach to geopolitics.

Youngs (2012) define geo-economics as the use of geopolitical or military power to achieve economic goals. Thirlwell (2010) sees it as the interconnection of international economics, geopolitics, and strategy. Lorot (2001) emphasizes on trade and protection of domestic industries without considering geopolitical aspects. Bremmer (2010) narrows the application of the term to the traditional study of international trade and sanctions. Blackwill and Harris (2016) describe geo-economics as the use of economic instruments to defend national interests and produce beneficial geopolitical outcomes, as well as the impact of other countries' economic actions on a country's geopolitical objectives. Scholvin and Wigell (2018) define geo-economics as the application of economic power tools to achieve strategic goals.

With the rise of geo-economics, geographic regions—unlike during the Cold War—became defined from another dimension: the distribution of energy-producing resources, primarily oil and gas. Energy emerged as a key variable influencing strategic planning (Ezzati, 2005). In the twenty-first century, geopolitical and geostrategic regions are those with abundant energy resources and substantial gross national product. Thus, when Cold War strategic regions (geopolitical) align with economic factors (geo-economic), these regions gain irreplaceable international positions and play a pivotal role in shaping global strategies. In other words, energy has assumed a geo-economic dimension, becoming the most influential variable in relations among major powers (Nami et al., 2009).

From a geo-economic perspective, the world's regions are significant insofar as they possess economic roles. Accordingly, the twenty-first century world is divided into six regions: North America, Western Europe, Southeast Asia, the Moscow-Leningrad axis, India, and the Middle East (Persian Gulf), each of which constitutes a geo-economic power. The first five regions mainly export manufactured goods, while the Middle East (Persian Gulf) exports raw materials (Akhbari, 2004).

2.6 Differences between the Geopolitical and Geo-economic Approaches

Although geo-economics is considered a branch of geopolitics that emphasizes on its economic dimension, yet the two approaches differ in several respects. Geo-economics is a process largely beyond the sole control of national governments and it is often driven by private sector economic initiatives at international level. In geo-economics, entrepreneurs act as key players, whereas in geopolitics, states are the primary actors (Mokhtari Hoshi, 2018).

Due to the multiplicity of actors at various levels, geo-economics is more complex than geopolitics. The use of military power to achieve economic goals is a feature of geopolitics, not geo-economics (Clinton, 2011). The logic of geopolitics is predominantly zero-sum, while geo-economics follows a positive-sum logic—where all parties can benefit (Mandelbaum, 2014). Geopolitics primarily relies on hard power, whereas geo-economics mainly employs soft power to advance interests. The audiences for geopolitical discourse are mainly intelligent agencies, military officers, politicians, and government officials, whereas geo-economic discourse is primarily directed at private sector executives, seeking to expand their businesses internationally (Mokhtari Hoshi, 2018).

2.7 Geo-economic Tools

Seven economic tools are commonly used in the geo-economic approach which include trade policies, investment policies, economic sanctions, cyberattacks, economic aid, monetary and fiscal policies, national policies governing energy, and commodities (Mokhtari Hoshi, 2018). Below comes a brief explanation of these tools:

- *Trade policies*: The concept constitutes economic warfare among nations and includes import regulations and tariffs, subsidies, export support, dumping, and protective measures. For instance, Russia's trade blockade of Georgia, involving closure of air, sea, road, rail routes, and postal communications, as well as similar tactics against Moldova and Ukraine which aimed at deterring these countries from signing agreements with the European Union, are among the geo-economic tools (Papava, 2012). The recent tariff war initiated by Donald Trump exemplifies this tool.
- *Investment policies*: The notion refers to the permissibility or restriction of foreign asset ownership within a country, involving the openness of national stock exchanges (Mokhtari Hoshi, 2018).
- *Economic sanctions*: The impact of sanctions, fundamentally depends on two variables: 1) the size of the domestic market and 2) a country's share of the global market for certain goods. Some countries monopolize production of specific goods, so sanctioning them leaves no alternative suppliers (Blackwill and Harris, 2016).
- *Cyberattacks*: In order to become qualified as a geo-economic tool, cyberattacks must meet two criteria: first, since geo-economics relates to state behavior, the actors behind cyberattacks must be state-sponsored or state-funded; second, the attacks must aim at economic influence and penetration (Blackwill and Harris, 2016). Beyond massive intellectual property theft, geo-economic cyber capabilities target private companies while seeking to undermine entire sectors of national economies and disable critical electronic infrastructure such as banking systems (Danzig, 2014). The energy sector is a particularly attractive target. The infamous "Night Dragon" cyberattack by China, which is considered the most destructive cyberattack on U.S. energy targets, spied on five major Western U.S. energy firms from 2008 to 2011, stealing hundreds of gigabytes of sensitive financial, bidding, and oil and gas operations data (Clayton and Segal, 2013).
- *Economic aid*: The economic or military aid along with bilateral development assistance and humanitarian aid targeting strategic influence constitute straightforward geo-economic tools. Military and humanitarian aids are broad geo-economic instruments, since money is fungible, allowing recipient countries to alter or store its use (Blackwill and Harris, 2016). Timely military aid can have significant geopolitical effects, such as the Saudi Arabia's $3 billion aid package to Lebanon in 2013, aimed at strengthening Lebanon's alignment with the Saudi Arabia and countering Hezbollah (Barnard, 2014).
- *Monetary and fiscal policies:* Changes in a country's financial management profoundly affect national power and global standing (Suri, 2014). Monetary and fiscal policies influence foreign investors' willingness and the cost-effectiveness of imports and exports, and it ultimately affect national power (Mokhtari Hoshi, 2018).

- *National energy and commodity policies:* Countries use energy and commodities to achieve geopolitical objectives. For example, in 2006 and 2008, Russia suspended gas exports to parts of the Europe, due to political disputes. Russia's use of energy and commodities as geopolitical tools is unique. Many Central Asian countries sign energy agreements with China to balance their relations with Russia (Blackwill and Harris, 2016).

Geo-economic power and its utilization represent a critical dimension in current international relations. While traditional geopolitical perspectives emphasize the U.S. military dominance as an unchallenged hegemon, the geo-economic view reveals a decline in the U.S. influence, considering the world moving toward multipolarity and a gradual reduction in the America's share of global economy. In international relations, the geo-economic perspective fosters a "soft balance" through economic means (Mokhtari Hoshi, 2018).

3 A Review of the Empirical Literature on the Geopolitics of Energy Transition in the Persian Gulf

Reviewing the existing literature provides an opportunity to reflect on previous studies, thereby laying the groundwork for advancing knowledge and better identifying the strengths, weaknesses, and expected innovations of the present research. Correspondingly, the current study reviews selected literature on the geopolitics and geo-economics of energy transition both globally and within the scope of the Persian Gulf region.

Hashemi (2011) identifies major obstacles to sustainable security formation in the Persian Gulf, including the dominance of threats, competition, conflicts, and hostility patterns among the security actors in the region, as well as arms races and political-ideological disputes at the regional level. Further, he points out that as an intervening actor in the Persian Gulf security complex, the United States has hindered the development of regional cooperation and in fact, its policies have exacerbated competition and hostilities. Given these internal and external barriers to establishing sustainable security, Hashemi proposes a participatory and cooperative security model and related mechanisms to improve security conditions in the Persian Gulf.

Luomi (2015) examines how resource-rich countries within the Gulf Cooperation Council (GCC) can consolidate their position in international green economy relations. He particularly focuses on the United Arab Emirates' efforts to acquire actionable tools for transitioning into a national green energy economy. The UAE has actively embraced the "win-win" aspects of the green economy agenda, and it has initiated numerous partnerships and programs. Lowmi confirms that the UAE's success in sustainable energy stems from the top-level political support, enhancing its global influence through engagement in international initiatives.

From Griffiths' (2017a, 2017b) perspective, the driving forces behind the evolution of energy policy in the Middle East and North Africa (MENA) region are energy security and the decrease in energy costs. He emphasizes that while renewables are the key global diversification strategy in the region, there remains significant interest in nuclear energy and coal to complement increased natural gas usage in electricity generation. Regional energy cooperation is essential, but it has to be approached thoughtfully and realistically. The energy transition in MENA will be challenging, yet inevitable.

O'Sullivan et al. (2017) discuss seven mechanisms through which renewables can shape the geopolitics of energy transition: (1) the formation of cartels over critical renewable technology materials; (2) the potential conflicts over technology transfer between developing and developed countries and over renewable energy infrastructure; (3) the "resource curse" may be affected as oil-producing countries lose high rents; (4) the geopolitical complexity of electrical interconnections that not only can increase vulnerability, but it can also enhance interdependence by reducing conflict risks; (5) the reduced fossil fuel consumption may trigger political reforms and economic diversification and political instability in fuel exporters; (6) the renewables can mitigate climate-change-related conflicts and instability; and (7) the renewables can enhance sustainable energy access and contribute to stability solutions.

Hache (2018) argues that the transition to renewables will gradually bring an end to the geopolitics of fossil fuels. However, new challenges arising from energy transition policies may paradoxically increase the complexity of energy geopolitics. Local and decentralized relationships add new geopolitical layers to traditional energy actors, while technical, economic, sociological, behavioral, and legal dimensions further complicate this emerging puzzle. A substantial increase in renewables will create new and unexpected interdependencies, such as the dependence on critical materials, new geopolitics of patents, and renewable energy diplomacy.

Stratfor (2018) acknowledges a significant geopolitical shift from the current energy geopolitical scenario, asserting that the main losers of the energy transition will be traditional oil exporters such as Venezuela, Kazakhstan, and the Persian Gulf countries. He argues that by encouraging regional grid integration, renewables promote greater cooperation among states. However, risks such as cyberattacks and supply disruptions of minerals pose challenges to clean technology. Additionally, trading issues like intellectual property theft, dumping, and local content requirements could become sources of international conflicts, hence weakening the global trade regime.

Luomi (2018) outlines several key challenges for the UAE and other Persian Gulf energy exporters in transitioning to sustainable energy: maintaining or increasing oil exports at competitive prices for a sufficient period; raising the share of higher-value oil-based exports to sustain government revenues and broader economic transition; meeting growing domestic energy demand without compromising environmental sustainability; and developing comprehensive and outward-looking energy diplomacy strategies based on domestic energy agendas and actively engaging with a global environment moving away from the hydrocarbons.

The International Renewable Energy Agency (IRENA, 2019) provides a comprehensive assessment from the geopolitics of the global energy transition, confirming that global power structures and arrangements will change in multiple ways and the dynamics of intrastate relations will also be transformed. Power will become more decentralized and dispersed. Countries investing in renewable technologies will increase their global influence, while those which are heavily dependent on fossil fuel revenues will face fundamental challenges to their economic and social models.

Goldthau and Westphal (2019) emphasize that the global energy transition does not signal the end of oil-producing countries. Instead, a shift to low-carbon consumption may create new multilateral monopolies and further market concentration among fewer crude oil suppliers. They hold that the rapid commitment to decarbonization and building a sustainable energy future necessitates readiness for a dual challenge: (1) managing a rapidly changing energy system to ensure benefits for human security and economic prosperity and (2) balancing the post-fossil fuel political (geographical) order.

Goldthau et al. (2019) present four different scenarios for the energy transition and its geopolitical impacts by 2030:

- Scenario 1 ("The Great Green Deal"): Oil-producing countries are rewarded for a smooth transition to a sustainable economy, resulting in a win-win for climate and security with low geopolitical friction.
- Scenario 2 ("Technological Progress"): Fossil fuel producers must rapidly adapt to declining demand, potentially increasing tensions in some regions.
- Scenario 3 ("Dirty Nationalism"): Priority is given to self-sufficiency and the domestic energy sources over imports.
- Scenario 4 ("Business as Usual"): Existing economic and geopolitical imbalances worsen, increasing energy inequality, with oil producers in the Middle East, Russia, and Africa facing political turmoil due to depleted state revenues.

Orland (2019) addresses four emerging myths in the geopolitics of renewables: competition over critical materials, new resource curse, disruption of electricity as a geopolitical weapon, and cybersecurity as a geopolitical risk. He confirms that the renewable energy resources are abundant but dispersed, making the technologies for collection, storage, and transport increasingly important during the energy transition. Hence, international energy competition may shift away from the control over physical resources and their transport routes, toward the technology and intellectual property rights.

Tagliapietra (2019) reviews ambitious economic reforms undertaken by hydrocarbon producers in the MENA region since the 2014 oil price decline and offers a positive outlook on their implementation. Besides the market volatility risks, two other arguments for the economic diversification are stressed: the uncertainty about the global energy transition speed and the urgent need to create jobs for large, young populations. Consequently, the global energy transition may become a positive driver for hydrocarbons in the MENA region, promoting economic diversification as an inevitable path to ensure future prosperity in any future scenario, including a low-carbon world.

Hafner and Wochner (2020) highlight four main drivers of change in the global energy system (global energy demand, climate policies, market-driven digitalization, technological innovations). They argue that under a "weak global climate policy" scenario, energy-exporting countries (the Persian Gulf States, Russia, and the United States) will remain strong, whereas under a "global climate action" scenario, traditional fossil fuel producers (the Persian Gulf States and Russia) must rapidly diversify their economies and shift from fossil fuel exports to hydrogen exports to remain internationally relevant.

Norouzizadeh and Goodarzi (2021) conclude that Iran's strategic location among three major energy consumer hubs (the European Union, the Indian subcontinent, and China) connects the Persian Gulf energy corridor to consumption areas, linking energy security with national interests. This connection makes these hubs more sensitive to Iran's national security and economic interests. From a geo-economic perspective, this nexus could foster economic partnerships and development and consequently enhance Iran's national security coefficient.

Daei Karimzadeh et al. (2021) analyze the interrelationship between clean energy, domestic and foreign capital development, economic growth, and environmental quality in a group of developing countries from 1995 to 2012. They find that clean energy projects have lower returns and higher financing costs compared to other energy projects in the developing countries. Due to underdeveloped financial institutions and limited access to necessary capital, investment in clean energy projects has been limited, hindering CO2 emission reductions.

Al-Sarifi and Mansouri (2022) investigate the reasons behind the insufficient adoption of renewable energy in GCC countries, identifying technical and economic feasibility as primary factors in slowing renewable energy technology uptake. They highlight high hydrocarbon subsidies, low electricity tariffs, fragmented energy policies, lack of dedicated regulators, and regulatory frameworks for renewables and highly controlled electricity markets as major barriers to renewable energy adoption in the GCC.

The dependence of major global economic and political powers on the Persian Gulf's energy resources underscores the region's crucial role as a primary global energy supplier. Therefore, ensuring the stability and security of energy supply and demand in the Persian Gulf seems essential. The region also plays a vital role in transiting energy from the Caspian Sea to the global markets. The Caspian countries—such as Azerbaijan, Kazakhstan, and Turkmenistan—possess significant oil and gas reserves, but they face export challenges due to the lack of access to deep water ports. Consequently, transit routes through the Persian Gulf countries represent an ideal export pathway for the Caspian energy to reach the global markets (Alizadeh et al., 2024).

Analyzing the geopolitical implications of shared oil resources between Iran and Iraq, Raisolsadat (2024) concludes that Iran must carefully assess its geopolitical position and strive to maintain its share and wealth in shared fields by developing relations with Iraq, while investing on its oil industry and converting potential threats into new opportunities through a cooperation that can maximize benefits. Factors affecting these geopolitics include regional competition, unilateral field development, close economic cooperation, regional disputes, Iran's economic growth and sanction relief, diverse trade partners, foreign investment absorption disparities, Iran's investment capacity, geopolitical convergence in the Strait of Hormuz, joint investments, and diplomatic instability.

The present study distinguishes itself by providing a foresight-based analysis of the geopolitical and geo-economic positioning of the Persian Gulf countries in global energy transition. Examining the challenges and opportunities ahead for these countries, the chapter aims to guide policymakers in charting an appropriate path for energy transition.

4 The Geopolitical and Geo-economic Significance of the Persian Gulf in Energy Transition

The Persian Gulf, endowed with abundant energy resources, represents a unique model of a geopolitical, geo-economic, and geostrategic region. Beyond its accessibility to the Indian Ocean, it is simultaneously connected to several strategic regions including the Indian subcontinent, the Central Asia, the Caucasus, and the European Union. Among the strategic advantages of the Persian Gulf is the Strait of Hormuz, which is situated along the vital oil transit route essential to the West, where the district lies on the Rimland and serves as a crisis diffusion point. It is a critical theater for the Indian Ocean operations, providing logistics services and supply facilities for naval forces, and complements land power (Goodarzi & Mohammadzadeh Ebrahimi, 2017).

In terms of strategic reserves; according to the 2021 annual report by British Petroleum (commonly known as the "Statistical Review of World Energy"), the Persian Gulf region holds approximately 2830 billion barrels of proven oil reserves—accounting for 48% of the world's total. Of this amount, about 157.8 billion barrels or 9.1% of global reserves, belong to Iran (British Petroleum, 2021). Among the 15 countries with the largest proven oil reserves worldwide, six are located in the Persian Gulf region (Table 1). These six countries collectively hold over 65% of OPEC's oil reserves (OPEC, 2019). From an energy transit perspective, around 35% of all oil transported by tankers and 20% of global oil supply pass through the Persian Gulf waterways and the strategic Strait of Hormuz (Ghanbari, 2018).

Regarding natural gas reserves, out of the global total of 188.1 trillion cubic meters of proven reserves, 74.7 trillion cubic meters (39.8%) are located in the Persian Gulf region. Of this, approximately 32.1 trillion cubic meters; equivalent to 17.1% of the world's total, belong to Iran (British Petroleum, 2021).

The discovery of gas fields in the Persian Gulf, along with the greater environmental compatibility of natural gas, the global rise in oil prices, the decline in oil reserves, the Kyoto Protocol (and its mandates for clean fuel usage), and the rapid development of emerging and Southeast Asian economies have increased the geopolitical-economic significance of the Persian Gulf throughout the late twentieth century. Moreover, geopolitical tensions between Russia and the Europe (especially following the Russia-Ukraine war), the suspension of the Northern European gas pipeline through Ukraine

Table 1 Proven oil reserves of the top 15 countries worldwide in 2022

Global share	Reserves (billion barrels)	Region	Country	Rank
21.3%	300.9	–	Venezuela	1
19%	266.5	Persian Gulf	Saudi Arabia	2
18%	209	Persian Gulf	Iran	3
9%	169.7	–	Canada	4
8.26%	142.5	Persian Gulf	Iraq	5
7.47%	101.5	Persian Gulf	Kuwait	6
7.02%	97.8	Persian Gulf	United Arab Emirates	7
5.33%	80.0	–	Russia	8
3.38%	48.4	–	Libya	9
2.69%	37.1	–	Nigeria	10
2.57%	36.5	–	United States	11
2.15%	30.0	–	Kazakhstan	12
1.82%	25.6	–	China	13
1.8%	25.2	Persian Gulf	Qatar	14
0.95%	12.7	–	Brazil	15

Source: https://www.statista.com and research findings

and volatility in global oil markets, have elevated the importance of Persian Gulf gas reserves for the European Union. Consequently, the region assumes a special geo-economic role in the twenty-first century, where geopolitical factors intertwine with economic interests, that in turn gives shape to global strategic policies (Nami et al., 2009).

The security of the Persian Gulf—due to its vast oil and gas reserves, strategic waterways, and regional consumer markets—is of paramount significance to global powers. It reflects the intersection of geographic determinants with political behaviors, regional power dynamics, and the level of regional tensions (Akhbari, 2004). In other words, the region's issues represent overlapping interests of external actors, closely linked with power structures within regional states (Nami et al., 2009). Currently, there is a growing presence of external actors like China—emerging as a global power—in the Persian Gulf. Additionally, the oil demand from the United States and the Asia-Pacific region has led to direct competition over global oil resources and energy security (Salameh, 2003). Indeed, the Persian Gulf represents a strategic arena where the United States confronts emerging centers of power within the new global order.

4.1 The Geopolitical and Geo-economic Indicators of Energy Transition in the Persian Gulf

The Persian Gulf region serves both as a global center for oil exports and a key natural gas supplier. Its infrastructure, economies, political systems, and international relations are profoundly shaped by hydrocarbon wealth. However, with its predominantly hot, semi-arid to arid climate, the region is vulnerable to climate change impacts. Nonetheless, the Persian Gulf holds significant potential for low-carbon energy transition through renewable energies—primarily solar—and geological and technological assets conducive to carbon capture, utilization, and storage (CCUS).

Despite hosting substantial global economic resources, geopolitical conflicts—responsible for most military confrontations over the past three decades—have hindered long-term strategic cohesion among the Persian Gulf countries. Hence, the region's strategic location, extensive economic and strategic resources (notably vast oil and gas reserves), consumer markets, unforeseen crises, conflicting actors, and cultural and ideological divisions constitute the key geopolitical and geo-economic indices of the Persian Gulf (Aminian, 2005).

Factors shaping the geopolitical energy transition in the Persian Gulf include ethnic-sectarian composition, political regimes, ideology, hydrocarbon endowments, non-hydrocarbon resources, economic development levels, and national wealth and international alliances. This transition is intertwined with a geo-economic shift focusing on changing oil and gas markets—from traditional consumers in the USA, Europe, and developed Asia toward the developing Asian countries, particularly China and India. This shift accompanies political trends such as the potential decline of the U.S. influence in the Persian Gulf and the assertiveness of regional powers like Iran, the Saudi Arabia, and the UAE along with the increasing involvement of Russia and possibly China and India in the future. These transformations occur alongside the global trends, including the movement toward free trade, the rise of populist economic and social policies, and geopolitical bloc fragmentation; all of which complicate the energy transition (Bazilian et al., 2019).

Hydrocarbon resources are unevenly distributed across the Persian Gulf. Some countries (mainly GCC members) possess large resources with small populations, whereas others like Iraq and Iran hold significant resources, while having larger populations (Mohaddes & Raissi, 2019).

Persian Gulf oil producers have developing economies vulnerable to external geopolitical pressures. Their heavy reliance on oil renders their economies fragile and susceptible to external and internal instability (Olanipekun & Alola, 2020). Politically, many face corruption and internal instability. Oil price shocks, revenue fluctuations, and political disputes over rent distribution and resource control contribute to fuel geopolitical unrest. The management and exploitation of shared energy fields as transboundary resources also present significant challenges to all stakeholders (Guo, 2012).

Energy trade integration in the region remains limited. As a result of political tensions, sanctions, and high domestic consumption, Iran has been unable to export natural gas to its Persian Gulf neighbors. The region's most successful pipeline is the Dolphin pipeline, running from Qatar to the UAE and Oman (KAPSARC, 2018).

4.2 The Geopolitical and Geo-economic Position of the Persian Gulf Countries in Energy Transition

The Persian Gulf region is undergoing a transition from its long-standing reliance on abundant fossil fuel reserves to a more diversified and sustainable energy mix, including renewable resources. This transformation is accompanied by a complex interplay of institutional, economic, and infrastructural factors that shape the region's future energy outlook. The vast oil and natural gas reserves of the Persian Gulf have been historically the cornerstone of economic growth and a foundation of geopolitical influence. However, this dependence has generated significant environmental challenges and has exposed regional economies to the volatility of global energy markets (Mills, 2020; Albaker et al., 2023). Rising domestic energy demand coupled with the severe economic and environmental consequences of continuous fossil fuel dependency and has underscored the strategic imperative of renewable energies. This shift not only represents an environmental reorientation, but it is also considered a strategic economic realignment. It presents an opportunity to redirect crude oil exports toward higher-value products, maximizing economic returns from the region's resource wealth (World Bank, 2023).

The transition to renewables in the Persian Gulf offers a viable and competitive alternative that can substantially reduce the region's carbon footprint, enhance energy security, and represent a crucial step toward sustainability and energy independence. Leveraging the geographic and climatic advantages of the Persian Gulf—particularly for solar and wind energy—to reduce carbon emissions, to increase energy security, and to stimulate economic growth, requires overcoming institutional barriers, including regulatory challenges, fragmented policy environments, and financing difficulties for green energy projects (Terrapon-Pfaff et al., 2022; Albaker et al., 2023).

The following section examines the geopolitical and geo-economic status of the Persian Gulf countries.

4.2.1 Iran

Iran possesses the world's fourth-largest proven crude oil reserves (over 83.6 billion barrels) and the second-largest natural gas reserves (approximately 34 trillion cubic meters) (USEIA, 2015, 2016). Consequently, Iran holds the largest hydrocarbon reserves worldwide. Geopolitically speaking, Iran's position between the Persian Gulf and the Caspian Sea—two of the world's critical energy hubs—and its access to the Strait of Hormuz, as the most strategic corridor for crude oil and LNG transportation throughout the world, underscores its influence. Furthermore, Iran's access to warm waters via the Sea of Oman amplifies its significance in the global energy landscape. Owing to these geopolitical and natural advantages, Iran is consistently regarded as a key player in the energy transition, particularly within the

Persian Gulf region as playing a pivotal role in ensuring global energy supply security.

Iran's unique geopolitical location, its vast oil and gas resources and geographic proximity to open waters and the strategic Strait of Hormuz provide it with a quasi-monopoly in supplying oil and gas for the Asian countries, compared to competitors such as Turkmenistan, Qatar, and Russia. Additionally, Iran's transit position at the international crossroads connecting Africa to the Asia and Asia to the Europe confers further geopolitical advantages. Iran facilitates access to open waters for Central Asian and the Caucasus countries, significantly influencing energy swap agreements and fuel supplies to producers in the Central Asia (e.g., Afghanistan and Pakistan) (Sheikh Attar, 2005). Among possible routes, Iran offers the shortest, most cost-effective and secure pathways to open waters. The transit of oil and gas pipelines through Iranian territory further expands Iran's geo-economic cooperation with the Central Asian and the Caucasus States. Energy collaborations stimulate broader economic cooperation and contribute to Iran's geopolitical integration with the Caspian region. Emphasizing the point that energy, economic cooperation, and broad political coordination can foster deep confidence-building mechanisms in the region (Sariolghalam, 1999).

Having been situated south of the Persian Gulf—the heartland of the world's fossil energy—and north of the Caspian Sea, Iran is considered the world's secondary energy priority. This geopolitical and geo-economic linkage between the Caspian Sea and Central Asia, along with Iran's status in the Persian Gulf (controlling half of this strategic region), expands Iran's role through Asia and the Europe (Mojtahedzadeh, 2000). Given that China and the Europe are the main twenty-first century competitors to the United States in seeking secure and uninterrupted energy supplies, Iran's geopolitical and geo-economic standing positions make it a prime energy supplier for these powers.

Iran's role is further reinforced by the 28 shared oil and gas fields and 15 joint reservoirs with its neighbors in the Persian Gulf. Regarding all, 15 reservoirs are offshore in the Persian Gulf and 13 are onshore. Shared fields include 12 blocks on the border with Iraq, 7 with the UAE, 4 with the Saudi Arabia, 2 each with Qatar and Oman, and one with Kuwait and Turkmenistan (Seif & Agha Mousa Tehrani, 2014; see Table 2).

Among these fields, the super-giant South Pars Gas Field is Iran's most significant offshore gas field and one of the largest globally, with an in-place gas volume of 13,130 billion cubic meters. Iran's total gas in-place reserves stand at 28 trillion cubic meters with nearly 50% (about 8% of global gas reserves) located in South Pars. The field also contains gas condensates equivalent to approximately 18 billion barrels (ibid).

South Pars is currently the only field in Iran governed by buyback contracts. In contrast, the Persian Gulf countries have long engaged in extensive development of shared resources through cooperation with international companies and the adoption of advanced technologies. For example, Qatar began exploiting South Pars in 1992 and by 2000 was producing daily 130,000 barrels of condensate, one billion cubic feet of gas, and 175,000 barrels of oil from the field. Similarly, other Persian

Table 2 Iran's shared hydrocarbon fields with Persian Gulf countries

Countries	Shared oil/gas fields
Iran-Iraq	Dehloran, Paydar Gharb, Naft Shahr, Azadegan, Yadavaran, Azar
Iran-Saudi Arabia	Esfandiar, Forouzan, Farzad A Gas Fields, Farzad B Gas Fields
Iran-UAE	Salman Oil and Gas Field, Farzam Oil Field, Nosrat Oil Field, Mubarak Oil Field
Iran-Kuwait	Arash Gas Field
Iran-Oman	Hengam Oil and Gas Field
Iran-Qatar	South Pars Gas Field, Rashadat Oil Field, South Pars Oil Layer

*Source:*Seif and Agha Mousa Tehrani (2014)

Gulf States leverage foreign investments and international expertise, coupled with political flexibility to exploit their energy resources, efficiently (Alizadeh et al., 2024).

4.2.2 Iraq

Iraq holds approximately 8.37% of the world's proven oil reserves and 1.86% of proven natural gas reserves. In 2020, Iraq's oil production and consumption were approximately 4.114 million and 628 thousand barrels per day, respectively, provided that its natural gas production and consumption were 10.5 and 20.8 billion cubic meters (BP, 2021). Iraq ranks as the second-largest crude oil producer within OPEC, following the Saudi Arabia. The country possesses the world's fifth-largest proven crude oil reserves, estimated at 145 billion barrels, accounting for 17% of the Middle East's and 8% of the world's proven oil reserves. The Iraqi economy is heavily dependent on oil export revenues; according to the International Monetary Fund (IMF), oil exports constituted approximately 91% of the total government revenues in 2018.

From exporting perspective, Iraq is the world's fifth-largest oil exporter with a volume of 3.583 million barrels per day. In 2019, about 88% of Iraq's maritime exports were shipped through the southern Gulf terminals, exporting both light and heavy crude from Basra. Northern Iraqi oil is transported via pipeline to the Turkish port of Ceyhan for export. Asia—mainly India, China, and the South Korea—has been the primary destination for Iraqi oil, absorbing 62% of Iraq's oil exports in 2019. China and India each imported approximately one million barrels per day (around half of Iraq's total exports), that makes them to be considered as Iraq's largest buyers annually. Outside Asia, the United States imported 331 thousand barrels per day (8% of Iraq's total exports), while the European countries accounted for 24% of Iraq's oil exports.

Iraq ranks eleventh in proven natural gas reserves, globally. Approximately three-quarters of its natural gas reserves are associated gas, predominantly located in southern Iraq. Since 2017, Iraq has been a net importer of natural gas. The bulk of Iraq's oil reserves are situated in the northern Kurdish region and in the southern and southeastern parts of the country (BP, 2021).

Numerous oil and gas fields extend across approximately 1500 kilometers along the Iran-Iraq border, from the southernmost point of the Shatt al-Arab waterway to the Turkish border in the Dalamper Mountains (Khatinoglu, 2014). The concept of constructing an oil pipeline between Iraq and Iran was discussed in December 2003 (Cordesman, 2005). In July 2005, a memorandum of understanding was signed to build a pipeline allowing Iraqi crude oil from the southern Basra fields to be refined in Iranian refineries and facilities in southwestern Abadan (Howard, 2007). In August 2007, an agreement on a crude oil and petroleum product swap scheme between Iran and Iraq was reached (Katzman, 2007). This plan involved a twin pipeline system: one line transporting 350,000 barrels per day of Iraqi crude from Basra to the Abadan refinery, and the other transporting 150,000 barrels per day of refined petroleum products from Abadan back to Basra (Shana, 2007). Iraq's oil export through Iranian ports and oil islands further underscores the strategic importance of the Strait of Hormuz as the world's most critical oil chokepoint.

After years of instability and insecurity, Iraq is emerging as a key player in the international energy supply landscape. Recent years have witnessed significant increases in Iraq's oil production and exports through cooperation with international companies. Iraq's strategy to diversify its oil export routes is a principal component of its energy policy, though it faces considerable obstacles and challenges in implementation.

4.2.3 The Gulf Cooperation Council (GCC)

The six Gulf Cooperation Council member states (the Saudi Arabia, the United Arab Emirates, Qatar, Kuwait, Oman, and Bahrain) collectively possess over 3000 kilometers of coastline and account for nearly one-third of the world's oil and more than one-fifth of global proven natural gas reserves. Out of the total amount of 1383 billion barrels of proven oil reserves worldwide, the GCC holds 495 billion barrels (approximately 33% of global proven reserves). Considering natural gas from a global total of 6609 trillion cubic meters, the GCC's proven reserves amount to 1483 trillion cubic meters. The Saudi Arabia alone accounts for over 200 billion barrels, representing 58% of GCC oil reserves and more than half of its total proven oil reserves with Kuwait and the UAE, holding approximately 20% and 19% of the GCC's proven oil reserves, respectively. Other GCC members such as Bahrain, Oman, and Qatar possess comparatively smaller shares, collectively accounting for about 7% of GCC oil reserves.

Despite its smaller size among the GCC members, Qatar holds more than 740 trillion cubic meters (60%) of the GCC's proven natural gas reserves. It ranks as the world's third largest holder of natural gas reserves, after Iran and Russia and in recent years, Qatar has become the world's largest LNG exporter. The Saudi Arabia and the UAE hold 19% and 14% of proven natural gas reserves, respectively, ranking them as the second and third largest gas holders among the GCC countries (QNB, 2012).

After the Saudi Arabia, the UAE and Kuwait are among the world's top ten oil producers, with oil comprising a major portion of their exports. Oman and Bahrain have the smallest oil reserves among the GCC members and correspondingly minimal oil export shares.

The Saudi Arabia controls over half of the Gulf's oil reserves, while the other GCC members have significantly smaller reserves. Bahrain faces natural resource constraints with relatively low per capita oil reserves in Bahrain and Oman. Apart from Qatar, which has the largest gas reserves, the Saudi Arabia, Bahrain, and Oman also have comparatively low natural gas reserves. Thus, disparities in the distribution of natural resources—oil and gas—across the GCC geographic environment are evident (Sturm & Siegfried, 2005).

The UAE is rich in oil, yet it still suffers from natural gas shortages like many GCC neighbors. With rapid population growth, household energy demand—largely met by gas—is increasing rapidly. Qatar, as the holder of massive gas reserves, is a natural regional gas supplier, however following political disputes with the Saudi Arabia, the UAE, and other GCC states have limited its ability to supply gas to neighbors. These obstacles have spurred the GCC governments, particularly the UAE to seek access to nuclear and renewable energy technologies to develop their domestic power sectors. For instance, a bilateral agreement between the UAE and South Korea, established in 2009, provides the UAE with nuclear technology access. Meanwhile, Russia and China actively seek to expand their influence in the region by marketing nuclear technology to the Saudi Arabia. In exchange for technology access from strategic partners, the GCC countries can leverage their oil wealth as a bargaining tool. The UAE's strategic partners in Asia—China, India, South Korea, and Japan—are major consumers of its oil and provide vital technology access in return (Griffiths, 2019).

The oil sector accounts for approximately 45% of the GCC's total GDP, highlighting the deep dependence of these countries on fossil fuels. As the share of non-oil sector in GDP grows, economic diversification increases, reducing vulnerability to oil price volatility and enabling more stable revenue growth (QNB, 2012).

The uneven distribution of natural resources may contribute to divergence among the GCC members in the short term. However, oil resource limitations in the long-term economic outlook will inevitably compel these countries to undertake reforms aimed at reducing dependence on oil revenues and advancing economic diversification.

4.3 The Geopolitical Risks of Energy Transition for Persian Gulf Countries

The vulnerability of Persian Gulf countries toward the energy transition depends on two factors: the share of government revenues derived from fossil fuel production and exports and the economy's capacity to generate income from alternative sources.

Gross Domestic Product (GDP) per capita serves as an indicator of a local economy's resilience to revenue declines. Even for wealthy countries, reduced oil revenues pose challenges, even though the risk of widespread poverty and civil unrest is lower than in poorer states. Typically, a high GDP per capita correlates with diversified income sources beyond oil and gas exports. The presence of refineries, oil service companies, and jobs in other sectors mitigates the impact of reduced fossil fuel revenue. Moreover, as more countries adopt carbon trading schemes, some energy-sector jobs—such as refining—may relocate from industrialized nations to oil-exporting regions like the Persian Gulf, where carbon prices are minimal or zero. Thus, some oil producers can offset declining oil and gas rents by increasing revenue from refining and processing activities (Klement, 2021).

With its very high GDP per capita, Qatar is likely the least vulnerable among the oil-producing countries. Other relatively resilient oil producers are the Saudi Arabia, Kuwait, and the UAE. Despite the heavy reliance on fossil fuel rents, these countries have relatively high GDP per capita. However, income inequality is significant in many and GDP per capita is not evenly distributed, that in turn increases vulnerability. Iraq remains heavily dependent on fossil fuel exports, but continues to experience poverty, creating fertile ground for terrorist organizations and a potential trigger for civil war with possible spillover effects on neighboring countries. Qatar's very low official youth unemployment rate renders it relatively insulated from energy transition risks. The Saudi Arabia, with a youth unemployment rate of 16.1%, is borderline; in contrast, the youth unemployment exceeds 30% in Iran and Iraq, placing these countries at high risk of social unrest or even conflict should their economies weaken (ibid).

5 The Geopolitical Challenges and Opportunities of Energy Transition in the Persian Gulf

Energy transition in the Persian Gulf region, as a central hub of global energy dynamics, has led to the emergence of various challenges. The responses of the countries in this region to these challenges revolve around four main axes: (1) restructuring their economies to cope with lower oil prices in the short-term and the long-term decline of hydrocarbon rents; (2) making efforts to safeguard the future of hydrocarbon industries; (3) shifting gradually, but accelerated toward re-equipping domestic energy systems for a lower carbon future; and (4) addressing the geo-economic transition accompanied by regional convergence (Hafner & Tagliapietra, 2020).

The energy transition has also created geopolitical opportunities for the Persian Gulf countries. These challenges and opportunities are summarized in Table 3 and are briefly discussed below.

5.1 *Oil Rent and Economic Diversification*

5.1.1 Challenge: Oil Rent

A defining characteristic of the Persian Gulf States lies in their heavy dependence on oil rents. The "rentier state" theory was first proposed by Mahdavy (1970). According to this theory, the states that are endowed with abundant natural resources rely less on taxing their citizens and more on allocating or distributing revenues from these resources. This situation leads to an oversized and often inefficient bureaucracy, while simultaneously diminishing incentives for hard work and government accountability. Rent-seeking behavior is part of a broader phenomenon known as the "resource curse," which describes various negative impacts of heavy reliance on natural resource revenues. These adverse effects include a lack of competitiveness in non-resource sectors and manufactured exports; lower GDP growth rates; overvalued exchange rates; high macroeconomic volatility; weak and corrupt institutions; a tendency toward authoritarianism; external and civil-military conflicts; and deficiencies in democracy, human rights, and gender equality.

5.1.2 Opportunity: Economic Diversification

One of the most critical structural economic problems among the Persian Gulf countries is the excessive reliance on hydrocarbon export revenues or in other words, the absence or weakness of economic diversification. This dependence makes these countries vulnerable to the oil price volatility.

According to Hvidt (2013), economic diversification has undergone several phases in the Persian Gulf. In the 1970s, fears of resource depletion in the near future prevailed. High oil prices at that time provided ample financial resources to invest in new industries, which was also enticing for the rent-seeking bureaucrats

Table 3 Geopolitical challenges and opportunities of the energy transition in Persian Gulf countries

No.	Challenges	Opportunities	Researchers
1	Oil rent and resource curse	Economic diversification	Mahdavy (1970), Hvidt (2013), Karsh and Rautsi (2008)
2	Oil demand peak	Economic restructuring and resilience through value-added production	Depledge (2008), Dale and Fattouh (2018), Bazilian et al. (2019), Bazilian and Howells (2019)
3	Climate change	Transition to low-carbon energy systems	Lowe (2019), Hafner and Tagliapietra (2020)
4	Regional cultural, economic, political, and territorial conflicts	Regional convergence	Alizadeh et al. (2024), Jafari Valdani (1995), Zeinlabedin (2004), Mills (2020), Nami (2007), Hashemi (2011), Raphael and Stokes (2011), Eslami (2012)

Source: Research findings

and merchants. During the 1980s and 1990s, low oil prices raised awareness about the need to find alternative revenue sources. The 2000s witnessed renewed oil revenues, enabling investments in infrastructure, real estate, and energy-intensive industries such as aluminum, steel, cement, and petrochemicals, often supported by cheap and subsidized energy. The Saudi Arabia developed more advanced petrochemical operations through companies like the Saudi Basic Industries Corporation (SABIC). Meanwhile; under the sanctions pressure, Iran developed industries less correlated with global oil prices to meet domestic needs and produce export goods.

In the 2010s, sovereign wealth funds were established, especially in Iran, the UAE, Kuwait, and Qatar to save surplus oil revenues with multiple objectives to prevent upward pressure on fixed exchange rates, to buffer macroeconomic, to prevent fiscal volatility from oil price fluctuations, to save for a declining oil revenues future, and to strategically invest in domestic and international economies.

The Persian Gulf countries have also outlined visions for diversification extending at least up to 2030 and have taken significant steps toward these goals. The Saudi Arabia's Vision 2030 initiated under Crown Prince Mohammed bin Salman is among the most recent and influential plans. However, its surprisingly limited focus on the energy sector with more emphasis on technology, tourism, and social transformation is notable. Currently, Iran has a relatively diversified economy with sanctions driving greater self-sufficiency and less dependency on oil revenues. Iraq's bureaucratic and sectarian system struggles to improve performance in oil, gas, and electricity sectors with limited progress.

Reversing the "resource curse" and rent-seeking in Persian Gulf countries depend on building strong and capable institutions. Reduced dependence on resource rents may decrease the military competition and internal conflicts. However, in the medium term, economic stress and struggles over remaining rents could lead to more violent confrontations, as exemplified by Saddam Hussein's 1990 invasion of Kuwait amid the financial crises (Karsh & Rautsi, 2008).

Most Persian Gulf countries' economic diversification programs aim to increase private sector participation, create jobs, and build human capital, further to expand commerce, business services, logistics, tourism, and manufacturing. In addition, expanding investments in renewable energy can support Persian Gulf States' diversification efforts and job creation by encouraging investment and participation of small and medium enterprises along the value chain (IRENA, 2020).

5.2 *The Climate Change and Transition to Low-Carbon and Renewable Energy Systems*

5.2.1 Challenge: Climate Change

A primary challenge for several GCC countries—such as the Saudi Arabia, the United Arab Emirates, and Kuwait—is how to maximize the value of their hydrocarbon resources in a world increasingly constrained by climate change, while competing with non-OPEC countries. In addition to facing climate-related challenges, Iraq and Iran grapple with political and security issues that hinder effective long-term planning. Smaller producers, including Oman and Bahrain, face the intermediate challenge of maximizing production, rationalizing domestic consumption and controlling costs through measures such as new exploration, enhanced recovery, and unconventional resources. Major gas holders—Qatar and Iran—are in a relatively better position due to the significantly lower carbon content of natural gas and its comparatively cleaner environmental footprint. Nevertheless, they face the long-term challenges of securing demand by ensuring gas remains cost-competitive against renewables, while reducing or eliminating its carbon footprint, at the same time. The energy-intensive industrial sectors in the region are also confronted with the climate actions implemented in key export markets; particularly the Europe, which may include carbon border taxes on imports from countries lacking equivalent carbon pricing mechanisms (Lowe, 2019).

The Arab countries in Persian Gulf currently hold the world's highest per capita emitters of greenhouse gases (GHGs), as nearly all energy demands (water, electricity, industry, transportation) are overwhelmingly met by the oil and gas. Furthermore, the 2019 Global Air Quality Index ranked Bahrain, Kuwait, and the UAE among the ten most polluted countries, globally (IQAir, 2019). These findings pose severe public health and climate concerns, underscoring the urgent need to develop alternative energy sources to reduce emissions (Omri & Bilaid, 2020).

5.2.2 Opportunity: Transition to Low-Carbon and Renewable Energy Systems

Renewable energy presents an opportunity for the Persian Gulf States to address emerging energy security challenges, rising GHG emissions, and deteriorating air quality and the adverse impacts of climate change. Table 4 summarizes the preventive actions undertaken by the Persian Gulf countries in response to the climate challenges.

The Persian Gulf States have articulated ambitious long-term economic diversification goals that integrate environmental sustainability as a core pillar. These objectives encompass air quality, public health, water supply, waste management, biodiversity, fisheries, climate change mitigation, and pollution control. For example, the Saudi Arabia's Vision 2030 puts its central focus on sustainability, committing to provide "a collective and responsible approach to confronting current and future energy and climate challenges." Bahrain's 2030 Economic Vision emphasizes that "economic growth should never come at the expense of the environment and the long-term well-being of our people." Kuwait Vision 2035 pledges "ensuring efficient environmental regulations and sustainability within the country." Qatar's National Vision 2030 asserts that the "economic development and environmental protection are dual imperatives, neither to be sacrificed for the other." Oman's development plan advances three interrelated national environmental goals: environmental protection, crisis risk management, and the promotion of science,

Table 4 Geopolitical actions of the persian gulf states in the energy transition

No.	Geopolitical actions in the energy transition	Country/countries
1	Engaging in international climate diplomacy; promoting the adoption of electric vehicles	United Arab Emirates
2	Enhancing energy efficiency in both production and consumption; substituting fossil fuels with renewable energy; reducing gas flaring and leakage; land-use changes; reducing overall greenhouse gas emissions below average levels	Iran, Iraq
3	Implementing carbon capture and storage (CCS) strategies	United Arab Emirates, Saudi Arabia, Qatar
4	Promoting the use of hydrogen as a clean fuel	United Arab Emirates, Saudi Arabia, Qatar

Source: Research findings

technology, and innovation (Al-Sarihi, 2018). Iran's 20-Year Vision Plan aimed to supply 10% of its electricity generation from renewable sources by 2025 (Iran 20-Year Vision Document, 2005–2025).

Deploying renewable energy technologies throughout the Persian Gulf not only supports growing domestic energy demand, but it also frees up fossil fuels for downstream economic diversification projects and enhances export capacity. Investments in the renewables help Persian Gulf States contribute to global GHG emission reductions and mitigate economic risks related to the climate change (Praveen et al., 2020).

The UAE is a regional leader in the renewable energy adoption, accounting for 68% of the region's installed renewable capacity, followed by the Saudi Arabia (16%) and Kuwait (9%). Moreover, the Persian Gulf countries have increasingly pursued greenhouse gas emission reduction schemes, often aligned with renewable energy targets. For instance, the Saudi Arabia has set a goal to avoid up to 278 million tons of CO2 equivalent annually by 2030. Oman committed to a 7% reduction in GHG emissions by 2030 in its second Nationally Determined Contribution (NDC).

The UAE adopted its National Energy Strategy 2050 in 2017, targeting 50% of its energy needs from clean sources (44% renewables and 6% nuclear) and a 70% reduction in carbon emissions. The UAE's early renewable energy expansion was facilitated by the industrial-scale renewable energy auctions, led by Dubai since 2015. The Mohammed bin Rashid Al Maktoum Solar Park's first independent power producer (IPP) contract was awarded through such auctions with Dubai Electricity and Water Authority (DEWA) holding a 51% stake in the consortium (Griffiths, 2017a, 2017b). Furthermore, the UAE has embedded climate change prominently in its international diplomacy and it has supported carbon capture and storage (CCS) inclusion within the Clean Development Mechanism (Hafner & Tagliapietra, 2020).

Bahrain launched its Economic Vision 2030 in 2008, aiming to reduce oil dependency and transition toward sustainability. This vision targets the installation of 700 MW of renewable energy capacity by 2030. Kuwait has set goals to increase the share of renewables in its energy mix to 10% by 2020 and 15% by 2030. The

Shagaya Solar Power Plant; whose first phase became operational in 2019, represents Kuwait's flagship renewable energy project.

Oman has implemented policies supporting the adoption of the renewable energy technologies both at small and large scales. For instance, at the small scale in 2013, the Public Authority for Regulation of Electricity and Water (formerly the Electricity Regulatory Authority) introduced its first policy to encourage renewable energy installations in rural areas. This policy led to the establishment of the 303 kW Mazionah solar pilot project and other rural projects such as the 500-kW wind pilot project on Masirah Island (Al-Sarihi & Cherni, 2018). Moreover, in 2017, Oman introduced a policy enabling individuals—including homeowners and industrial and commercial entities—to generate electricity from renewable sources like solar power and sell excess energy back to distribution companies (Viswanathan, 2020).

Qatar has set a target to meet 20% of its electricity demand from the renewable sources by 2030. It is the only Persian Gulf country with a polysilicon manufacturing plant—a critical component in various photovoltaic (PV) technologies. Qatar Solar Technologies (QSTec), located in the Ras Laffan Industrial City (approximately 80 km north of Doha), is a joint venture between Qatar Solar (a subsidiary of Qatar Foundation), the German company Solar World AG and Qatar Development Bank. Moreover, Qatar is the only Persian Gulf State operating a waste-to-energy facility, the 30 MW Mesaieed plant. While the project was expected to be operational by the end of 2020, only the first phase of the 800 MW Al Kharsaah photovoltaic solar project reached financial close in the late 2020 (Thompson, 2020).

The Saudi Arabia's announced energy mix includes a target of 50% renewables and 50% natural gas by 2030. The country possesses the highest solar energy potential in the region and ranks 13th globally for onshore wind energy production (Al-Ghamdi, 2020). The Saudi Arabia's renewable energy capacity reached 700 MW by 2021, comprising 400 MW of wind power (Dumat Al-Jandal project) and 300 MW of photovoltaic power (Sakaka project), which achieved a record low solar PV tariff of $0.0234 per kWh. During its G20 presidency, the Saudi Arabia proposed the activation of a Circular Carbon Economy (CCE) framework, endorsed by all G20 members as an integrated and practical approach to managing greenhouse gas emissions. The CCE is based on three environmental protection strategies—reduce, remove, and reuse and recycle—and supports a fourth strategy aiming to eliminate accumulated emissions in the atmosphere.

The Saudi Aramco is the most advanced in climate-aligned demand-side thinking, among national oil companies in the region. The company has significantly invested in research and development to improve engine efficiency, including pioneering fundamental projects that could extend the competitiveness of oil-based transportation relative to electric vehicles, while reducing greenhouse gas emissions. Aramco also supports carbon capture and storage (CCS) policies (UNFCCC, 2015a). Besides ADNOC and Qatar Petroleum, Aramco has launched large-scale carbon capture and storage facilities that inject CO2 from gas processing or industrial plants into underground reservoirs for safe disposal or enhanced oil recovery. Hydrogen has recently attracted growing attention as a clean fuel. Both the "blue hydrogen," produced from fossil fuels with carbon capture and storage and the "green hydrogen," produced via water electrolysis powered by low-carbon electricity, represent promising potential in the Persian Gulf region (Hafner & Tagliapietra, 2020).

Currently, the renewable energy accounts for less than 2% of Iran's energy consumption mix. However, positive trends toward clean energy transition are emerging. Recognizing the importance of renewables in the energy transition era, Iran has focused on electrification across various economic sectors. The country's energy policy is shifting from oil dependency toward a diversified energy portfolio with more sustainable resources (Solaymani, 2021). Acknowledging the sector's potential, Iranian policymakers have developed programs to capitalize on it. Within the framework of the Seventh Development Plan, Iran prioritizes the renewable energy-sector development, emphasizing the removal of barriers and establishing appropriate mechanisms to increase the renewable energy generation by 12,000 MW during the planned period through public and private sector participation (IRENA, 2020). However, international sanctions are expected to make financing the renewable projects challenging. The renewable energy market in Iran will mainly be driven by the ongoing hydropower projects, projected to add nearly 1650 MW to the national capacity over the forecast period. In addition to hydropower, Iran is planning to expand its solar capacity, further supporting the renewable energy growth (Modor Intelligence, 2021).

Iraq faces challenges in transitioning to renewables due to its inherent reliance on fossil fuels in its energy infrastructure. Currently, 98% of Iraq's electricity production comes from non-renewable sources with only 2% derived from the renewables, like wind and solar. For a successful energy transition, Iraq requires substantial renewable energy generation capacity to meet consumer demand. Policies that lower the cost of renewables and promote the installation of renewable energy generators—such as carbon taxes, investment attraction, renewable promotion, and expanded research and education—can facilitate a just transition in Iraq. Carbon and value-added taxes can increase the cost of non-renewable energy, encouraging both consumers and producers to adopt cleaner alternatives like the renewables. A combination of these policies could promote energy transition by making fossil fuels relatively more expensive than the cleaner renewable sources (Harsha, 2025).

Both Iran and Iraq have submitted their Nationally Determined Contributions (NDCs), which include energy efficiency improvements in production and consumption; achievements in renewable and occasionally nuclear energy; fuel substitution; strengthening of public transportation; reduction of gas flaring and leakage; land-use changes; and overall greenhouse gas emissions reductions below business-as-usual (BAU) levels. Iraq has committed to reducing approximately 90 million tons of greenhouse gases between 2020 and 2035, a 14% reduction compared to BAU (UNFCCC, 2015b). Iran has pledged unilateral reductions of up to 12%; and with international assistance, up to 16% (4% below BAU) (UNFCCC, 2015c).

5.3 Peak Oil Demand/Economic Restructuring and Resilience

5.3.1 Challenge: Peak Oil Demand

Peak oil demand refers to the near-term decline in global oil demand driven by the expansion of electric vehicles, improved efficiency, environmental pressures, and greenhouse gas (GHG) emission constraints. Global efforts to reduce GHG emissions through policies that aimed at lowering hydrocarbon consumption could directly result in economic losses due to the decreased oil and gas demand and consequently reduced oil export revenues (IEA, 2019). The Persian Gulf countries still need to fully internalize the implications of peak oil demand. In 2015, the Saudi Arabia and other OPEC producers significantly increased production to engage in a "price war" aimed at capturing market share, but non-OPEC production—especially the U.S. shale oil—prevented this strategy from succeeding. The abundance of cheap feedstock has also sparked a renaissance in the U.S. petrochemical sector, posing another challenge to the Persian Gulf's oil and gas industry. Meanwhile, the short-term budgetary needs of OPEC countries may inhibit pursuing a high-volume, low-price strategy designed to maximize production and displace competitors on the cusp of peak demand (Dale & Fatouh, 2018).

5.3.2 Opportunity: Economic Restructuring and Resilience Through Value Creation

The value creation strategy dates back to 1960s in Iran, 1970s in Iraq, and early 1980s in the Saudi Arabia, but it has been pursued more rigorously and persistently in recent years. Part of this increased focus on value creation involves "local value addition," which seeks to enhance the capacity of domestic companies or joint ventures to supply equipment to the national oil industry. Localization efforts, including the strengthening skill development and employing nationals instead of expatriates, have also been pursued.

Value creation primarily occurs outside the upstream oil sector. The Persian Gulf national oil companies have made relatively limited investments in the international upstream sector due to extensive low-cost domestic resources and in some cases, insufficient technical and managerial skills. Primarily through Aramco and the Saudi Basic Industries Corporation (SABIC), the Saudi Arabia has become a leader in this arena. Qatar Petroleum, under CEO Saad Al-Kaabi, has adopted a strategy of acquiring stakes in international oil companies' expiring fields. Kuwait Petroleum Corporation (KPC) and Petroleum Development Oman (PDO) have also been active, but to a lesser extent.

Another aspect of value creation involves a shift toward the downstream sector including refining, petrochemicals, tankers, storage, trading, and fuel retailing. Petrochemicals are viewed as one of the most promising domains for the future oil demand, as requisition typically grows faster than GDP in emerging economies and the alternatives such as bio-based materials remain relatively costly and limited in supply. Petrochemical production emits some greenhouse gases, but the products themselves do not release GHGs unless decomposed or burned. Currently, new petrochemical strategies focus on large-scale integrated refining and petrochemical complexes, epitomized by Aramco/SABIC's proposed direct crude-to-chemicals plant in Yanbu on the Red Sea coast. Specialty chemicals within the value chain are being upgraded to support local industries such as automotive parts manufacturing. These plants improve profit margins and market compatibility, while being significantly more complex to build and operate.

Within gas sector, Aramco acquired a stake in Sempra Energy's Gulf Coast export facilities (25% of LNG Port Arthur) (Saudi Aramco, 2019). Iran began exporting gas to Iraq in June 2017 (EIA, 2019). Iraq is gradually advancing in reducing gas flaring and increasing electricity production. Ultimately, Iraq could connect itself to the GCC grid, by becoming a key gas and electricity corridor linking Iran and the Persian Gulf in the east, Turkey in the north, and the Eastern Mediterranean in the west.

5.4 *Regional Conflicts in Culture, Economy, Politics, and Territory/Regional Convergence*

5.4.1 Challenge: Regional Conflicts

In the recent years, Persian Gulf countries have sought to diversify their economies by reducing dependence on oil and gas, instead investing in renewable energy and new energy technologies. These efforts require enhanced cooperation and convergence among these countries, which would increase regional stability and sustainable development. However, multiple factors—including cultural, economic, political, and territorial disputes among the Persian Gulf States, as well as the intervention of international powers—have hindered collaborative activities and led to divergence within the region (Alizadeh et al., 2024). Some of these territorial and border disputes among the Persian Gulf countries are summarized in Table 5.

Iran has reached formal agreements with Oman, Qatar, Bahrain, and the Saudi Arabia regarding its borders in the Persian Gulf. Iran and Dubai have delineated their maritime boundaries, yet Iran and the UAE have remained without a formal maritime boundary due to the UAE's territorial claims over the three islands. Additionally, the maritime boundaries between Iran and Iraq and between Iran and Kuwait remain undefined, serving as sources of tension and threat (Karimipoor, 2000). As the Iran-Iraq maritime boundary has not been demarcated on the one side, and the Iraq-Kuwait maritime boundary on the other, the exact location of the tripoint remains uncertain (Nami, 2007).

These disputes remain as significant factors contributing to the divergence and negative security perceptions among Persian Gulf countries, constituting major obstacles to institutionalizing intra-regional security mechanisms. They have led to

Table 5 Territorial and border disputes among Persian Gulf countries

Maritime and river border disputes	Land border and island ownership disputes
Maritime border between Iran and UAE (except Iran-Dubai maritime boundary)	Islands of Tunb and Abu Musa between Iran and UAE
Maritime border in the Persian Gulf, Sea of Oman, and Musandam Peninsula between UAE and Oman	Land border in parts of Ras Al Khaimah and Sharjah between UAE and Oman
Maritime border between Bahrain and Qatar	Dispute between Bahrain and Qatar over the Hawar Islands
Arvand River between Iran and Iraq	Iraq and Kuwait over Warbah and Bubiyan islands
Maritime border between Iran and Kuwait	Saudi Arabia and Kuwait over Qarwah and Umm al-Maradim islands
Maritime border in Salwa Gulf and Khor al-Adid between Saudi Arabia and Qatar	Multiple territorial disputes between Saudi Arabia and Yemen
Maritime borders between UAE and Saudi Arabia	UAE and Qatar over Halul Island and other islands in Khor al-Adid
Maritime borders (except Abu Dhabi-Dubai)	Territorial disputes among the seven emirates of the UAE, numbering twelve

Source: Jafari Valdani (1995/1374), Zainlabedin (2004)

specific geopolitical conflicts, including the Gulf Wars: the Iran-Iraq War (1980–1988), Saddam Hussein's invasion of Kuwait and the subsequent U.S.-led liberation (1990–1991), and the U.S. invasion of Iraq, the ensuing civil war and the conflict with ISIS (2003–present). These incidents have been accompanied by varying degrees of insurgencies, territorial disputes, revolutions, coups—especially during the Arab Spring (2011)—severe international sanctions (notably against Iran and Iraq), and state repression (Hashemi, 2011).

Persian Gulf countries also have complex political and institutional histories. Conflicts in the region have repeatedly threatened global oil and gas supplies. The global economic significance of the region, alongside the presence of small wealthy states reliant on external security patrons, has led to repeated interventions by the United States, Russia, and the European countries. "Resource regionalism" within countries has fueled conflicts and separatism over resource-rich areas, such as the Kurdish region (Mills, 2020).

The most critical challenge to energy cooperation and transit in the Persian Gulf in recent years has been the tension between Iran and the Saudi Arabia, rooted in divergent ideological foundations. The result of this tension has been a diplomatic crisis throughout the Persian Gulf region. Efforts to expand spheres of influence and proxy wars have threatened energy production and transit; thus, confrontational approaches have led to the economic sanctions and the loss of economic partners, the reducing economic power, the diminishing geopolitical weight, and the increasing national security vulnerabilities. Beyond economic issues arising from oil and gas resources, the ethnic and sectarian diversities in the region have intensified territorial disputes, producing enduring conflicts. These prolonged conflicts have destabilized the region and have fostered divergence among its states. These territorial and border disputes become even more acute, when regional or extra-regional powers take sides, as most notably witnessed in the dispute between Iran and the UAE over the three islands. Consequently, the mutual perceptions of threat and insecurity remain amongst the primary obstacles to regional integration (Alizadeh et al., 2024).

5.4.2 Opportunity: Regional Convergence of the Persian Gulf States

Energy and its various political and economic dimensions have been historically central to international developments and trends, while their significance in international relations is steadily increasing. In other words, energy has become a core element of power in international relations and it plays a pivotal role in linking different domains of national and transnational politics and economics (Eslami, 2012).

Through economic and technical cooperation, harmonization of energy policies, joint energy security efforts, and attempts to diversify economies, energy can serve as a key driver of regional integration (Alizadeh et al., 2024).

Possessing abundant underground resources—particularly energy resources, which fuel the global industrial economy—can provide each political entity in the international system with leverage and bargaining power in global competitive landscape. Given today's world's reliance on energy carriers (oil and natural gas) and the lack of near-term substitutes, such as solar and wind power, energy diplomacy has become one of the most important and effective tools in power presentation. Governments endowed with significant natural resources can exploit oil or gas politically (Niakooei & Karimi Pour, 2015).

In the new structure of international political economy, energy is considered as one of the most significant and effective power instruments among the industrialized countries and regions such as the European Union, China, India, Southeast Asia, and North America. There is no foreseeable escape from this dependency for at least several decades. The importance of energy is such that the consumer countries accompanying the producing countries and transit routes, consider energy sources as strategic targets and components of their national security interests (Raphael & Stokes, 2011).

6 Concluding Remarks

The international decarbonization policies and advances in low-carbon technologies will have profound geopolitical implications by reshaping the global energy architecture. A large-scale transition to low-carbon energy will affect the global energy system, impact economies, and change political dynamics both within and among countries.

With the advent of geo-economic era in global governance, the Persian Gulf has emerged as a critical zone for control and geopolitical leverage. Although the eight

Persian Gulf countries share a common geopolitical and geo-economic energy domain and possess the necessary capacities and geographical proximity for the developments and exchanges, they have been unable to fully capitalize on these potentials, so far. The main factors overshadowing the region's economic variables are political, ideological disputes, and territorial conflicts.

As a result of underperformance and failure to seize global opportunities, the region has not yet evolved into a true geo-economic hub and holds a marginal share in global equations relative to its geopolitical status—primarily limited to energy exports. Therefore, these countries must activate their role in the global geo-economic arena by leveraging their vast energy reserves in support of national and regional capabilities to strengthen their geo-economic position, in the context of globalization.

Another determinant of the Persian Gulf's geopolitical and geo-economic significance to the world lies in its proximity to the Sea of Oman, the Red Sea, and the Indian Ocean. The strategic importance of the Persian Gulf security has led major powers to control regional actors and influence the trajectory of regional events simultaneously, hence ultimately securing economic resources under their sway.

Intervention by extra-regional powers has hindered the convergence of the Persian Gulf countries in their transition to sustainable energy. The success of the energy transition demands cooperation and mutual understanding among countries, globally—especially among fossil fuel producers. Given the globalization trends, this region can enhance its geo-economic performance for the development, progress, and competition with other countries, thereby fostering regional convergence in energy transition.

Although the Persian Gulf States have, over past decades, been producers, refiners, and exporters of hydrocarbon-based products, they have been deeply impacted by the global economy's reliance on fossil fuels. They are currently striving to move away from hydrocarbons and join the global decarbonization movement in the energy sector. These countries are advancing toward reducing fossil fuel dependency and adopting green energy at varying paces. Among them, the Saudi Arabia, the UAE, and Oman stand out as the regional and global leaders driving a more accelerated energy transition. Accordingly, several policy recommendations can be made:

While all Persian Gulf countries have announced ambitious renewable energy targets, still some lack allocated institutions with clear mandates and regulatory frameworks to oversee renewable energy deployment and achieve their targeted goals. Establishing such dedicated agencies would reduce institutional barriers—including streamlining governance, permitting and approving processes—thereby facilitating renewable energy project development.

A dedicated renewable energy authority would enhance coordination in energy transition efforts and promote the sharing of knowledge, lessons learned, experiences, and resource flows among stakeholders.

Hydrocarbon pricing reforms not only improve the competitiveness of renewable energy sources and promote efficient energy use, but they also alleviate fiscal pressures on Persian Gulf States. However, it is crucial to carefully consider hydrocarbon pricing policies and their potential impacts on low-income consumers, particularly in the residential sector.

Direct cash transfers or low-interest loans could be effective policy tools to offset the high upfront investment costs in renewable energy. Subsidies supporting mid-to large-scale renewable energy asset investments can create competitive environments for the renewable projects and conventional energy supply technologies.

Another important aspect of increasing renewable energy demand is raising public awareness about the new renewable energy technologies.

At the national level, Persian Gulf countries should focus on providing financial support for local renewable energy technology development to reduce dependence on imports. This is particularly significant, because most imported renewable technologies underperform within the Persian Gulf's harsh environment characterized by heat, humidity, and dust. Most importantly, the institutional framework needed to support innovation and foster collaboration among all stakeholders—including academia, private sector, and government—must be strengthened.

References

Akhbari, M. (2004). *The geopolitical structure of the world and its impact on the Middle East. In: Proceedings of the First Scientific Congress of the Iranian Geopolitics Association*. Geographical Organization.

Albaker, A., Abbasi, K. R., Haddad, A. M., Radulescu, M., Manescu, C., & Bondac, G. T. (2023). Analyzing the impact of renewable energy and green innovation on carbon emissions in the MENA region. *Energies, 16*(16), 6053. https://doi.org/10.3390/en16166053

Al-Ghamdi, A. (2020). *Saudi Arabia energy report*. Riyadh, Saudi Arabia.

Alizadeh, A., Ghalandari, Y., & Kabiri, H. (2024). The Role and position of the energy component on the convergence of the countries of the Persian Gulf region. *Research on Global Relations, 1*(3), 205–241. https://doi.org/10.22054/jrgr.2024.79188.1078

Al-Sarihi, A.(2018) Prospects for Climate Change Integration in GCC economic diversification strategies; *LSE Middle East Centre Working Paper* 20; Kuwait Programme; LSE Middle East Centre, London, UK.

Al-Sarihi, A., & Cherni, J. A. (2018). Assessing strengths and weaknesses of renewable energy initiatives in Oman: an analysis with strategic niche management. *Energy Transit, 2*, 15–29. https://doi.org/10.1007/s41825-018-0008-9

Al-Sarihi, A., & Mansouri, N. (2022). Renewable energy development in the Gulf Cooperation Council Countries: Status, Barriers, and Policy Options. *Energies, 15*, 1923. https://doi.org/10.3390/en15051923

Aminian, B. (2005). NATO expansion and persistence: U.S. hegemony. *Geopolitics Quarterly, 2*. Winter.

Barnard, A. (2014), Saudis' Grant to Lebanon Is Seen as Message to U.S., New York Times, January 6, 2014.

Bayram, I. S., & Ustun, T. S. (2017). A survey on behind the meter energy management systems in smart grid. *Renewable and Sustainable Energy Reviews, 72*, 1208–1232. https://doi.org/10.1016/j.rser.2016.10.034

Bazilian, M., & Howells, M. (2019). Preface to the special issue on 'The geopolitics of the energy transition'. *Energy Strategy Reviews, 26*. https://doi.org/10.1016/j.esr.2019.100413

Bazilian, M., Bradshaw, M., Goldthau, A., & Westphal, K. (2019). Model and manage the changing geopolitics of energy. *Nature, 569*(7754), 29–31. https://doi.org/10.1038/d41586-019-01312-5

Berryman, J. (2012). Geopolitics and Russian foreign policy. *International Politics, 49*(4), 530–544. https://doi.org/10.1057/ip.2012.15

Blackwill, R. D., & Harris, J. M. (2016). *War by other means*. Harvard University Press..
Bremmer, I. (2010). *The End of the free market: who wins the war between states and corporations?* Portfolio.
British Petroleum (BP). (2021). energy economics/statistical -review/bp-stats-review. https://www.bp.com/content/dam/bp/business-sites/en/global/corporate/pdfs.
Brown, S. (1991). Explaining the Transformation of World Politics. *International Journal: Canada's Journal of Global Policy Analysis, 46*(2), 207–219. https://doi.org/10.1177/002070209104600201
Cahnman, W. J. (1943). Concepts of Geopolitics. *American Sociological Review, 8*(1), 55–59.
Chen, B., Xiong, R., Li, H., Sun, Q., & Yang, J. (2019). Pathways for Sustainable Energy Transition. *Journal of Cleaner Production, 228*, 1564–1571. https://doi.org/10.1016/j.jclepro.2019.04.372
Clayton, B., & Segal, A. (2013). Addressing Cyber Threats to Oil and Gas Supplies. *Council on Foreign Relations Energy Brief, 2013*, 2.
Clinton, H. (2011). Economic Statecraft, Speech delivered at the Economic Club of New York, October 14, 2011.
Cordesman, A. H. (2005) The changing balance of US and global dependence on middle eastern energy exports (pp. 1–40) Working Paper. Washington, DC: Centre for Strategic and International Studies (CSIS).
Criekemans, D. (2018). Geopolitics of the renewable energy game and its potential impact upon global power relations. In D. Scholten (Ed.), *The geopolitics of renewables* (pp. 37–74). Springer.
Daei Karimzadeh, S., Sheikh Bahaei, A., & Ghobadi, S. (2021). Interaction of clean energy, domestic and foreign capital, economic growth, and environmental quality in selected developing countries using GMM approach. *Energy Economics Research Journal of Iran, 10*(40), 11–37.
Dale, S., & Fattouh, B. (2018). Peak Oil Demand and Long-Run Oil Prices, The Oxford Institute for Energy Studies, Energy Insight: 25, January 2018. https://www.oxfordenergy.org/wpcms/wp-content/uploads/2018/01.
Danzig, R. (2014). Surviving on a Diet of Poisoned Fruit: Reducing the National Security Risks of America's Cyber Dependencies. *Center for a New American Security, 2014*, 8.
Depledge, J. (2008). Striving for No: Saudi Arabia in the Climate Change Regime. *Global Environmental Politics, 8*(4), 9–35. https://doi.org/10.1162/glep.2008.8.4.9
Ebrahimi, M., & Rahmani, D. (2019). A Five-Dimensional Approach to Sustainability for Prioritizing Energy Production Systems Using a Revised GRA Method: A Case Study. *Renewable Energy, 135*(C), 345–354. https://doi.org/10.1016/j.renene.2018.12.008
Eslami, M. (2012). Iran-Russia Energy Diplomacy: Grounds for Convergence and Divergence. *Strategy, 21*(3), 189–220.
Ezzati, E. (2005). *Energy geo-economy and its security implications for Iran, Pakistan, and India*. Center for Political and International Studies.
Ezzati, E. (2009). *Strategic geography of Iran*. Geographical Organization of the Armed Forces.
Foxon, T. J. (2011). A coevolutionary framework for analysing a transition to a sustainable low carbon economy. *Ecological Economics, 70*(12), 2258–2267. https://doi.org/10.1016/j.ecolecon.2011.07.014
Ghanbari, L. (2018). *Geo-economy, energy security, and energy diplomacy* (Vol. 1). Ava Publishing.
Goldthau A, Westphal K (2019) Why the Global Energy Transition does not mean the End of the Petrostate. Global Policy, Policy Insights.
Goldthau, A., Westphal, K., Bazilian, M., & Bradshaw, M. (2019). How the energy transition will reshape geopolitics. *Nature, 669*, 29–31.
Goodarzi, M., & Mohammadzadeh Ebrahimi, F. (2017). The geopolitical and geo-economic position of the Strait of Hormuz in Iran's regional policy. *Global Politics Quarterly, 6*(3), 103–124.
Griffiths, S. (2017a). A review and assessment of energy policy in the Middle East and North Africa region. *Energy Policy, 102*(2017), 249–269. https://doi.org/10.1016/j.enpol.2016.12.023
Griffiths, S. (2017b). Renewable energy policy trends and recommendations for GCC countries. *Energy Transit, 1*, 3. https://doi.org/10.1007/s41825-017-0003-6
Griffiths, S. (2019). Energy diplomacy in a time of energy transition. *Energy Strategy Reviews, 26*, 100386. https://doi.org/10.1016/j.esr.2019.100386

Guo, R. (2012). *Cross -border resource management* (2nd ed.). Elsevier.
Hache, E. (2018). Do renewable energies improve energy security in the long run? *International Economics, 156*(C), 127–135.156. https://doi.org/10.1016/j.inteco.2018.01.005
Hafner, M., & Wochner, A. (2020). How tectonic shifts in global energy are affecting global governance. In L. Grigoriev & A. Pabst (Eds.), *Global governance in transformation* (pp. 147–162). Springer.
Hafner, M. and Tagliapietra, S. (eds.). (2020). The Geopolitics of the Global Energy Transition, Lecture Notes in Energy 73, https://doi.org/10.1007/978-3-030-39066-2_6.
Harsha, J. E. (2025). "A Path for a Post-Oil Iraq: A Green Transition Strategy to Prepare Iraq for Climate Change" (2025). Student Research Submissions. 635. https://scholar.umw.edu/student_research/635
Hashemi, F. (2011). Sustainable security in the Persian Gulf: Barriers and mechanisms. *Geopolitics Quarterly, 7*(1), 136–167.
Högselius, P. (2019). *Energy and geopolitics*. Routledge.
Howard, R. (2007). *Iran oil: The new Middle East challenge to America*. I.B. Tauris.
Hvidt, M., (2013), Economic diversification in GCC countries: Past record and future trends, LSE Kuwait Programme on Development, Governance and Globalisation in the Gulf States, Number 27. http://eprints.lse.ac.uk/55252/1/Hvidt%20final%20paper%2020.11.17_v0.2.pdf
International Renewable Energy Agency (IRENA). (2019). A New World. The Geopolitics of the Energy Transformation. https://www.irena.org/publications/2019/Jan/A-New-World-The-Geopolitics-of-the-Energy-Transformation.
IQAir. (2019). Available online: https://www.iqair.com/ world-most-polluted-countries (accessed on 27 December 2020).
IRENA. (2018). Energy Transition. Available online at: https://www.irena.org/energytransition (accessed on 10.02.2022).
IRENA. (2019). "A New World: The Geopolitics of the Energy Transformation." Global Commission on the Geopolitics of Energy Transformation, International Renewable Energy Agency, Abu Dhabi, January.
IRENA. (2020). Global Renewables Outlook. Energy Transformation 2050; International Renewable Energy Agency: Abu Dhabi, United Arab Emirates,. World's Most Polluted Countries 2019 (PM2.5). World Air Quality Index2020.
Ivleva, D., & Tänzler, D. (2019). Geopolitics of decarbonisation: Towards an analytical framework. *Climate Diplomacy*.
Jafari Valdani, A. (1995). *Border changes and their geopolitical role in the Persian Gulf*. Ghoomes Publishing.
Janparvar, M. (2017). *Geopolitics for Everyone*. SAMT Publishing.
Kabeyi, M. J. B., & Olanrewaju, O. A. (2022). Sustainable energy transition for renewable and low carbon grid electricity generation and supply. *Frontiers in Energy Research, 9*, 743114. https://doi.org/10.3389/fenrg.2021.743114
KAPSARC. (2018). Electricity Market Integration in the GCC and MENA: Imperatives and Challenges, July 2018. https://www.kapsarc.org/research/publications/electricity-market-integrationin-the-gcc-and-mena-imperatives-and-challenges/.
Karimipoor, Y. (2000). *An Introduction to Iran and its neighbors source pf stress and threat*. vbJihad Publications of Tarbiat Moalem University.
Karsh, E., & Rautsi, I. (2008). Why Saddam Hussein invaded Kuwait. *Survival, 33*(1), 18–30. https://doi.org/10.1080/00396339108442571
Katzman, K. (2007). Iran's activities and influence in Iraq. Congressional Research Service (CRS) Report for Congress, pp. 1–6. Retrieved June 23, 2016, from http://fpc.state.gov/documents/organization/96430.pdf
Khatinoglu, D. (2014) Iran's "espionage" claims toward Gazprom, CNPC. Trend News Agency. Retrieved March 23, 2015, from http://en.trend.az/iran/2276667.html.
Klement, J. (2021). The Interplay between Geopolitics, Economics, and Investments. CFA Institute Research Foundation, ISBN 978-1-952927-06-5, www.cfainstitute.org.

Lorot, P. (2001). La geoeconomie, nouvelle grammaire des rivalites internationals. *L'information géographique, 65*(1), 43–52. https://doi.org/10.3406/ingeo.2001.2733
Lovins, A. B. (1978). Soft Energy Technologies. *Annual Review of Energy, 3*, 477–517. https://doi.org/10.1146/annurev.eg.03.110178.002401
Lowe, S. (2019). Border Carbon Adjustment: How to get it right, Centre for European Reform (CER), 7 October 2019. https://www.cer.eu/in-the-press/border-carbon-adjustment-how-get-it-right.
Luomi, M. (2015). The international relations of the green economy in the gulf: lessons from the UAE's state-led energy transition. Oxford Institute for Energy Studies (OIES), OIES paper: MEP 12, May 2015.
Luomi, M. (2018) The foreign relations of energy transitions – framing the issue for the UAE. Emirates Diplomatic Academy (EDA), EDA Insight, December 2018.
Luttwak, E. (1990). From Geopolitics to Geo-Economics: Logic of Conflict, Grammar of Commerce. *National Interest, 20*, 17–23.
Mahdavy, H. (1970). Patterns and problems of economic development in rentier states: the case of Iran. In M. A. Cook (Ed.), *Studies in Economic History of the Middle East* (p. 466). Oxford University Press.
Mandelbaum, M. (2014). *The road to global prosperity* (pp. xvi–xvii). Simon and Schuster.
Markand, J., Raven, R., & Truffer, B. (2012). Sustainability transitions: An emerging field of research and its prospects. *Research Policy, 41*, 955–967. https://doi.org/10.1016/j.respol.2012.02.013
Mills, R. (2020). A fine balance: The geopolitics of the global energy transition in MENA. In Lecture Notes in Energy (pp. 115–150). Springer. https://doi.org/10.1007/978-3-030-39066-2_6
Modor Intelligence. (2021). Iran power market—growth, trends, covid-19 impact, and forecasts (2022-2027). Retrieved from: B2n.ir/w52178.
Mohaddes, K., & Raissi, M. (2019). The US oil supply revolution and the global economy. *Empirical Economics, 57*, 1515–1546. https://doi.org/10.1007/s00181-018-1505-9
Mojtahedzadeh, P. (1975). *Historical geography of the Persian Gulf.* Tehran University Press.
Mojtahedzadeh, P. (2000). *Geopolitical ideas and Iranian realities*. Ney Publishing.
Mojtahedzadeh, P. (2002). *Political geography and geographic politics*. SAMT Publishing.
Mokhtari Hoshi, H. (2018). Explaining the concept of geo-economics and recommendations for Iran. *Geopolitics Quarterly, 14*(2), 56–82.
Nami, M. H. (2007). *Iran and Kuwait's Maritim boundary issues*. Armed Forces Geographical Organisation.
Nami, M. H. (2019). Geopolitics of the Persian Gulf: Historical and future challenges. *Persian Gulf Studies Journal, 4*(4), 16.
Nami, M. H., et al. (2009). Analyzing Iran's geo-economic position in the Middle East. *Geopolitics Quarterly, 5*(2), 41–65.
Niakooei, S. A., & Karimi Pour, D. (2015). Israel's energy diplomacy: Foundations and regional goals. *International Political Studies Quarterly, 7*(22), 27–58.
Norouzizadeh, F., & Goodarzi, M. (2021). The role of geopolitical and geo-economic energy transit (oil and gas) in the Persian Gulf and its impact on Iran's national security. *Islamic World Political Studies Quarterly, 11*(4), 99–120.
O'Sullivan, M., Overland, I., Sandalow, D. (2017). The geopolitics of renewable energy. Columbia Center on Global Energy Policy & Harvard Belfer Center for Science and International Affairs, Working paper, July 2017.
Olanipekun, I. O., & Alola, A. A. (2020). Crude oil production in the Persian Gulf amidst geopolitical risk, cost of damage and resources rents: Is there asymmetric inference? *Resources Policy, 69*, 101873. https://doi.org/10.1016/j.resourpol.2020.1018
Olayele. (2015). The geopolitics of oil and gas. *International Association for Energy Economics*.
Omri, A., & Belaïd, F. (2020). Does renewable energy modulate the negative effect of environmental issues on the socio-economic welfare? *Journal of Environmental Management, 278*, 111483. https://doi.org/10.1016/j.jenvman.2020.111483
OPEC. (2019). World Oil Outlook 2019. https://www.opec.org/opec_web/en/publications/340.htm.

Overland, I. (2019). The geopolitics of renewable energy: debunking four emerging myths. *Energy Research & Social Science, 49*, 37–40. https://doi.org/10.1016/j.erss.2018.10.018

Overland, I. (2015). Future petroleum geopolitics: Consequences of climate policy and unconventional oil and gas. In *Handbook of Clean Energy Systems* (pp. 1–29). https://doi.org/10.1002/9781118991978.hces203

Papava, V. (2012). Economic component of the Russian-Georgian Conflict. *The Caucasus & Globalization*, 6 (1), https://ssrn.com/abstract=2182507 or https://doi.org/10.2139/ssrn.2182507

Praveen, R., Keloth, V., Abo-Khalil, A. G., Alghamdi, A. S., Eltamaly, A. M., & Tlili, I. (2020). An insight to the energy policy of GCC countries to meet renewable energy targets of 2030. *Energy Policy, 147*, 111864. https://doi.org/10.1016/j.enpol.2020.111864

Qi, L., & Liu, X. (2024). Measuring energy transition away from fossil fuels: A new index. *Renewable and Sustainable Energy Reviews, 200*, 1–15.

QNB. (2012). *GCC Economic Insight*. Qatar National Bank SAQ.

Raeesolsadat, M. T. (2024). Geopolitical implications of shared oil resources between Iran and Iraq. *Asia-Africa Relations Scientific Journal, 1*(1).

Raphael, S., & Stokes, D. (2011). Globalizing West African oil: US 'energy security' and the global economy. *International Affairs, 87*(4), 903–921. https://doi.org/10.1111/j.1468-2346.2011.01010.x

Salameh, M. (2003). Quest for middle east oil: The us versus the Asian– pacific region. *Energy Policy, 31*.

Samadi, A. H. (2025). Identifying institutional barriers to energy transition in Iran to increase energy security. Research Project, National Science Foundation of Iran, Presidential Office.

Sariolghalam, M. (1999). Effects of the Soviet Union's collapse on the Third World. *Foreign Policy Journal, 4*. Tehran: Center for Strategic Research.

Scholten, D., & Bosman, R. (2016). The geopolitics of renewables; exploring the political implications of renewable energy systems. *Technological Forecasting and Social Change, 103*, 273–283. https://doi.org/10.1016/j.techfore.2015.10.014

Scholvin, S., & Wigell, M. (2018). Power politics by economic means: Geoeconomics as an analytical approach and foreign policy practice. *Comparative Strategy, 37*(1), 73–84. https://doi.org/10.1080/01495933.2018.1419729

Seif, A. M., & Agha Mousa Tehrani, R. (2014). *Oil and gas economy (shared fields)*. Supreme National Defense University.

Shana. (2007, September 15) 2 pipelines to be built between Abadan, Basra. Petro Energy Information Network. Retrieved May 16, 2015, from http://www.shana.ir/en/newsagency/114417/2-Pipelines-to-Be-Built-Between-Abadan-Basra

Sharma, G. D., Verma, M., Taheri, B., Chopra, R., & Parihar, J. S. (2023). Socioeconomic aspects of hydrogen energy: an integrative review. *Technological Forecasting and Social Change, 192*, 122574. https://doi.org/10.1016/j.techfore.2023.122574

Sheikh Attar, A. (2005). *Energy diplomacy and national security*. Ministry of Foreign Affairs Publishing.

Shum, R. Y. (2019). Heliopolitics: The international political economy of solar supply chains. *Energy Strategy Reviews, 26*, 100390. https://doi.org/10.1016/j.esr.2019.100390

Solaymani, S. (2021). A review on energy and renewable energy policies in Iran. *Sustainability, 13*(13), 7328. https://doi.org/10.3390/su13137328

Stratfor. (2018). How renewable energy will change geopolitics. Strat for assessments, https://worldview.stratfor.com/article/how-renewable-energy-will-change-geopolitics. Accessed 27 June.

Sturm, M., & Siegfried, N. (2005). *Regional monetary integration in the member states of the Gulf Cooperation Council* (Occasional Paper No. 31). European Central Bank. europa.eu.

Suri, J. (2014). "State Finance and National Power: Great Britain, China, and the United States in Historical Perspective," Tobin Project discussion paper on "Sustainable National Security Strategy," January 2014.

Tagliapietra, S. (2019). The impact of the global energy transition on MENA oil and gas producers. *Energy Strategy Reviews, 26*, 100397. https://doi.org/10.1016/j.jfueco.2022.100065

Takase, M., Aboah, M., & Kipkoech, R. (2022). A review on renewable energy potentials and energy usage statistics in Ghana. *Fuel Communications, 11*, 100065. https://doi.org/10.1016/j.jfueco.2022.100065

Terrapon-Pfaff, J., Prantner, M., & Ersoy, S. R. (2022). Risikobewertung und Risikokostenanalyse der MENA-Region. MENA-Fuels: Teilbericht, 8.

Thirlwell, M. (2010). The Return of Geo- economics. Interpreter, Lowy Institute for International Policy, May 24, 2010.

Thompson, M. (2020). Al Kharsaah: How Low Can Solar Tariff Bids go? TXF. Available online: https://www.txfnews.com/News/Article/7038/Al-Kharsaah-How-low-can-solar-tariff-bids-go (accessed on 20 December 2020).

UFCCC. (2015a). "Intended Nationally Determined Contribution – Kingdom of Saudi Arabia", November 2015. https://www4.unfccc.int/sites/ndcstaging/PublishedDocuments/Saudi%20Arabia%20First/KSA-INDCs%20English.pdf.

UFCCC. (2015b). "Intended Nationally Determined Contribution – Iraq", 10 November 2015. https://www4.unfccc.int/sites/submissions/INDC/Published%20Documents/Iraq/1/INDC-Iraq.pdf.

UFCCC. (2015c). "Intended Nationally Determined Contribution – Iran", 19 November 2015. https://www4.unfccc.int/sites/submissions/INDC/Published%20Documents/Iran/1/INDC%20Iran%20Final%20Text.pdf.

USEIA. (2015). Country analysis br ief: Iran. Retrieved September 16, 2015,from http://www.eia.gov/beta/international/analysis.cfm?iso=IRN.

USEIA. (2016). Country analysis brief: Iraq. Retrieved June 23, 2016, from https://www.eia.gov/beta/international/analysis.cfm?iso=IRQ.

Viswanathan, G. "Sahim" Scheme to Power Homes by Solar Energy, Times of Oman. Available online: http://timesofoman.com/article/109724/Oman/Solar-energy-initiative\T1\textquoterightSahim\T1\textquoteright-launched-in-Oman (accessed on 20 December 2020).

World Bank. (2023). World development indicators. Retrieved from https://databank.worldbank.org/source/world-development-indicator.

Youngs, R. (2012). Geo-economic futures. In A. Martinegue & R. Youngs (Eds.), Challenges for European foreign policy in 2012: What kind of geo-economic Europe? Madrid: FRIDE.

Zainlabedin, Y. (2004). Political Geography and seas Management with emphasis on maritime border, Ph.D. thesis, Islamic Azad University, Science and Research Branch of Tehran.

Zinecker, A., et al. (2018) Real People, Real Change: Strategies for a Just Energy Transition. GSI Report. International institute for Sustainable Development, Winnepeg, Canada.

The Expanse of the Persian Sea in the Most Authoritative Geographical and Historical Sources of the Ninth and Tenth Centuries CE

S. Abolghasem Foroozani

Abstract Outstanding Muslim geographers and historians who have compiled their works on geography and history in the Third and Fourth centuries AH (Ninth and Tenth Centuries CE) have expressed different opinions about the extent and boundaries of the Persian Sea (the Persian Gulf). In the current study, after expressing the opinions of prominent geographers such as Ibn Khordadbeh, Abu Zeyd Balkhi, Istakhri, and Maqdasi and the unknown author of the book *Hodoud al-Alam Men al-Mashreq Ilal-Maqreb*, regarding the extent and boundaries of the Persian Sea, attention has been paid to the explanations of celebrated historians such as Ibn Yaqubi and Abu al-Hasan Masoudi, concerning the boundaries and the depths of the Persian Sea's maritime extent. According to the viewpoints of great geographers and historians of the third and fourth centuries AH, the present research has concluded that the Persian Gulf was only a part of a greater sea, which was located in the south of Iran under the name of the Persian Sea.

Keywords *Masaalek va Mamaalek [The Routes and the Kingdoms]* the Persian Sea · *Ashkal al-Alam [The World's Images]* Khalij al-Farsi · *Morooj al-dhahab [The Golden Meadow]*

1 Background

"Why are you thoughtful?"

With this question posed by Abu Ali ibn Hazem (a renowned merchant whose merchant ships sailed the vast seas), Abu Abdullah Muhammad ibn Ahmad al-Maqdisi (a prominent geographer of the fourth century A.H.) emerged from the world of thought. It is worth mentioning that in that moment, the author of the famous book *Ahsan al-Taqasim fi Ma'rifah al-Aqalim* was on the coast of Aden

S. A. Foroozani (✉)
Professor of History, Shiraz University, Shiraz, Iran

N. Faghih et al. (eds.), *The Persian Gulf and Islands*, Perspectives on Development in the Middle East and North Africa (MENA) Region,
https://doi.org/10.1007/978-3-032-27910-1_5

(located in the country of Yemen) gazing at the sea and lost in thoughts (Maqdasi, 1361).

In response to the question asked, Maqdasi said: "May God help the Sheikh, I'm wandering on this sea with all the differences in it." Then Maqdasi asked Abu Ali ibn Hazem to help him out of his doubts based on his knowledge. To explain his viewpoint to Maqdasi, the experienced navigator (Abu Ali ibn Hazem) "smoothed the sand with his hand and drew the sea map on it" (Maqdasi, 1361, p. 16).

The sea map that Abu Ali ibn Hazem drew was the scheme of the Indian Ocean and its related seas and gulfs. However, contrary to Maqdasi's imagination, the sea map that Abu Ali ibn Hazem presented was neither in the form of a teilsani[1] nor in the form of a bird. In fact, what had caused Maqdasi wandering was the numerous explanations of the sea he was looking at, as well as the various shapes that the cartographers had presented in drawing that sea. Among other things, some people considered that sea to be like a garment that surrounded China and Abyssinia, extending to Qolzom (the Red Sea) from one side and to Abadan (in the Persian Gulf) from the other side.

But Abu Zeyd Balkhi (the great geographer of the third century A.H.) has described the aforementioned sea (the Indian Ocean) "like a bird whose beak is in the Red Sea, its neck in Iraq, and its tail between Abyssinia and China" (Maqdasi, 1361, pp. 15–16). The reason beyond these differences about the sea, which the Iranians called the "Green Sea" and the Tazys called its equivalent in their language "Bahru-al-Akhdar" and the Romans called it "the Eastern Ocean," (Minorsky, 1372, p. 91) was that, according to the book *Hodoud al-Alam Men al-Mashreq Ilal-Maqreb* (compiled in 372 A.H.): "No one has crossed this sea, and no one knows where it ends" (Minorsky, 1372, p. 91).

This ambiguity existed not only about the Green Sea but also about the other seas. According to Abu al-Hasan Ali Masoudi in his book *Al-Tanbih va Al-Ashraf*, "earlier and later scholars differed about the number of seas, their area, length, width, continuity, discontinuity, tides and other characteristics" (Masoudi, 1349, p. 50). It is also worth noting that, especially in various geographical sources, there is disagreement not only regarding the shape, number, and area of large and small seas, but also about their names. Of course, this is not so surprising since according to Le Strange, "a sea has sometimes several different names that are adapted from the large cities and countries that are located on its shores…" (1364, p. 25). In the meantime, some purposes (such as creating a change in cultural essence) as well as the political goals and interests in not using the real names of some marine surface tolls (like the seas, lakes, bays, and rivers) cannot be ignored.[2]

[1] Jafar Sho'ar has written the following about amulets in his footnotes and comments on the book *Surat Al-Arz [The Earth Shape]*: A long, loose garment thrown over the shoulders. A type of short green woolen cloak with a hood worn by Persian and Zoroastrian elders and scholars, similar to the Christian censer (Ibn Huqal, 1345).

[2] It is worth noting that, after entering the land of the Transoxiana the Arab armies called the great river "Wah Rut" "Jeyhun" and the river "Gulzarion" or Chach, "Seyhun" (Forouzani, 1381, p. 32).

2 Authoritative Geographical and Historical Sources

The intentional use of fake names for the mentioned water tolls, especially in recent centuries, is one of the cases that should not be ignored. Reasoned responsiveness is one of the solutions in confronting such issues. Accordingly, specific references to the contents of authentic and reliable historical and geographical books in the desired field make our reasons justified and documented. What is examined in the current research, following the authentic geographical and historical sources written in the third and fourth centuries A.H., is that the Persian Sea is a name that was applied to a highly extended marine zone, and the area that is known today as the Persian Gulf is only a part of the Persian Sea.

Abu Ishaq Ebrahim Estakhri, (died in 346 A.H.) wrote a book on geography in Arabic, titled *Masaalek va Mamaalek*, which has fortunately survived the ravages of time. There are also two translations of this book in Persian.[3] In the translation of the book *Masaalek al-Mamaalek* by Estakhri made by Mohammad Ibn Asad Tostari, it is stated that: "Know that the Persian Sea is a branch of the Mohit Sea[4]" (Estakhri, 1373, p. 107). In the mentioned book; in describing the Mohit Sea, it is stated that this sea "emerges from Sin (China) and passes through the city of Waq Waq[5] until it reaches the borders of the cities of Sindh, India and Kerman until it reaches Persia" (Estakhri, 1373, p. 107).

Concerning the Mohit Sea, in the book *Al-Tanbih va Al-Ashraf*, it is said that "for most people, the Sea of Mohit is the head and source of all other seas, from which all branches out and many have called it Al-Akhdar, and in Greek it is called the Ocean and according to Ptolemy and others, most of its surroundings are unknown" (Masoudi, 1349, p. 64). In the book *Hodoud al-Alam Men al-Mashreq Ilal-Maqreb*, after explaining the Eastern Ocean (Al-Akhdar) and the Western Ocean, a sea known as the "Great Sea" is mentioned and its boundaries are noted:

> "The eastern limit of this sea is connected to the Eastern Ocean... and the northern limit of this sea should start from China and pass through the cities of India and the cities of Sindh and pass through the borders of Kerman and Pars and also the borders of Khuzestan and the

---

The Arab also called the Arvand River, the Tigris. Referring to this issue, Ferdowsi wrote, "If you do not know how to be a warrior, call the Arvand River the Tigris" (Ferdowsi, 1363, p.48).

[3] It worth mentioning that both translations of the mentioned book were published by Iraj Afshar. Iraj Afshar published one of the translations under the title *Mamaalek va Masaalek [The Countries and Routes]*. (Estakhri, 1373).

The other translation of Estakhri's book *Masaalek al-Mamaalek*, whose translator is unknown, has been published under the title *Masaalek va Mamaalek [The Routes and Countries]* (Estakhri, 1340).

[4] A Sea which has covered the lands around the world (the great ocean)

Ibn Balkhi wrote about the Persian Sea and the Mohit Sea: "This Persian Sea is a branch of a great sea which is called the Green Sea and is also called the Mohit Sea. The countries of Sin [China], Sindh [Pakistan], India, Oman, Aden, Zanzibar, Basra and other places are located on the shores of this sea" (Ibn Balkhi, 1363, p. 153).

[5] Zakaria Qazvini (d. 682 A.H.) has provided valuable information in his work about Waq Waq, an archipelago located in the China Sea, and the reason beyond such a naming (Qazvini, 1371).

> borders of Basra and the southern limit of this sea should start from Jabal al-Ta'en[6] and pass through the area of Zaij[7] and reach the area of Zangistan and Abyssinia and the western limit of this sea is the Gulf..." (Minorsky, 1372, pp. 93–94).

The author of the book *Hodoud al-Alam Men al-Mashreq Ilal-Maqreb,* after explaining the Great Sea (Bahr el azam) points out that the mentioned sea has five gulfs. He points out to the Persian Gulf as one of those five gulfs and says: "... and the fourth is called the Persian Gulf which starts from Pars with a narrow width until it reaches the borders of Sindh" (Minorsky, 1372, pp. 94–95). The author of the mentioned book also points out that "everywhere in this great sea is called by the city and the area that it is connected to" (Minorsky, 1372, p. 95).

The book *Masaalek va Mamaalek* by Ibn Khordadbeh (died around 300 A.H.) is one of the oldest Muslim books on geography, written in Arabic. In this book, in a section entitled "The Route from Basra to the East along the Persian Coast," important islands located in the Persian Sea (on the route from Basra to the East) and major cities placed on the coast of that sea are discussed (Ibn Khordadbeh, pp. 61–62). Ibn Khordadbeh's writings on the distances of the areas in question come as following:

> "From Basra to the island of Kharg is fifty leagues… from Kharg to the island of Lavan is eighty leagues… from Lavan to the island of Ebron[8] is seven leagues… from Ebron to the island of Khin is seven leagues… from Khin[9] to the island of Kis [Kish] is seven leagues… from Kis to the island of Ibn Kawan[10] is 18 leagues… from the island of Ibn Kawan to Ormuz [Hormuz] is seven leagues "From Ormuz to Thara[11] is seven days' journey, and this place is the border between Fars and Sindh. From Thara to Daybol[12] is eight days' journey. From Daybol[13] to the mouth of Mehran, the Indus River is 2 farsakhs (12 kilometers) on the sea coast" (Ibn Khordadbeh, 1370, pp. 46–47).

[6]Concerning Jabal al-Ta'in, the author of the book *Hodoud al-Alam Men al-Mashreq Ilal- Maqreb* quotes: "but the first mountain in the eastern direction is the mountain that we called al-Ta'in fi al-Bahr, which is half on land and half in the sea." In the commentary to the aforementioned book, "al-Ta'in fi al-Bahr" is most likely understood to mean the one that protrudes into the sea (Minorsky, 1372, pp. 121–122).

[7]Zaij (Zabih = Zabij) is an island located below the equator that today corresponds to the island of Java (Minorsky, 1372, p. 94).

[8]According to Le Strange, "the island of Ebron is undoubtedly the same as the present-day Hendorabi" (Le Strange, 1364, p. 282).

[9]As Ibn Khardadbeh noted, Khin was located seven miles from the island of Kish. Le Strange has also solely quoted that Khin was located near Kish (Le Strange, 1364).

[10]According to Le Strange, Ibn Kawan Island is apparently the same as Qeshm Island. Qeshm Island was also known as Tavilleh [long] Island (Le Strange, 1364).

[11]This place was probably located in the Tis or Tiz Mokran region because, as mentioned in the text, Ibn Khordadbeh considered it the border between Fars and Sindh.

[12]Daybol was a prosperous city, a commercial center and a port in the Sindh region (Ibn Huqal, 1345).

[13]About the Mehran River, Zakaria Qazvini quotes: "... It is a river whose width is as wide as the Tigris or greater, coming from the east and going south to the west at the Persian Sea following the end of Indus" (Qazvini, 1371, p. 120).

3 Further Authoritative Sources

Hence, if based on the writings of some sources that will be pointed in the following lines, we assume the coastal areas of the Indus land to be along the Persian Sea and consider the Mehran River estuary on the coast of the Persian Sea, which is two Farsang (12 kilometers) from Dibal, to be the eastern border of the Persian Sea, the aforementioned sea extended to distant areas, eastward. The reason for this statement is that, according to the writings of Ibn Khordad, Dibal was located 8 days' journey from Thara. However, if we consider the extent of the Persian Sea only to the borders of the Indus land, Thara, which was located 7 days' journey from Ormuz (Hormuz), is believed to be the final point of the Persian Sea from the east. Thus, the Persian Sea also had a much larger area than the area that is called the Persian Gulf in the contemporary times.

In the book *Al-Aelaq al-Nafisa*, written in Arabic by Ibn Rustah in the late third century A.H., it is stated that there is a gulf branching from the Indian Ocean in the Persian region, which is called the Persian Gulf. Ibn Rustah estimated the length of the gulf at one thousand four hundred miles and its width as five hundred miles (Ibn Rustah, 1897).

From what is stated in another part of the book *Al-Aelaq al-Nafisa*, it is clear that by mentioning Fars region, Ibn Rostah means all of the coastal lands of Iran (not only the Fars province). Citing to expert scholars, he notes that Tigris al-Awra (= the blind Tigris, whose ancient and Persian name is the Bahmanshir River and whose Arabic name is Shatt al-Arab) (Le Strange, 1364), is the beginning of the Persian Sea, and Tiz Mokran, which is the beginning of the Indus land, is considered the end of the intended sea from the east. Continuing his discussion on the boundaries of the Persian Sea, Ibn Rustah argues that this sea continues from the mouth of Tigris al-Awra to Aden from the west, and from the east, the provinces of Fars, Kerman and Mokran are on the coast of the Persian Sea. The author of *Al-Aelaq al-Nafisa* holds that the Persian Sea borders with the Arab provinces of Bahrain, Oman, Muscat, and Socotra[14] up to Aden from the west. Ibn Rustah says that Adan is the last region of the Arabian Peninsula and there is a place known as Al-Duwarij.[15] And there is a marine route that connects to the sea of Jeddah and Egypt (Ibn Rustah, 1897).

In one of the oldest historical works available, written by Ibn Vadheh Yaqubi (died after 278 A.H.) known as *Tarikh Yaqubi*, the Ras al-Jamha region (located between Oman and Aden) is considered the end point of the Persian Sea[16] (Ibn

---

Masoudi notes about the Mehran River: "The Mehran River flows into the sea about two farsakhs from Daybol, which is on the coast of the Indus" (Masoudi, 1349, p. 54).

[14] Socotra, also known as Socotra, Socotra, and Scutari, is an island located in southern Arabia, near the coast of the Arabian Peninsula (Qarchanlou, 1380).

[15] No information was found about Al-Duraj in geographical sources, but according to what Ibn Rustah wrote (and what has been quoted in this study), the mentioned place was near Aden (in Yemen) (Ibn Rustah, 1897).

[16] The author of Nukhbat al-Dahr Fi Aja'ib. al-Barr va al-Bahr also considers Jamhah to be a black, tall and elongated mountain that was considered the border of the Persian Sea (Ansari Dameshqi, 1357).

Yaqubi, 1993). This is confirmed by Abu al-Hasan Masoudi (died in 345 A.H.) in his book *Morooj al-dhahab* as follows:

"The beginning of the Persian Sea is from the Khashabat of Basra[17] and the place known as Kankalas, where wooden markers for ships have been placed in the sea, and from there to Oman it is three hundred farsang, and the coast of Persia and the land of Bahrain is in this part, and from Oman, whose center is Sohaar (Suhar),[18] which the Iranians call Mezon, to the village of Muscat, where the ship owners get fresh water from the wells there. It is fifty farsakh. And from Muscat to Ras al-Jammah it is fifty farsakh, and this is the end of the Persian Sea, which is four hundred farsakh distance that has been determined by sailors and ship owners[19]" (Masoudi, 1365, p. 147).

Ibn Huqal, in his geographical work called *Surat al-Arz*, talks about the extent of the Persian Sea: "this sea extends from the borders of the Indus and Kerman to Fars" (Ibn Huqal, 1345, p. 46). He states that the Persian Sea encompasses most of the Arab world and expresses the belief that Qolzam is part of the Persian Sea, saying, "Qolzam ends at Ileh,[20] then it goes around the borders of the Arab world and from there to Abbadan [Abadan] and after crossing the Tigris it reaches Mahruban[21] and then to Janaba [Ganawah]. Then it passes through the banks of Fars towards Siraf and extends to the shores of Hormouz [Hormuz] behind Kerman and reaches Dibal and the shores of Multan, which is the Indus shore and in here the border of the Islamic world ends. Then it passes through the shores of India, crosses the shores of Tibet and reaches the land of China" (Sirafi, 1381, p. 2; Ibn Huqal, 1345, p. 1).

---

[17] About the Khashabat Maqdasi says: "Khashabat is attributed to Basra, it is rare and very dangerous. The logs are fixed there and houses are built on them. At night, the owners of the houses light fires so that the ships do not come close" (Maqdasi, 1361, p. 18).

Jeyhani notes that Al-Khashab, which is located about six miles from Ibadan, is located where the Tigris flows into the sea. Because there is a fear that ships will run aground there, "there are logs on the ground in the middle of the water, and there is a watchtower built there, listening during the day and making a fire at night so that the way to the Tigris is clear" (Jeyhani, 1386, p. 57).

[18] In both the Arabic text and the Persian translation of the book *Morooj al-dhahab*, the center of Oman is written as Sinjar, which is incorrect, and the center of Oman was Sohar (Suhar) (Maqdasi, 1361).

More information (Qarchanlou, 1380)

[19] Regarding Ras-al-Jumha, which is also known as Ras-al-Jumhamah and Ras-al-Jumjumah, Masoudi said:

"Ras-al-Jumha is a mountain from the land of Shihr, Ahqaf, and Raml, which has joined the land of Yemen, part of which is under the sea, and it is not known where it ends under the water..." (Masoudi, 1365, pp. 147–148).

[20] Ileh, which is known today as the Port of Aqaba, is located at the end of the Gulf of Aqaba and is considered a magnificent port on the Red Sea (Qarchanlou, 1380).

[21] Mahroyan, which is also mentioned in various sources as Mahroyan and Mahi-Royan, according to Hamdollah Mostowfi: "It is a city by the sea... It has a hot and stinking air, but it is a city of the sea, so whoever goes to the sea from the way of Fars to the way of Khuzestan, and whoever goes to the sea from Basra and Khuzestan, their passage was through there" (Mostowfi, 1362, p. 131).

Ibn Huqal's explanations about the Persian Sea are comprehensive and noteworthy. In another part of his book, he fully describes the size of the Persian Sea and its marine features, noting:

"The part of the Persian Sea where Qolzom is located is called the Qolzom Sea until it reaches the borders of Yemen's interior... Then it turns away from the Qolzom Sea to the other side... The part of the Persian Sea opposite Yemen's interior is called the Aden Sea, and after that it is the Zanj Sea until it reaches the borders of Oman by turning towards the Persian Sea... If you pass through Oman and leave the borders of Islam and come near Sarandib,[22] that part is also called the Persian Sea" (Ibn Huqal, 1345, pp. 3–4). In another part of his contents about the Persian Sea, Ibn Huqal has considered the end of the mentioned sea to be the boundary of China (Ibn Huqal, 1345).

Abu al-Ghasem Jeyhani, the author of the book *Ashkal al-Alam*, also agrees with the opinion of the author of *Surat al-Arz*. He considered the Persian Sea to be a highly vast expanse of water, only a part of which encompassed the entire Arab land and the Red Sea (Qolzom) was considered one of its branches. The author of *Ashkal al-Alam* describes the expanse of the Persian Sea as following:

"First, from Abbadan, and that is where the rest of the water that remains in the Tigris flows into the sea, then it flows from Abbadan to Bahrain and Oman, then it returns and flows along the banks of Mahrah,[23] Hadramaut[24] and Adan, and along the coasts of Yemen to Jeddah, then it flows over Al-Jaad,[25] Madyan [Midian][26] and Ileh. And here the boundaries of the Arab land are cut off by the sea, and this place in the Persian Sea is like a tenon and is known as the Qolzom [Red Sea]" (Jeyhani, p. 43).

Based on what has been mentioned, in his book *Ashkal al-Alam,* Jeyhani has considered the Red Sea to be a part of the Persian Sea. In another part of his work about the Persian Sea and its boundaries, he writes:

---

[22] According to the author of the book *Hodoud al-Alam Men al-Mashreq Ilal- Maqreb,* "Serendib is in the south of China and is on the border between India and China, on the shores of the sea, and it has many regions" (Minorsky, 1372, p. 187).

More information (Ibn khordadbeh, 1370, pp. 48–52)

[23] Estakhri has considered Mahrah as the areas related to Yemen (Estakhri, 1373).

[24] Jeyhani notes about Hadramaut: "Hadramaut is on the eastern side of Aden, near the sea" (Jeyhani, 1386, p. 50).

The author of *Hodoud al-Alam Men al-Mashreq Ilal- Maqreb* believes that "Hadramaut is a prosperous and green region within which are cities" (Minorsky, 1372, p. 438).

[25] In another part of the book *Ashkal al-Alam*, a place called "Al-Jar" is mentioned, which is very likely the same place called "Al-Jaad" in the text used in this study. Referring to Al-Jar, the author of *Ashkal al-Alam* quotes: "Al-Jar is supposedly from Medina and is a populated place, and many merchants travel from Jeddah and from there to the Tigris and the sea is three or four levels" (Jeyhani, 1386, p. 46).

[26] Maqdasi quotes: "Madyan is on the border of Hejaz" (Maqdasi, 1361, p. 251).

Jeyhani wrote about Madyan that "Madyan is on the Red Sea and is larger than Tabuk" (Jeyhani, 1386, p.47).

Qarchanlou says that Madyan is "located on the eastern coast of the Red Sea in the Hejaz region" (Qarchanlou, 1380, p. 157).

> "First, we move from the Qolzom [Red Sea]. Its shore is towards the east until it reaches Ileh, then it flows over the Arab land to Abbadan as we have described, and it extends the width of the Tigris to Mahruyan and Janaba. "So it passes through Fars and Siraf to the coasts of Hormuz and Kerman to Daybol and the shores of Multan and Sindh. The boundary of the cities of Islam extends to the coasts of India [and from there] to the coasts of Tibet and extends to China" (Jeyhani, 1386, p. 50).

In another part of the aforementioned book, the author of *Ashkal al-Alam* writes: "thus when you pass through Oman and cut the boundaries of Islam along the coast until you reach near Sarandib, it is called the Persian Sea" (Jeyhani, 1386, p. 50).

In addition to the mentioned authors, Abu Abdullah Ahmad Maqdasi has discussed the Persian Sea in his book *Ahsan al-Taghasim fi Maerefate al-Aghalim* based on which we can understand that from the perspective of people contemporary to Maqdasi, a vast expanse of water was known as the Persian Sea, and the Persian Gulf was only a part of it. Maqdasi states: "Don't you see that most people call this sea the Persian Sea up to the borders of Yemen, and most shipbuilders and sailors are Persian?" (Maqdasi, 1361, p. 26).

In almost all geographical sources, the Persian Sea waters formed not only the southern borders of the provinces of Fars and Khuzestan, but they also included the southern borders of the provinces of Kerman, Mokran, and Sindh. For instance, pointing out the borders of the province of Sindh, Maqdasi says: "To the east is the Persian Sea, to the west is Kerman and the Sistan Desert and its environs, to the north are the lands of India, and to the south is the desert between Mokran and the Qofs Mountains, and behind it is the Persian Sea. The Persian Sea encompasses the east and south of this land from behind the desert, because this sea goes from Seymour in the east of the "Tiz" Mokran to this desert, bypassing the cities of Kerman and Fars" (Maqdasi, 1361, p. 26).

Now that we have expressed the different opinions about the extent of the Persian Sea based on important geographical and historical sources from the third and fourth centuries A.H., we must address the point why the mentioned sea was known as the Pars Sea. Concerning the reason for such naming, Estakhri notes:

> "And this sea is attributed to Persia from all other countries because, since this sea branches off from the surrounding area to Persia, no country is more populated than this, and its kings and leaders have continuously dominated and conquered the far and near surroundings and the surrounding areas of that sea in warfare and combat to this day" (Estakhri, 1373, p. 107).

This topic is expressed in an almost similar way by Ibn Huqal in his book *Surat al-Arz*, believing that the Persian Sea:

> "is called by the name of Persia among other countries, because Persia is more populated than all these countries and its kings had more dominion in ancient times and now they're dominant over all the far and near shores of this sea" (Ibn Huqal, 1345, p. 46).

4 Conclusion

Following the previous pointes and according to some of the most authentic geographical and historical sources related to the third and fourth centuries A.H., there are various views about the extent of the Persian Sea. For instance, some of the noted sources consider the eastern limit of the Persian Sea to be limited to the coast of Mokran, some consider the mouth of the Mehran River into the sea two miles from Daybol (in the land of Sindh) as the easternmost part of the Persian Sea, and some consider the territory of the Persian Sea to be as far as Sarandib (Ceylon = Sri Lanka).

Concerning the western limit of the Persian Sea, there is no significant difference in the used sources in the way that the Basra Basin, the Tigris River (Bahmanshir River), and Abadan (Abadan); all of which are located in the same area adjacent to each other are considered the westernmost point of the mentioned sea. However, while some geographical and historical sources consider the Ras al-Jamha region (located between Oman and Aden) to be the southern end of the Persian Sea, other used sources in the current research consider the Red Sea (Dar al-Qolzom) to be a part of the Persian Sea. Despite all the differences and diversity of views regarding the extent of the Persian Sea, it is interesting to note that all of the sources that are used in this discussion (which enjoy outstanding scientific importance and credibility) share a common point, and that is the name of the Persian Sea, which is used for a vast expanse of water; of which the Persian Gulf is only a part. The question that arises here is why the name Persian Sea is applied to an area much beyond what is known today as the Persian Gulf in all the authentic geographical and historical sources related to the third and fourth centuries A.H.?

Answering this question is not so difficult. In fact, the authors of these noted sources have admitted to the fact that the Persian Sea, which took its name from its most important adjacent province (Pars), covered a much broader area than the coastal lands of Pars province. They knew it very well that the Persian Sea is a name that has been given to an expanse of water far beyond the Persian Gulf, since ancient times. This expanse of water, which is located throughout southern Iran and within the territory of this vast and ancient country, extended at least from Bahmanshir River to the coastal waters of Sindh province.

References

Ansari Dameshqi, S. M. b. A. (1357). *Nokhbat al-Dahr fi Ajayeb al-Bar va al-Bahr [Elite of the age in the wonders of the land and sea] (S. H. Tabibian, Trans.).* Farhangestan Adab va Honar Iran.

Estakhri, A. E. (1373). *Mamaalek va Masaalek [The Kingdoms and the Routes]* (M. A. A. Tostari, Trans.). يرج افشار،ابه كوشش Bonyad-e Moqufat-e Dr. Mahmoud Afshar Yazdi.

Estakhri, A. E. (1340). *Masaalek va Mamaalek [The Routes and the Kingdoms]* (I. Afshar, Ed.). Bongah Tarjomeh va Nashr Ketab.

Ferdowsi, A. (1363). In J. Mohle (Ed.), *Shahnameh Ferdowsi [Ferdowsi's Shahnameh]* (3rd ed.). Sherkat Sahami Ketab haye Jibi.

Forouzani, S. A. (1381). *Tarikh-e Tahavolat Siyasi, Ejtemaei, Eqtesadi va Farhangi Iran dar Dore Samanian [The Iran's History of Political, Social, Economical and Cultural Changes in the Samanid's Period]*. Samt Publication.

Ibn Balkhi. (1363). In G. Lestrange & R. A. Nickleson (Eds.), *Farsnameh* (Vol. 2). Donyaye Ketab Publication..

Ibn Huqal, (1345). Surat al-Arz [The Earth Shape] (J. Sho'ar, Trans.). Bonyad Farhang Iran Publication.

Ibn Rustah, Abi Ali Ahmad bin Omar (1897). Al-Aelaq al-Nafisa [Precious relationships] Bril Publication.

Jeyhani, A. A. (1386). Ashkal al-Alam [The World's Images] (A. A. S. Kateb, Trans.). (F. Mansouri Ed.). Beh Nashr Publication.

Minorsky, V. (Ed.). (1372). *Hodoud al-Alam Men al-Mashreq Ilal- Maqreb [The Borders of the World from the East to the West]* (Mirhossein Shaah, Trans.). (M. Mirahmadi & Gh. Varham, Eds.). Al-Zahra University Publication.

Le Strange, G. (1364). Joqrafiay-e Tarikhi Sarzamin haye Khelafat Sharqi [Historical Geography of the Eastern Caliphate Lands] (2nd ed.). (M. Erfan, Trans.). Elmi va Farhangi Publication.

Masoudi, A. A. H. (1349). *Al-Tanbih va al-Ashraf [Warning and Supervisions]* (A. Payandeh Trans.). Bongah-e Tarjomeh va Nashr-e Ketab.

Masoudi, A. A. H. (1365). Morooj al-dhahab [The Golden Meadow] (Abulghasem Payandeh Trans.). Vol. 2. Elmi va Farhangi Publication.

Maqdasi, A. A. M. A. (1361). *Ahsan al-Taghasim fi Maerefate al-Aghalim [The Best Classification in Recognizing Countries]* (Alinaghi Monzavi Trans.). Sherkat Moaelfan va Moterajeman Iran.

Mostowfi, H. (1362). In G. Le Strange (Ed.), *Nuzhat al-Qulub [The Hearts' Bliss]*. Donyaye Ketab.

Qarchanlou, H. (1380). *Joqrafiay-e Tarikhi Keshvar haye Eslami [Historical Geography of the Islamic Countries]*. Samt Publication.

Qazvini, Z. M. M. (1371). Asaar al-Belaad va Akhbar al-Ebaad [The Countries' Secrets and the People's News] (M. M . Abdolrahman, Trans.). (S. M. Shahmoradi, Ed.). Tehran University Publication.

Sirafi, S. T. (1381). Selselat al-Tavaarikh (Akhbar al-Sin va al-Hend) [Historical Series: The News of the China & India] (A. H. Sirafi, Ed.). (H. Qarchanlou, Trans.). Asatir Publication.

Yaqubi, A. A. Y. (1993). *Tarikh al-Yaqubi [The Yaqubi History]* Moasesat al-Elmi lel-Matbooat

The Historical Geography of Makran

S. Abolghasem Foroozani

Abstract Makran (Mokran, Mekran or Makorran (in Balouchi dialect)—all pronunciations are correct.) is one of the most prominent regions of Iran, located in the south of Baluchistan and on the northern coast of the Sea of Oman (Makran). The special geographical location of Makran has long promoted the economic base for this part of Iran and the ports located there have possessed a privileged commercial status along with significant economic prosperity throughout history. Makran enjoys several thousand years of history and a valuable civilization. There are various opinions about the lexical origin of Makran and the extent of that land, as well as its administrative and political conjunction with neighboring states. Also, more accurate information is required concerning the cities, ports, and settlements related to Makran and its historical geography. Referring to the original historical and geographical sources as well as the new studies, some of the existing ambiguities about the historical geography of the land of Makran have been resolved in the current research.

Keywords Mokran · Gedrosia · Baluchistan · Tiz · Panjbur

1 Introduction

There are many disagreements among the experts regarding the name of the land of Mokran, its geographical location, its boundaries, the cities, ports, and settlements related to that province, as well as the administrative and political connection of that area to other neighboring provinces. In this study, which has been done with the aim of dispelling some of these researchers' opinions and proving or disproving some of the other expert views based on the authentic historical and geographical sources, it seems inevitable to address peripheral, yet related topics to this research. Hence, at

S. A. Foroozani (✉)
Professor of History, Shiraz University, Shiraz, Iran

N. Faghih et al. (eds.), *The Persian Gulf and Islands*, Perspectives on Development in the Middle East and North Africa (MENA) Region,
https://doi.org/10.1007/978-3-032-27910-1_6

first, Makran in the contemporary era has been briefly discussed, and then various opinions about the name of Makran and its lexical origin, from the very distant past to the several centuries after the arrival of Islam in Iran, have been reviewed and examined. The boundaries of the Makran province, which are considered in two parts: Makran in ancient times and Makran in the Islamic realm, are among the topics that have been investigated based on reliable geographical sources and scientific research. Also, following the title of important cities, ports, and settlements of Makran, the specific importance of some significant areas of that province has been discussed, while seeking to find the true pronunciation of the names of cities and settlements located in Makran. In the last section of this chapter, the social, economic, cultural and religious conditions of Makran province have been examined with regard to the available information in the original sources. Finally, based on the aforementioned topics, the findings of the research have been presented in a general conclusion.

2 A Brief Overview of Makran in the Contemporary Times

Mokran is a land located in the south of Baluchistan. On his commentary on the book *Tarikh-e Beyhaqi [The Beyhaqi History]*, [Saeed Nafisi] refers to Adib Pishavari's quotes about Mokran's territory: "it is a province limited to the east of Kerman and the south of Sistan, the north of the Indian Ocean and the west of Sindh and the Qosdar country" (Beyhaqi, 1319, p. 1068). Makran, which, as we will see in the following pages, has enjoyed an impressive expanse in the past, and nowadays it is located in a not so large area, while in a very valuable geographical status and this has been very effective for the economic prosperity of that land from the past to the present. Currently, Makran is limited to Saravan and Bampur in the north, to the Sea of Oman in the south, to Kalat (in Pakistan) in the east, and to Bashagard in the west (Dehkhoda, 1377, p. 21392). Since administratively this land is considered part of Baluchistan in the country divisions of Iran, it is necessary to be aware of the fact that "the present Baluchistan of Iran is a part of the land of ancient Baluchistan, that has been limited to Afghanistan from the north, from the east to the Indus River, from the south to the coast of the Sea of Oman and from the west to the border of Kerman." According to the book Introduction on the Historical Geography of Iran, Baluchistan is "an ancient land with ancient monuments that has a historical identity of five thousand years … It is a mountainous region with desert and dry climate conditions located in the southeast of the Iranian plateau" (Beik Mohammadi, 1377, p. 198).

During Nasir al-Din Shah's reign (1264–1313 A.H.), the British colonial government that dominated India sent General Goldsmith to Iran at the head of a delegation to determine the border of its empire with Iran. Finally, following Nasir al-Din Shah's acceptance of Goldsmith's proposal, "the land of Kalat was separated from Iran under the name of British Baluchistan and annexed to the territory of (Greater) India, and the present border of Iran and Pakistan was determined from the port of

Gwatr to the east of Kohak." A few years later (1870–1871 A.D.), the northern part of that section, i.e., the distance between Kohak and Malek Siah (the common border of the three countries of Iran, Afghanistan, and Pakistan), was also demarcated by a delegation headed by Goldsmith (Beik Mohammadi, 1377, p. 164).

3 Various Viewpoints Concerning the Name of Makran and Its Lexical Origin

In the distant past, the Sumerians lived at the head of the Persian Gulf and on both sides of the Shatt al-Arab, and the Akkadians lived in the northeast of their habitat. According to the findings of American archaeologists, the Sumerian civilization dates back to more than 3000 years BC. As, according to the existing inscriptions, one of the Sumerian pates (rulers) named "Ennatum" fought against the Elamites around 3000 years BC (Pirnia, 1362a, pp. 25–21), it can be concluded that the Sumerians had succeeded in forming a ruling dynasty at least 3000 years BC. During the Sumerians' reign, the Persian Gulf coasts were occupied by them (Pirnia, 1362a, p. 22). Accordingly, it can be said that the historical period of the Persian Gulf begins with the reign of the Sumerians.

In Sumerian and Akkadian inscriptions, the two regions named Makkan and Mellukhah have been mentioned many times. The book *Tarikh-e Khalij Fars va Mamaalek Hamjavar [The History of the Persian Gulf and Adjacent Countries]* quotes, considering the point that the names of the two mentioned regions are often mentioned together, and it is possible that those regions had been close to each other geographically. Researchers and archaeologists believe that Makkan is the Oman region located in the south of the Persian Gulf (Vosouqi, 1384, pp. 24–26). Donald Hawley emphasizes that "the location of Magan and Melukha, that are usually mentioned together in the tablets, has not been precisely determined and finding their location has been facing difficulty," he notes: Deylamun (Teylamun), is "generally considered to be the present-day Bahrain," and it is believed to be the closest region to Mesopotamia, and Melukha is considered the farthest land from there (Mesopotamia), and Magan is presumed to be a land between Deylamun and Melukha. He reminds us that Magan is mostly considered to be the same country as Oman. Hawley's work states that: "The geographical continuity and the combination of the names Magan and Melukha in bold letters and obtained in the tablets does not indicate their geographical proximity. Magan may have been a center for distributing goods (Melukha)" (Hawley, 1377, p. 29).

It worth pointing out that "mankind's traditional geography in ancient times called the current area of the Sea of Oman and the Persian Gulf and the eastern parts of Oman in the Indian Ocean, the Persian Sea" (Vosouqi, 1384, p. 35). The name Makkan was slightly changed to Mekka during the Achaemenid period and was also used with the same pronunciation in Greek texts, and Herodotus referred to Mecca as Myciens and included it among the 14th Achaemenid province (Vosouqi, 1384,

p. 26). The book *Historical Geography of Islamic Countries* notes that the Babylonian word Mekka means house (settlement) (Qarchanlou, 1380, p. 181). In an inscription left by Darius I of Achaemenid dynasty in Bisotun, located 30 km from Kermanshah, on a stone tablet located at an altitude of 105 m in the Zagros Mountains (Dandamayev, 1373, p. 24), Maka is mentioned as one of the twenty-three countries that had been under Darius's jurisdiction (until then) (ibid.: 343). In Naqsh-e Rustam, placed three-quarters of a mile from Persepolis, an inscription is written above the entrance to the tomb of Darius I of Achaemenid dynasty in three languages: Old Persian, Elamite, and Assyrian, counting other provinces under the command of that king, in addition to Persia and also points out to one of the countries that was under Darius' control as "Makia" (Machia). Considering the geographical location of Makya, Pirnia states: "Makya has been compared to Western Tripoli and Burqa because the Greek called the people of this country Makwes" (Pirnia, 1362a, pp. 117–121). It should be noted that Western Tripoli and Burqa are now part of Libya (Mahjoub & Yavari, 1362, pp. 295–294). Also, it worth noting that Burqa is currently known as Benghazi (Pirnia, 1362a, p. 100) and it (Benghazi) is now considered as one of the most populous cities in Libya (Mahjoub & Yavari, 1362, p. 294). Pirnia has expressed another opinion about Makya in his book *Iran-e Bastan [The Ancient Iran (Detailed History of Ancient Iran)]*. He asserts that the location of "Makya" with Makya is also not known for certain; some compare it to Mokran, while others compare it to Western Tripoli and Burqa. The first opinion is more powerful (Pirnia, 1362b, *Iran-e Bastan*, p. 1454).

Regarding Melukh, it should be said that some researchers consider Molukh to include the northern shores of the Persian Gulf and the coast of Iran to the east of the Indus Valley, but the famous Sumerian scholar Kramer, "considered the land of Melukh to correspond to Abyssinia and the shores of the Red Sea," referring to two Sumerian and Akkadian inscriptions. Likewise, since the shores of the Red Sea are mentioned in Assyrian inscriptions as Melukh, "the correspondence of this name to the current land of Abyssinia seems more probable" (Vosouqi, 1384, p. 26).

The name Makan that primarily appears in Sumerian and Akkadian inscriptions is indicative of this land's antiquity. The name of this state first appears in the surviving inscriptions of Darius I during the Achaemenid era, and "it seems that the name Mekka or Mecca or Mikoy has been applied to both sides of the shores of the Persian Gulf, the boundary between the present-day United Arab Emirates—ancient Oman—and the shores facing the island of Kish during the Achaemenid era." It is worth noting that in the early years of Darius I's reign, the four provinces of Aseh Garneh (at the southeastern end of the central Iranian desert), Zarangeh (Sistan), Yautiyeh = Yutiyeh (current Larestan), and Mecca (in the coastal parts of the Persian Gulf) were forced to pay huge tributes due to the widespread riots, and they were also degraded in terms of administrative status and became a part of the State of Harahutish, whose inhabitants were loyal to Darius (Vosouqi, 1384, pp. 37–39).

Pirnia has adapted "Harkhuvatish" to Rakhj (southern Afghanistan to Kandahar) (Pirnia, 1362a, p. 1118). However, according to the book *Tarikh-e Khalij Fars va Mamaalek Hamjavar*, up to the time when Darius had added the Indus region and its surroundings to his possessions; a state called Harahutish (Harahvatish) was located in the south easternmost part of the Achaemenid territory and "its area was almost the same as the State of Mokran in later periods" (Vosouqi, 1384, p. 36). It is necessary to explain that during the time of Darius in 512 BC. The Iranians crossed the Indus River and annexed part of Western India to the territory of Iran. After this conquest, on the orders of Darius, ships commanded by a Greek named Scylax (with the aim of familiarizing with the water passages) set off for the Sea of Oman. According to Herodotus, this delegation "flowed down the Indus River and passed the coasts of present-day Baluchistan and Mokran," then passed through the coasts of Arabia and entered the Red Sea from Bab al-Mandab (Pirnia, 1362b, *Iran-e Bastan*, p. 630–629).

During the time of Alexander the Great, one of his generals, Nearchus, was commissioned to identify the coasts of the Persian Gulf. "His journey began from the coasts of the present-day Baluchistan. First, he passed through the region of Gedrosia" (Vosouqi, 1384: 43). Nearchus referred to the coasts of Gedrosia in his travelogue as the "Fish-eating Coasts." According to T. W. Haig, an English orientalist, the coastal region of Baluchistan was called Gedrosia (Beyhaqi, 1319, p. 1083). Bartold believes that "it is clear that the Aryans occupied the coastal region (north of the Persian Sea) after Kerman, and apparently this province got its Greek name Gedrosia from the name of that branch of the Iranian nation that Herodotus called the Drusiai." He, who considers Gedrosia to be the same as Makran, notes that this province took its name from the Drusiaivi tribe, and considers that tribe to be among the Persians (Bartold, 1358: 158–168).

Haig believes that the Greeks referred to the coastal region of Baluchistan as the abode of fish-eaters (Ichtyophage) (Beyhaqi, 1319, p. 1083). According to the book *Tatbiq-e Loqat Joqrafiaei Qadim va Jadid Iran [Matching old and new geographical terms of Iran]*, "Ichsiophakorum" or "Ichsiophakorum," which means fish-eater in Greek, was the name that the Greeks applied to a tribe that lived on the coast of the Makran Sea (Oman) and that their food and their livestock food was fish (Etemad al-Saltaneh, 1363, p. 80). Referring to Barthold, Makran is not a name that was given to this region by an Aryan tribe and according to scholars, the word Makran is derived from the name of a Dravidian tribe that the Greeks called Makai or Mokai and is called Maka and Masia in cuneiform inscriptions. In the book of Stephan Byzantium, a Greek geographer, the name of the province does not appear in the form of Makareh (Bartold, 1358, p. 168). According to Haig, the translation of the Greek word Ichtyophage, which in Persian means "fish-eater," "has caused an amusement in the derivation of its current name and with greater probability [the word] traces back to a Dravidian origin" (Beyhaqi, 1319, p. 1083).

According to the book *Moqadamei bar Joqrafiaye Tarikhi Iran [An Introduction on Historical Geography of Iran]*, the present-day Baluchistan consisted of two parts in the past: "one was the southern coastal region called Maka or Makuran, which researchers have interpreted as fish-eating, and the other was the central and northern regions called Gedrosia, where its center was Pahreh or Fahraj, the plain of Iranshahr and the current Bampour" (Bei Mohammadi, 1377, pp. 199–198). Muslim authors have also referred to Makran in their books as Makuran (Bartold, 1358, p. 168) while presenting various opinions about the derivation of the word

Makran. Considering Yaqut Homavi's contemplation on the word Makran to be pronounced with the vowel O on the first letter, which is M and the silence of K letter [Mokran], he has pointed out that in Arabic poetry, Kaf Makran is used in the stressed form. Yaqut has suggested that Makran is the plural of Makr. He also refers to Hamza (Esfahani) asserting that perhaps Makran was originally Maah Kerman, which was then shortened to Makran. Yaqut also mentioned that Makran is attributed to Makran ibn Farak ibn Sam ibn Noah, and he (Makran) was the brother of Kerman (Al-Homavi, 1995, pp. 180–179). In his commentary on the book of *Tarikh-e Beyhaqi*, Saeed Nafisi has noted that "the things that Yaqut said about the derivation of the word Makran are clearly incorrect and even childish," and he rejected Yaqut's views by citing some reasons (Beyhaqi, 1319, pp. 1070–1071). According to Saeed Nafisi, in the book *Ganj Danesh* (compiled by Mohammad Taghi Hakim), Makran is attributed to Makran ibn Hital (Beyhaqi, 1319, pp. 1083–1082).

4 The Boundaries of Makran Province

4.1 Mokran in Ancient Times

As previously noted, Makran was the name of the coastal areas of Gedrosia (Baluchistan), yet except for its southern areas, which were limited to the Mokran Sea (Oman) and its northern areas, which extended to the central areas of Gedrosia; its eastern and western boundaries were not precisely defined. Following Ibn Khordadbeh's views, Saeed Nafisi believes that "apparently, the land of Makran formed an independent region with the land of Indus, that was part of Iran, during the Sasanian era." Nafisi, refers to the writings of Ibn Khordadbeh, quoting that Ardashir Babakan (the founder of the Sasanian dynasty) divided his country into 33 regions and called the ruler of each of those regions, who were reigning based on hereditary government, a king. According to Saeed Nafisi, "the region that was later called Makran and in recent times has become more commonly known as Baluchistan, was finally divided between Iran, English India and today's Pakistan. Concerning the recorded list by Ibn Khordadbeh, the area was divided into three regions during the Sassanid period." Nafisi mentioned the three regions as: "One is the Makran region, whose ruler was called Makran Shah, and the other is the region of the nomadic nomads, whose title of king was recorded by Ibn Khordadbeh, Qofos Shah, and the third is the Qiqan region, which is the northern part of Makran and the current Baluchistan, adjacent to the land of Sindh, and its ruler was called Qiqan Shah" (Beyhaqi, 1319, pp. 1071–1072). In the book *Chech-Nameh*, it is noted that (Rai) Chech bin Silaij (the ruler of Sindh) took steps to define the boundaries of his kingdom and determined Kashmir as the eastern border of his territory and decided to define the boundaries of Makran. During the second year of the Hijri and when Iran's situation was chaotic and "the affairs of the monarchy had reached to a woman," upon learning of these circumstances, Chech "went to the land of Kerman, fully equipped ... From there he turned to the land of Makran." He determined a stream located between Makran and Kerman as the boundary between the two provinces and "planted more date palms the banks of the stream and specified that it was the boundary that was used during the reign of Chech ibn Silaj ibn Basas, the king of Sindh" (Koufi, 1384, pp. 48–49).

4.2 Makran in the Islamic Realm

Pursuant to *Tarikh-e Tabari [The Tabari History; History of the Messengers and Kings]*, several Arab generals were assigned to conquer some provinces of Iran in the year 23 A.H. Among them, Hakam bin Amru Taghlabi was assigned to conquer the land of Makran, and a general named Shahab bin Mokhareq joined him. There, Soheil bin Adi and Abdullah bin Abdullah, who had conquered Kerman, rushed to help Hakam bin Amr Taghlib. At that time, the people of Makran were preparing to confront the Arabs in a camp outside their city. When the Muslims reached the camp of the Makran people, the king of Sindh, whose name was Rasel, rushed to the aid of the Makranians, but in the battle that took place between the Muslims and the people of Makran, led by Rasel, at a distance that was few houses[1] to Mehran River, the Muslims were victorious; Rasil was defeated, and his camp was captured by the Muslims. In this war, many of Makran people were killed and the Muslims settled in Makran. After this victory, Hakam ibn Amru informed Caliph Omar about the incident and after learning about the characteristics of Makran, Omar "wrote to Hakam ibn Amru and Soheil that no one from your army should pass through Makran and stop on this side of the river" (Tabari, 1362: 5, 2017–2006). The story of Makran's occupation is mentioned in quite a different way in the book *Chech Nameh.* Accordingly, the beginning of the Muslim attack on Sindh happens in the 15th year of the Hijri during the caliphate of Omar ibn al-Khattab (13–23 A.H.) and when Chech ibn Silaj was the ruler (Rai) of Sindh. The wars between the Muslims and the people of Sindh continued for years (Koufi, 1384, pp. 83–72), but it seems that Makran was captured by the Arabs during their first attacks and became a center for the Arabs to invade Sindh. According to a narration, in the 23rd year of the Hijri, Makran was captured by the Muslims (Bahar, 1383, pp. 279–278).

During the caliphate of Valid ibn Abdulmalek Omavi (96–86 A.H.), his general, Hojaj ibn Yusuf (Thaqafi), "asked the caliph, Al-Walid, for an order to invade Sindh and India," the caliph initially opposed Hajjaj's request but granted it, eventually (Koufi, 1384, p. 91). At first, Hajjaj assigned a general named Badil ibn Tohfa to invade Sindh and India, but Badil failed to do anything about it and lost his life. After receiving the news of Badil's death, Hajjaj nominated his cousin and

[1] An old unit of measurement for distances. Each house is equal six Farsang.

son-in-law, Mohammad ibn Qasim, "to invade India and Sindh." as the time Mohammad ibn Qasim reached Makran on his way, a person named Mohammad ibn Harun was ruling there, it can be seen that Makran had been under the Muslim control for some time before that (Koufi, 1384: 99–91).

In his book *Al-Masaalek al-Mamaalek*, Ibn Khordadbeh has considered Makran to be one of the regions related to the land of Sindh (Ibn Khordadbeh, 1967: 242) Yaqubi has also listed Makran among the lands of Sindh in his book *Alboldan [The Countries]* (Yaqubi, 1356, p. 57). Likewise Estakhri has considered Makran to be one of the lands of Sindh about which he writes "Makran has a wide and spacious areas" (Estakhri, 1373, p. 179). Concerning the boundaries of Sindh, it is stated that "there is a region, the east of which is the Mehran River, the south of which is the Great Sea, the west of which is the region of Kerman, and the north of which is a desert that joins the borders of Khorasan" in the book *Hodoud al-Alam Men al-Mashreq Ilal-Maqreb [The Borders of the World from the East to the West]* (Minorsky, 1372, p. 362). It seems noteworthy to mention that Mehran River, which according to Estakhri is "a good, large and pleasant river … and is as large and swift as the Nile River," begins from the (southern slopes) of the mountains whose (northern slopes) are the source of the Jeyhun River, and from there it goes towards Multan and then enters Mansoura and after passing east of Deybol it flows into the sea (Estakhri, 1373, p. 183). In the book *Asaar al-Belaad va Akhbar al-Ebaad [The Countries' Secrets and the People's News]*, it is stated that "the width of Mehran River is as wide as the width of the Tigris or more" and this river finally "falls into the Persian Sea at the end of the Indus" (Qazvini, 1371, pp. 162–161). It is worth pointing that Mehran River is also called the Andes River.

Describing Sindh, Maqdasi accounts: "I have divided this land into five provinces. I have also added Makran, which is close and attached to it, so that the lands are connected to each other" (Maqdasi, 1361, p. 700). Ibn Huqal mentioned a desert that is "between Kerman, Makran, and Sindh". He has mentioned that this desert is "entirely inhabited and has tents and houses made of clay and other things" (Ibn Huqal, 1366: 141). In the book *Ashkal Al-Alam [The World's Images], Estakhari's* writings about Makran are repeated: "Makran is a large and spacious province and is mostly desert" (Jeyhani, 1368, p. 136). In the book *Al-Ansaab, Qadim laha Mohammad Ahmad Halaaq [Genealogy, Presented by Mohammad Ahmad Halaq]*, Makran is listed among the areas related to Kerman (Al-Sameani, 1999, p. 349). In the book *Asaar al-Belaad va Akhbar al-Ebaad*, it is stated that Makran "is a region between the land of Sindh and the land of Tiz, its cities and villages are many" (Qazvini, 1371, p. 359). Yaqut Homavi has mentioned that Makran is the name of a seashore (Al-Homavi, 1995, p. 179). In *Nuzhat al-Qulub [The Hearts' Bliss]*, Makran is considered an annex to Kerman, and about it (Makran) it is stated that "Makran is a vast province and is within the sphere of Kerman" (Mostowfi, 1362, p. 141).

5 Important Cities, Ports and Settlements of Makran

Before entering this discussion, it seems noteworthy to point out that due to the Arabicization of the names of the cities, ports, and settlements of Makran, awareness of the correct pronunciation of those names requires specific attention. Also, authors' mistakes in writing some names, as well as their inappropriate punctuation and finally some indiscretions of the editors in correcting the names, are problematic. As previously noted, Ibn Khordadbeh has considered Makran as one of the areas related to the land of Sindh. In another part of his book, he has listed the cities of Sindh as Qiqan, Bonneh, Makran, Mid, and Kandahar. While mentioning the distances between some cities of Sindh, Ibn Khordadbeh has accounted for settlements that are not in such detail in other sources. He has mentioned Fahraj, Tabaran, Basurjan (the central city of Kharun), the village of Yahya ibn Amru, Hazar, Madar, Musara, Darak Bamuyeh, Tajin, the Moqateat al-Balus district (areas ceded to the Baluch), Mount Maleh, Nakhl, Qalman, Saray Khalf, Fannazbur, His (Tis = Tiz), Qandabil, Saray Daran, Jathiya, and Qasdar, and has considered the distance from the beginning of Makran to Mansoura to be 385 farsakhs (Ibn Khordadbeh, 1967, pp. 54–56).

Regarding Fahraj, Yaqubi asserts: "The people call it Fahrah and it is the last city subordinate to Kerman and the governor of Makran claims that it is one of the districts of Makran." Yaqubi then mentions "Khoruj" as the first city of the districts of Makran and considers the city of Fannazbur as the largest city of Makran (Yaqubi, 1356, p. 62). According to Istakhri (Estakhri), the city of Kiz (Kij) has been the throne to the ruler of Makran and "it is a beautiful and pleasant city with many date palm trees and is the capital of Makran and its regions." Estakhri considers Kiz to be half the size of Multan. He also notes (Bandar) Tiz (= Tis, near Chabahar port) as the capital (bar-andaz) of Makran and considers it to be known as Tiz Makran. He has accounted Qanzbur (Fanzbur) as the largest city in Makran and mentioned "Beh," "Band," "Qasr-e-Gand," "Darak," and "Fahlahfarah" as small cities in Makran. Estakhri has also mentioned the city of Rask and villages called Qarh and Jadran, noting the distances between the different cities of that land as follows: from Tiz to Kiz five houses, from Kiz to Qanzbur two houses, from Qanzbur to Darq three houses, and from Darq to Rask three houses … (Estakhri, 1373, pp. 181–179).

Considering that the geographical book *Hodoud al-Alam Men al-Mashreq Ilal-Maqreb*, prepared by an unknown author in 372 A.H., is in Persian, perhaps the actual pronunciation of some of the names of the cities and settlements of Makran can be obtained from that book. About Tiz, which was one of the important ports of Makran, it is mentioned that it is the first city within the area of the Indus on the shores of the Great Sea and it is a tropical place in the mentioned work. In that book, other cities of Makran are also mentioned as follows: "Kiz, Kushk-e-Qand, Neh, Band, Dezak (Darak), Isfak, all these are cities of the limits of Makran … and the king of Makran resides in the city of Kij." Likewise, the author of *Hodoud al-Alam Men al-Mashreq Ilal-Maqreb* mentions that "Rask is the town [= center] of the district of Joruj." According to his writings, Meshki was a town in the desert, Panjbur was considered the most important city in Sindh, and Pahlpareh was considered a city in the Joruj region (Minorsky, 1372, pp. 364–365).

In the book *Ahsan al-Taghasim fi Maerefate al-Aghalim [The Best Classification in Recognizing Countries]*, the names of other settlements have been added to the entries of the book *Hodoud al-Alam Men al-Mashreq Ilal-Maqreb*. According to Maqdasi, the capital (center) is Makran, Banjpur, and Meshka, Gij (Kij), Sarai, Shahr, Barbour, Khawash, Damdan, Jalek, Dzak, Dasht Ali, Hayz (Tiz?). He refers to Ebrahim al-Farsi (Estakhri) pointing out to Kabertun and Rask, quoting about Rask: "this is the town of the village of Khruq, which also has Band, Qasr Qand, Isfaqah, Fahl Fahr, Qanbali, and Armabil" (Maqdasi, 1361, pp. 702–701). As it can be seen in the book *Ahsan al-Taghasim fi Maerefate al-Aghalim*, Qasr Qand is written instead of Kushak Qand, Isfaqah is written instead of Isfak, Fahl Fahr is written instead of Pahlpara and Meshka is written instead of Meshki. Saeed Nafisi believes that the original Persian form of Kiz and Kij must be considered Kizh (Beyhaqi, 1319, p. 1086). Barthold also has referred to Banjbur or Fenzbur as Panjpur (Bartold, 1358, p. 169). It seems necessary to explain that Banjbur (Fanzbur) is currently known as Panjgur (Le Strange, 1364, p. 352).

6 Social, Economic, Cultural, and Religious Conditions of the Makran Province

In *Nuzhat al-Qulub* it is stated that "Makran is a large country, the second largest in size, its area is 12 stages, its royal residence is Fanzbur [Banjabur] ... and it has many crops and buildings and countless villages" (Mostowfi, 1362, p. 262). Maqdasi has mentioned Banjpur as the city of Makran in which: "it has a fort made of mud, a moat. It is in the middle of a palm grove and has two gates called "Turan" and "Tiz." Concerning the water used by the people there, he quotes that it comes from a stream and their mosque is in the middle of the market. Regarding Tiz, Maqdasi notes that it is located on the shore of the sea and "it is full of palm groves, has several good caravanserai and a beautiful mosque" (Maqdasi, 1361, pp. 702–701). Estakhri has noted Tiz as the Tiz of Makran and considered that city as Mokran's port (Estakhri, 1373, p. 179). Maqdasi has also quoted Tiz as a famous shipping port (Maqdasi, 1361, pp. 704–703). The author of *Hodoud al-Alam Men al-Mashreq Ilal-Maqreb* has considered Rask as "a place of prosperity and many people and merchants" (Minorsky, 1372, p. 364). Estakhri has mentioned Kiz (Kij) as the throne to the Makran's ruler, quoting that: "it is a beautiful and pleasant city with many date palm trees and port of Makran and its surroundings," considering its area to be half of Multan (Estakhri, 1373, pp. 180–179).

According to the book *Hodoud al-Alam Men al-Mashreq Ilal-Maqreb*, "many merchants" are mentioned in the city of Rask, but Pahlpara is presented as a place with few blessings (Minorsky, 1372, p. 365). Estakhri also mentions the city of Rask and villages called Khorosh and Jadran, and writes about the Jadran product that: "there is unlimited Paniz (sugarcane) and sugarcane there, and all the sugarcane that falls in the horizon is higher than it, except for a little that falls from the area of the Maskan" (Estakhri, 1373, p. 180). It should be noted that the sugarcane (Fanidh) is the same as white sugar (Habibi, 1380, p. 214). Recalling that "Mashki" is one of the tropical regions, Estakhri points out that "there are all kinds of cold-hardy fruits there" (Estakhri, 1373, p. 180). According to Ibn Khordadbeh, the income of Makran was transferred to the applicants in exchange for receiving one million dirhams (from the Abbasid Caliph) (Ibn Khordadbeh, 1967, p. 242). Estakhri has accounted for the distances between different cities in Sindh, among which, the distance between some cities of Makran is as follows: from Tiz to Kij (Kij) is five houses, from Kij to Qanzbur (Panjbur) is two houses, from Qanzbur to "Darq" is three houses, and from "Darq" to "Rask" is three houses (Estakhri, 1373, p. 181).

It is important to note that due to water scarcity in the province of Makran, "mobile resident and nomadic people predominated in this province" (Bartold, 1358, p. 168). Also, according to Maqdasi, most of the areas of Makran were deserts and dry-land agriculture was prevalent in that land (Maqdasi, 1361, p. 711). Estakhari has quoted that "most of the time there [Makran] is in famine" (Estakhri, 1373, p. 179). He has also talked about the "blackness" of the people of Makran and has called the language of the people of the center there (Banjpur) the Baluchi language (Estakhri, 1373, p. 703). Regarding the language of the people of Makran, Estakhari has written that "the language of the people of Makran is Persian and Mokri" (Estakhri, 1373, p. 179). This issue has also been repeated by Abolghasem Jeyhani in his book *Ashkal Al-Alam* (Jeyhani, 1368, p. 136). It is very likely that the Mokri language was actually a dialect of Persian.

Concerning the religion of the people of Makran, as was previously pointed out, the people of that land resisted the Muslim armies, but they were eventually defeated by them and Makran was captured by the Muslims. Yaqut Homavi refers to this issue holding that Makran fell into the hands of the Muslims by force (through war) (Al-Homavi, 1995, p. 179). After the first decades of the first century A.H., Islam was naturally spread throughout that land. Maqdasi has pointed to Islam as the religion of the people of Banjpur (Maqdasi, 1361, p. 703). The existence of a beautiful mosque and fine caravanserai in "Tiz" (which were mentioned in the previous lines) is indicative of the spread of Islam in that famous port. Estakhri has noted a "pleasant and beautiful" region called Il, located between Kizkanan and Qandabil, as a place where "all the inhabitants are Muslims". Following what Maqdasi has written about the religious situation in Sindh (which also included Makran), it appears that in addition to the Sunni religion, which has been the religion of the majority of the people there, and the Shiite religion, that has been believed by the people of Multan, believers in religions that Maqdasi referred to as polytheism and idolatry have lived in Sindh (Maqdasi, 1361, pp. 700–713).

7 Conclusion

According to what has been mentioned earlier; Makran, a province located in the south of Baluchistan, has an ancient history. The historical era of the Persian Gulf began with the reign of the Sumerians more than 5000 years ago. In the remaining inscriptions from the Sumerian era, regions with the names Makan and Melukh are mentioned; about which there are different opinions. Although some researchers have considered Molukh to include the northern shores of the Persian Gulf and the coast of Iran to the east of the Indus Valley, but with regard to the previously noted reasons, it is more likely that Molukh can be adapted to Abyssinia. Concerning Makan it can be generally said that this word, which has come in the form of Mecca as the name related to one of the provinces under the Achaemenids, has been applied to both sides of the coasts of the Persian (Sea) Gulf. Although in the case of Gedrosia (Baluchistan), there's an acceptable theory that a tribe of Persians known as Drusyaiv gave their name to the region on the Persian coast after entering the region, but in the case of the name Makran, Haig and Barthold's views on Makran's derivation from the name of a Dravidian tribe seem significant. As we witnessed, Yaqut's opinion on the derivation of the word Makran was rejected. Considering the different views mentioned about the area of the Makran province in ancient times and also in the Islamic era, it can be noted that Makran was in the territory of the Achaemenids, prior to the conquest of Sindh, yet after Sindh was annexed to Iran, Makran was placed within the area of this province related to Iran. The area of Makran is diversely mentioned in different sources, but it is certain that Fanzbur (Banjabur = Panjbur), Kij (Kiz), Tiz (Tis), and Rask were among the important cities of Makran. Among the quoted cities, Tiz was of great commercial importance and Kij was famous for its date palm trees. Also, a village called Jadran was considered an important center of sugar production. Accordingly, the language of Makran people's was Persian and also Makrani (which was most likely a local dialect of Persian). Since this land was conquered by Muslims in the first decades of the first century A.H., it is certain that the spread of Islam there, was not unexpected. From what is written in the sources about the mosques and the caravanserai in the various cities, it can be seen that Islam gradually became the dominant religion of the people of Makran.

References

Al-Homavi, S. A. A. Y. (1995). *Mojam Alboldan [The dictionary of countries]*. Dar Sader Publication.

Al-Sameani, A. S.'a. A. b. M. (1999). *Al-Ansaab, Qadim laha Mohammad Ahmad Halaaq [Genealogy, presented by Mohammad Ahmad Halaq]*. Dar Ehya al-Taras al-Arabi.

Bahar, M. a.-S.'a. (Ed.). (1383). *Mojmal al-Tavaarikh va al-Qesas [All histories and stories]*. Donyaye Ketab.

Bartold, V. V. (1358). *Tazkere Joqrafiaye Tarikhi Iran [An historical geography of Iran]*. (H. Sardadvar, Trans. Toos Publication.

Beik Mohammadi, H. (1377). *Moqadamei bar Joqrafiaye Tarikhi Iran [An introduction on historical geography of Iran]*. Isfahan University Press.

Beyhaqi, A. M. b. H. (1319). In S. Nafisi (Ed.), *Tarikh-e Beyhaqi [Beyhaqi history]*. Ketabkhaneh Sanaei.

Bosworth, C. E. (1362). *Tarikh-e Qaznavian [The Ghaznavides]* (Vol. 2). (H. Anoosheh, Trans). Amirkabir Publication.

Dandamayev, M. (1373). *Iran dar Doran Nakhostin Padeshahan Hakhamaneshi [Iran during the Era of the First Achaemenid Kings]* (Vol. 2). (R. Arbab, Trans). Elmi va Farhangi Publication.

Dehkhoda, A. A. (1377). *Loqat Nameh [Dictionary]* (2nd ed.). Tehran University Press.

Estakhri, A. E. (1373). *Mamaalek va Masaalek [The Kingdoms and the Routes]* (M. A. A. Tostari, Trans.). به کوشش ایرج افشار، Bonyad-e Moqufat-e Dr. Mahmoud Afshar Yazdi.

Etemad al-Saltaneh, M. H. (1363). In M. H. Mohades (Ed.), *Tatbiq-e Loqat Joqrafiaei Qadim va Jadid Iran [Matching old and new geographical terms of Iran]*. Amirkabir Publication.

Habibi, A. H. (1380). *Tarikh-e Afghanistan bad az Eslam [The history of Afghanistan after Islam]* (Vol. 3). Afsoon Publication.

Hawley, D. (1377). *Daryaye Pars va Sarzamin haye Motesaleh [The Trucial states]*. (H. Zanganeh, Trans. Moasese Farhangi Hamsayeh.

Ibn Huqal. (1366). *Safarnameh (Iran in Surat al-Arz) [The earth shape]* (Vol. 2). (J. Sho'ar, Trans). Amirkabir Publication.

Jeyhani, A. A. (1368). *Ashkal Al-Alam [The World's images]*. (A. A. S. Kateb, Trans. Beh Nashr Publishing Company and Astan Quds Razavi Publications.

Khordadbeh, I. (1967). *Al-Masaalek al-Mamaalek*. Brill Publication.

Koufi, A. b. H. (1384). In D. Pooteh (Ed.), *Fat'h Nameh Send (Chech Nameh)*. Asatir Publication.

Le Strange, G. (1364). *Joqrafiay-e Tarikhi Sarzamin haye Khelafat Sharqi [Historical geography of the Eastern Caliphate Lands]* (2nd ed.). (M. Erfan, Trans). Elmi va Farhangi Publication.

Mahjoub, M., & Yavari, F. (1362). *Gita shenasi Keshvarha [The geography of countries]* (Vol. 2). Gita Shenasi Publication.

Maqdasi, A. A. M. b. A. (1361). *Ahsan al-Taghasim fi Maerefate al-Aghalim [The best classification in recognizing countries]*. (Alinaghi Monzavi Trans. Sherkat Moaelfan va Moterajeman Iran.

Minorsky, V. (1372). In M. Mirahmadi & G. Varham (Eds.), *Hodoud al-Alam Men al-Mashreq Ilal-Maqreb [The Borders of the World from the East to the West]*. (Mirhossein Shaah, Trans. Al-Zahra University Publication.

Mostowfi, H. (1362). In G. Le Strange (Ed.), *Nuzhat al-Qulub [The Hearts' Bliss]*. Donyaye Ketab.

Pirnia, H. (1362a). *Iran-e Bastani [The Ancient Iran]*. Donyaye Ketab.

Pirnia, H. (1362b). *Iran-e Bastan [The Ancient Iran (Detailed History of Ancient Iran)]* (Vol. 2). Ketab Forooshi Ibn Sina va Bongah Danesh.

Qarchanlou, H. (1380). *Joqrafiay-e Tarikhi Keshvar haye Eslami [Historical geography of the Islamic countries]*. Samt Publication.

Qazvini, Z. b. M. b. M. (1371). In S. M. Shahmoradi (Ed.), *Asaar al-Belaad va Akhbar al-Ebaad [The countries' secrets and the people's news]*. (M. M. Abdolrahman, Trans. Tehran University Publication.

Tabari, M. b. J. (1362). *Tarikh-e Tabari [The Tabari history; History of the messengers and kings]* (Vol. 2). (A. Payandeh, Trans). Asatir Publication.

Vosouqi, M. B. (1384). *Tarikh-e Khalij Fars va Mamaalek Hamjavar [The history of the Persian Gulf and adjacent countries]*. Samt Publication.

Yaqubi, Ibn Vazeh (1356). Alboldan [The countries] (3). (M. E. Ayati, Trans.). Bongah Tarjomeh va Nashr Ketab.

The International Military-Commercial Status of Siraf Port (On the Persian Gulf Coast), During the Buyid Era

S. Abolghasem Foroozani

Abstract Considering the realistic approaches of the Buyid rulers (especially Azad al-Dawla), the economic prosperity of the country and people's security and well-being were of particular importance. In the light of the Buyid government's deeds, industries developed significantly and agriculture flourished. This eventually led to the production of products in excess of domestic needs; as a result, the government paid attention to the export of those items. What is examined in this chapter is that during the period in question, the Samanid dominated an extensive area of the Silk Road and enjoyed the commercial benefits related to that trade highway. Accordingly, the Buyid paid great attention to the major trade routes in southern Iran, both on land and at sea. Due to its peculiar geographical location, the port of Siraf, which was an important center of trade exchanges, enjoyed increasing prosperity and became famous as an international trade center during the Buyid reign. This very significant port also turned into a major military base and played a fundamental role in establishing security in the Persian Gulf and a highly extensive domain for the adjacent seas. This chapter also explores the commercial and military development of the Siraf port during the Buyid rule.

Keywords The Buyid · Port of Siraf · The Persian Gulf · Trade · Security

In response to King Charles VI of France's letter, after expressing mutual friendship and proposing satisfaction with the French ruler's military victories, Amir Timur Gurkan (708–771 A.H.) demanded the establishment of business relations between his country and France. In part of that letter, we read:

> … Your merchants should be sent in such a way that their position will be strengthen and honored and no one will force or abuse them … (Qazvini, 1363, pp. 51–52).

S. A. Foroozani (✉)
Professor of History, Shiraz University, Shiraz, Iran

N. Faghih et al. (eds.), *The Persian Gulf and Islands*, Perspectives on Development in the Middle East and North Africa (MENA) Region,
https://doi.org/10.1007/978-3-032-27910-1_7

Concerning the aforementioned letter, Timur spoke of the obligation in mutual respect for merchants of the two countries and insisted on protecting their rights. Timur's emphasis on expanding trade relations and respecting the merchants' dignity and ensuring their legal security is because, from that great explorer's viewpoint, "the world is prosperous as a result of merchants" (Qazvini, 1363, pp. 51–52).

But Timur's statement about the dependence of the world's prosperity on merchants (and trade) is interesting only because it expresses a tyrant's warrior perspective on the importance of trade. Having succeeded in conquering countries by the power of the sword, he realistically believes that the secret of prosperity and well-being of his realm lies in the prevalence of commerce. This realistic view is undoubtedly due to the experiences that have their roots in centuries and ages and were formed on the basis of necessities that mankind has long been aware of.

Yet, trade, which was initially carried out in the form of exchanging goods with each other (barter), was transformed and facilitated in the course of human progress into exchanging goods for money (in its various forms). In this case, in most societies, especially when the population increased, people were faced with surplus products on the one hand and with great difficulties in providing some of the needed goods on the other. Thus, it became necessary for each society to establish relations with societies that would purchase surplus products and supply the items it demanded. In the meantime, a group engaged in buying and selling goods with other societies. Whereas the importance of trade increased, the mentioned group also enjoyed a more desirable social status. Thus, merchants became among the privileged people of society.

Archaeological excavations in some ancient hills such as Tape-e-Hisar,[1] Cheshme-Ali,[2] Tape-e-Sialk,[3] Tape-e-Gian,[4] and Tal-Bakun[5] have led to the discovery of artifacts with non-local origin. Undoubtedly, objects such as shells, agates, turquoise, rings of crystal and lapis lazuli, copper, bronze, gold, and silver had been brought to these regions from distant places. Also, a tablet from the Naramsin era found in Susa indicates the trade relations of different cities in the third millennium BC (Pirnia & Afsar, 1370).

Before the Achaemenid era, the Tigris and Euphrates rivers connected the marine route of the Indian Ocean and the Mediterranean Sea. During the time of Bakht-al-Nasr (561–604 BC), a port called "Teredon" on the Persian Gulf was a trade intermediary between India and the port of Tyrus (one of the Phoenician ports on the Mediterranean coast). In those days, trade goods were transported from India to Tarsus; from there they were transported via the Euphrates River to Syria, and then sent to Phoenicia and its ports, terrestrially (Pirnia & Afsar, 1370).

During the Achaemenid Empire, the aforementioned route was abandoned for various reasons and the "Indian Sea-Red Sea"[6] marine route was established instead

[1] Located near Damghan City.

[2] Located in Shahr-e Rei.

[3] Located near Kashan City.

[4] Located near Nahavand.

[5] Located near Persepolis.

[6] The reasons for the abandonment of the aforementioned road are explained in page 69 of the book *Rah va Robat [Routes and caravansary]*.

(Pirnia & Afsar, 1370, p. 69). Digging a canal that connected the Egyptian Nile River to the Red Sea was a valuable action that was carried out by the order of Darius I of the Achaemenid Empire. In this way, the Mediterranean Sea was connected to the Indian Ocean and the Persian Gulf (Zarrinkoob, 1363). Undoubtedly, digging the aforementioned canal played a significant role in facilitating trade relations. Alexander the Great's invasion of the East and the subsequent entry of Western merchants and craftsmen into the newly conquered territory in the East led to the expansion of trade exchanges between the East and the West. During the Seleucid era, trade also enjoyed a favorable boom and popularity. This dynasty made a significant effort in repairing and expanding Iran's great roads that connected the continents of Asia, Europe, and Africa. The Seleucids also developed maritime trade by establishing numerous ports in the Persian Gulf (Pirnia & Afsar, 1370).

During the Parthian era and following their growing power and territorial expansions, trade gradually benefited from high status. At that time, in the vast and wealthy empire of Roman Empire, special attention was paid to luxurious life and its manifestations. Accordingly, goods such as silk and silk fabrics, precious carpets, perfumes, jewelry, gold, silver, Chinese and Indian steel, spices, and ivory found many customers. The route that transported the aforementioned products from the east to the western lands passed through the Iranian plateau. Thus, Iran's roads and the marine route of the Persian Gulf and the Red Sea gained great economic importance, while the Parthians made great efforts to improve the roads and maintain merchants' order and comfort (Pirnia & Afsar, 1370).

During both the Parthian era and the Sassanid Empire, the monopoly of trade in the aforementioned goods, especially silk, was in the hands of the Iranians, and the Romans were unsuccessful in finding another way to have direct relations with China. The struggle between the Romans and the Persians for the control of trade routes continued until the end of the Sassanid Empire (Pirnia & Afsar, 1370). The route that connected China to Iran and continued from Iran to the city of Antioch (on the Mediterranean coast) is known as the Silk Road. The reason for this designation is that Chinese silk and silk products were exported to Rome through that route (Pirnia & Afsar, 1370).

An extended and significant part of the Silk Road was in the hands of the Sassanid and they received significant sums from merchants in exchange for granting permission for trading goods to pass through their territory. The Sassanid were also fully aware of the importance of the marine routes and established a great navy, using their Arab subjects' assistance (Pirnia & Afsar, 1370). They ensured the security of trade in the Persian Gulf and the Indian Ocean by suppressing the pirates.[7] Thus, Iranian merchant ships traveled throughout all eastern waters and Iranian ports in the Persian Gulf and the Sea of Oman gained great prosperity and prestige as a result of their economic activity. Naturally, during Iran's Muslim conquests, the trade faced stagnation for a while. But over time, the roads were made safe again

[7] For instance, the Sasanian king Shapur II (410–479 A.D.) sent troops to the island of Bahrain to suppress pirates who threatened the shipping lanes between the Persian Gulf and the Indian Ocean (Masoumi, 1352).

and the caravanserais were repaired and the caravans set off on the reconstructed roads and the trade was revived.

Among Iran's roads, two major highways were famous since the distant past: the Khorasan Highway and the Fars Highway. Although their locations have been changed due to the destruction of some cities or the collapse of bridges and the destruction of roads in the floodwaters, their main routes have not changed. Of course, the terminals have changed as a result of changes in the capital locations. For instance, sometimes Ctesiphon and sometimes Hamadan, sometimes Baghdad and once upon a time Maragheh and Sultanieh have become the terminals (Pirnia & Afsar, 1370).

During the first centuries of Hijri, the aforementioned roads were in the territory of governors, mostly of Arab descent, who were assigned by the caliphate to govern the northern or southern provinces of Iran. However, after the emergence of semi-independent and independent Iranian governments, those major and important roads came under the jurisdiction of new dynasties.

Now, considering the mentioned contents, we will discuss the topic of this chapter: From what date and due to what elements did Siraf[8,9] emerge as an important port in the Persian Gulf?

Since when and under what influences did that port become famous as one of the international trade centers?

What were the reasons for the development of Siraf during the Buyid era?

One can find qualified answers to some of these posed questions in the book "Historical Geography of Siraf" (Semsar, 1357, pp. 105–243). What has been added to the above discussions in this chapter is that: The Buyid realized the necessity of expanding foreign trade for the welfare of the people and the economic prosperity of their territory. This was while the Samanid had control over an important part of the profitable trade highway known as the Silk Road. Accordingly, the Buyid inevitably paid specific attention to maritime trade in addition to paying attention to the expansion of trade relations through the southern terrestrial routes (the Persian Highway). In line with the Buyid's proper attention to the maritime routes located in southern Iran, the important port of Siraf in the Persian Gulf gained a global status.

From the second half of the third century A.H. and after the emergence of the Samanid in the arena of political power and their territory expansion from Ray to Taraz (on the banks of the Seyhun River), a powerful government was established in an extended area of Iran (Frye, 1363). This government, which had a strong and efficient administrative system (Bartold, 1366), took the first step in forming a flourishing trade by establishing security in its territory. The determination of precise laws and regulations and the establishment of criteria that, in addition to observing the interests of the state, protected the security and legal rights of merchants, encouraged investors in commercial affairs.

[8] Siraf, or currently the Taheri Port, is located 250 kilometers east of Bushehr Port on the northern coast of the Persian Gulf (Masoumi, 1352).

[9] More information about the meaning of the word Siraf (Semsar, 1357). Ahmad Eqtedari has also provided valuable information about Siraf and its historical monuments (Eqtedari, 1357).

During the Samanid era and within their territory, Sogdian merchants held the first place in trade with China and Khwarezmian had a privileged position in trade with Eastern Europe (Frye, 1365). Also, trade exchanges between the nomads living in the northern lands of the Seyhun River and the people of the cities located south of the Seyhun River (which were in the possession of the Samanid) were popular (Bartold, 1366).[10] Further, good exchanges were running from the lands located north of the Seyhun River toward Khorasan and from there to the heart of the Abbasid Caliphate and also to the shores of the Mediterranean Sea. It is clear that the government received a great income from the transportation of goods (transit) through the roads located in the Samanid territory (Right of passage).

In 322 A.H., the central nucleus of the Buyid government was formed by Ali Buyid in Shiraz (Razi, 1376). The Buyid rule over Fars had not yet been established when the chaos caused by the murder of Mard-e-Awij Ziyari provided the newly founded Buyid government with a suitable opportunity to seize Isfahan. In 334 A.H., the Buyid government took advantage of the chaotic situation of the Abbasid Caliphate and marched on toward the center of the caliphate (Baghdad) (Razi, 1376). The capture of Baghdad by Ahmad Buyid brought about considerable power and prestige for the Buyid.

During that time, the Buyid government, which enjoyed wise and realistic ministers and knowledgeable agents, after establishing security in the country, placed economic prosperity and ensured the material well-being of the people at the top of its programs following their ministers' guidance. By paying attention to the factors that led to the economic prosperity of the society, various economic activities increased in most cities, especially Isfahan, Shiraz, Rey and Hamedan. The noted cities, with their important spinning and weaving workshops and centers for the production of pottery, metal products and other products, were among the reputable centers for the production of the necessities of their time.[11] In order to sell industrial products as well as agricultural, livestock, mineral, and other surplus goods and also to meet the mutual needs of different regions of the country, it was very necessary to pay attention to the promotion of internal trade.

But the foreign trade income for the Buyid government, through the collection of taxes on exported items and also the collection of customs duties on imported goods, also required special attention to foreign trade (Faghihi, 1365). In addition, the increasing luxury needs of the wealthy classes of society were met through the import of those goods from abroad.[12] More importantly, the authority in the area of neighboring seas, control over the maritime trade routes and the receipt of rights of passage from merchant ships (transit rights) were of undeniable importance from political, military, and economic dimensions.

---

[10] It is worth noting that Maqdasi has provided the best information about the commercial situation in Transoxiana (the lands north of the Jeyhoon River) during the Samanid era, in his book (Maqdasi, 1361).

[11] More information is available on this topic (Faghihi, 1365).

[12] That is why the goods imported to the great port of Siraf included: oud, ambergris, camphor, jewels, ivory, ebony, fragrant oils, etc. (Jeyhani, 1368, p. 125).

In such circumstances, Siraf, as the most important port of the Persian Gulf, came into the focus of the Buyid's attention. Considering the Buyid's goals in the Persian Gulf and other neighboring seas, Siraf not only gained importance from a commercial perspective, but it also became renowned as a major naval base. Undoubtedly, the famous shipyards of Siraf played a fundamental role in meeting the needs of the newly established Buyid navy (Jaish al-Maa).[13] It was also for this reason that Siraf played a major role as the base of military operations during the conquest of Oman by Ahmad Buyid (Mu'ad al-Dawla) in 355 A.H. According to the previous map, the military forces of Azad al-Dawla (who ruled the southern regions of Iran at that time) were stationed in Siraf to assist the armies of Ahmad Buyid, and with the alliance of these two Buyid Amirs, the land of Oman came under the control of the Buyid (Razi, 1376).

The conquest of Oman by the Buyid was a remarkable military operation, yet more importantly, this important maritime gorge became completely under the control of the Buyid by capturing the lands in the southern part of the Strait of Hormuz. Thus, the Buyid's authority in the Persian Gulf, the Sea of Oman, and the adjacent seas was established. International maritime trade in that area was under the control of the Buyid (Faghihi, 1365), and their government received a great income. Correspondingly, the port of Siraf, which was a flourishing commercial center and a strong military base for the Buyid, gained increasing significance and became famous in a short time as one of the most important international ports in the world trade arena.

References

Balkhi, I. (1363). In G. Lestrange & R. A. Nickleson (Eds.), *Farsnameh* (Vol. 2). Donyaye Ketab Publication.

Bartold, V. V. (1366). *Turkestan Nameh* (K. Keshavarz, Trans.). Agah Publication.

Eqtedari, A. (1357). *Asar-e Shahr haye Bastani Savahel va Jazayer Khalije Fars va Daryaye Oman [The remains of ancient cities on the coasts and islands of the Persian Gulf and the Sea of Oman]* (Vol. 2). Anjoman Asar Melli va Mafakher Farhangi Publication.

Faghihi, A. A. (1365). *Āl-e Būya (Nakhostin Selseleh Ghodratmand Shi'a) [Āl-e Būya (the first powerful Shiite dynasty)]*. Saba Publication.

Frye, R. N. (1363). *Tarikh-e Iran az Islam ta Salajeqe [The Cambridge History of Iran: The Period from the Arab Invasion to the Saljuqs]*. (H. Anoosheh, Trans (Vol. 4). Amirkabir Publication.

Frye, R. N. (1365). *Bukhara Dastavard-e Qoroon Vosta [Bukhara: A medieval achievement]*. (M. Mahmoodi, Trans.) (2nd ed.). Elmi va Farhangi Publication.

Jeyhani, A. A. (1368). *Ashkal Al-Alam [The World's Images]*. (A. A. S. Kateb, Trans.). Beh Nashr Publishing Company and Astan Quds Razavi Publications.

Maqdasi, A. A. M. A. (1361). *Ahsan al-Taqasim fi Ma'rifah al-Aqalim [The Best Division in Understanding Territories]*. (A. Monzavi, Trans.). Moalefan va Motarjeman-e Iran Company.

[13] Ibn Balkhi has noted the existence of warship construction centers in the port of Siraf (Ibn Balkhi, 1363).

Masoumi, Q. R. (1352). *Siraf (Bandar Taheri) [Siraf (Taheri Port)]*. Anjoman Asar Melli Publication.

Pirnia, M. K., & Afsar, K. (1370). *Rah va Robat [Routes and caravansary]*. National Cultural Heritage Organization and Armin Publications.

Qazvini, M. (1363). In A. Eqbal & E. Pourdavood (Eds.), *Bist Maqaleh [Twenty Articles]*. Donyaye Ketab.

Razi, I. M. (1376). *Tajareb Al-Omam [The People's Experiences]*. (A. Monzavi, Trans.). Toos Publication.

Semsar, M. H. (1357). *Joqrafiaye Tarikhi Siraf [Historical geography of Siraf]*. Anjoman Asar Melli Publication.

Zarrinkoob, A. H. (1363). *Tarikh-e Mardom Iran [The history of Iranian People (Iran before Islam)]*. Amirkabir Publication.

Entrepreneurial Ecosystems and Poverty Alleviation in Selected Persian Gulf States

Ali Hussein Samadi and Sara Togha

Abstract This chapter provides a concise overview of various poverty alleviation strategies, with particular emphasis on entrepreneurship as a participatory policy tool in combating poverty. Employing the Panel-Corrected Standard Errors (PCSE) method, the current study examines the entrepreneurial ecosystem impact on poverty alleviation in selected Persian Gulf countries (Iran, Oman, Bahrain, Iraq, Qatar, Kuwait, the United Arab Emirates, and Saudi Arabia) over the period of 2010–2022. The analysis investigates the effects of individual components of the entrepreneurial ecosystem on poverty alleviation and evaluates the relative contribution of each factor. The findings indicate that a robust entrepreneurial ecosystem, coupled with effective governance, has a significant and positive effect on poverty reduction in the Persian Gulf region. Furthermore, the results demonstrate that the government-led entrepreneurship programs and the early-stage entrepreneurship education exert the most positive influence, whereas the technology transfer appears to have the least favorable impact among the entrepreneurial ecosystem indicators in the selected countries.

Keywords Poverty Alleviation Strategies · Entrepreneurship · The Persian Gulf

1 Introduction

Poverty alleviation refers to a broad set of economic strategies aimed at enabling individuals to escape poverty, while reducing its overall prevalence within society (Ajakaiye & Olomola, 1999). It continues to represent one of the most pressing

---

A. H. Samadi (✉)
Professor of Economics, Shiraz University, Shiraz, Iran
e-mail: asamadi@rose.shirazu.ac.ir

S. Togha
Department of Economics, Shiraz University, Shiraz, Iran
e-mail: asamadi@rose.shirazu.ac.ir

N. Faghih et al. (eds.), *The Persian Gulf and Islands*, Perspectives on Development in the Middle East and North Africa (MENA) Region,
https://doi.org/10.1007/978-3-032-27910-1_8

challenges confronting nations worldwide. Achieving effective poverty alleviation requires the identification of existing assets, the development of innovative approaches for their optimal utilization, and the strengthening of distribution mechanisms to ensure a more equitable sharing of benefits (Clyde & Karnani, 2015). In addition, it involves addressing and dismantling socio-economic barriers that limit access to opportunities and essential resources (Begum & Abdin, 2015).

Poverty alleviation has rapidly emerged as a central area of inquiry across the social sciences, economics, and the management disciplines. This growing scholarly attention has been driven by the persistence and expansion of extreme poverty, alongside the mixed and often disappointing outcomes of various interventions, including foreign aid, microfinance initiatives, and the expansion of property rights. In many cases, these efforts have not only fallen short of effectively reducing extreme poverty, but they have also generated additional socio-economic challenges. Key approaches to poverty alleviation include enhancing individuals' knowledge and skills, improving access to educational resources, reducing levels of deprivation, and promoting public participation in decision-making processes. Achieving sustainable poverty alleviation further requires careful consideration of factors such as income growth, education, employment generation, entrepreneurial opportunities, well-being, living standards, skill development, savings, and investment (Abubakar & Mitra, 2013).

According to the Arab Development Portal,[1] per capita poverty rates across the Persian Gulf countries in 2022 ranged from 0.38% in Qatar to 32.11% in Iraq. Iraq and Iran recorded the highest per capita poverty rates, at 32.11% and 20%, respectively. Saudi Arabia and Oman ranked third and fourth, at 13.37% and 10.1%, respectively. By contrast, Qatar (0.38%) and Kuwait (1.39%) reported the lowest per capita poverty rates among the Persian Gulf countries. Evidence from this report, together with Global Development Indicators[2] covering the period from 2016 to 2022, suggests that per capita poverty rates in Iraq, Iran, Bahrain, and Kuwait exhibited a modest upward trend, whereas Saudi Arabia, Oman, the United Arab Emirates, and Qatar experienced a slight downward trend over the same period.

An examination of the Doing Business Index for the Persian Gulf countries, indicates that Kuwait achieved the highest score with an optimal value of 6.05, whereas the United Arab Emirates recorded the lowest score at 2.84, as reported by the Arab Development Portal in 2023. These findings suggest that Kuwait's legal and regulatory frameworks are largely aligned with or closely approximate to the international guidelines and standards. In contrast, the legal framework in the United Arab Emirates appears to operate at a basic or below-average level when assessed against the prevailing international benchmarks.

The Persian Gulf countries face distinctive challenges in poverty alleviation, largely stemming from their heavy dependence on oil revenues and the region's specific socio-economic dynamics. Despite being widely regarded as affluent due to their substantial hydrocarbon resources, these countries continue to experience

[1] http://arabdevelopmentportal.com

[2] See Appendix Error! Reference source not found.

notable levels of poverty. Moreover, poverty alleviation strategies in the Persian Gulf differ markedly from those implemented in regions such as Southeast Asia and Sub-Saharan Africa, reflecting variations in economic structures, governance systems, and social policy frameworks. Whereas the Persian Gulf countries often rely on oil wealth to finance direct income support and large-scale infrastructure development, Southeast Asian nations typically pursue more diversified and export-oriented economic strategies.[3]

In the Persian Gulf countries, a range of strategies has been implemented to address poverty, most of which are redistributive, structural-adjustment-oriented or supportive in nature. These approaches have largely concentrated on the income dimension of poverty, often overlooking its multidimensional characteristics. Consequently, there is a growing need to adopt strategies that address poverty in a more comprehensive manner. The entrepreneurial ecosystem, which encompasses multiple interconnected dimensions, exhibits features that can directly influence the non-income aspects of poverty, including the access to opportunities, skills development, and social inclusion (Forouharfar, 2018).

A substantial body of scholarly research has explored the multiple dimensions of poverty reduction. The contribution of entrepreneurship to poverty alleviation is summarized in Table 1, as documented in the existing literature.

Considerable progress has been made by researchers in identifying the underlying causes of poverty and developing strategies for its alleviation, including the institutional reforms, microfinance initiatives, innovation, and the creation of new investment opportunities (Khavul et al., 2013; Ault & Spicer, 2014; Chliova et al., 2015). Entrepreneurship has been widely recognized as one of the most effective approaches for addressing poverty on a global scale. Given the limited success of foreign aid and infrastructure-focused interventions in reducing poverty, examining the role of entrepreneurship has emerged as a critical area of scholarly inquiry (Mair & Marti, 2009; Yanya, 2012; Bruton et al., 2013; Álvarez & Barney, 2014; Sutter et al., 2019; Amorós et al., 2021; Blanco-Arana & Angulo-Guerrero, 2024).

A central challenge lies in understanding the complex relationship between entrepreneurship and poverty alleviation. Previous studies have often merely focused on one or two indicators of entrepreneurship, whereas the entrepreneurial ecosystem comprises multiple interconnected dimensions that can address diverse aspects of poverty, thereby enhancing its overall effectiveness. Accordingly, this chapter not only outlines the strategies for poverty alleviation, but it also underscores the critical role of the entrepreneurial ecosystem within this context. Furthermore, it evaluates the efficacy of individual indicators within the ecosystem in relation to their potential impact on poverty reduction.

The heavy reliance on oil revenues and the prevalent use of direct aid strategies have limited the focus on entrepreneurship as a central mechanism within participatory approaches to poverty alleviation in the Persian Gulf countries. Following the

---

[3] https://www.unescwa.org/publications/arab-business-legislative-frameworks-2023
https://www.unescwa.org/publications/poverty-in-the-gcc-countries-2010-2021

Table 1 The role of entrepreneurship in contributing to poverty alleviation

Contribution of entrepreneurship	Author(s)
Highlights the role of entrepreneurship in poverty reduction through the creation and transformation of socio-economic value	Hashim and Gaddefors (2023), Si et al. (2019)
Examines the effects of opportunity-driven, necessity-driven, and early-stage entrepreneurship on poverty alleviation	Amorós and Cristi (2011), Moradi et al. (2020), Amorós et al. (2021)
Emphasizes the importance of government involvement in fostering entrepreneurship and small business development, leading to improved employment opportunities for the poor	Mensah and Benedict (2010), Djankov et al. (2018), Nakara et al. (2021), Dugguh (2013), Azamat et al. (2023)
Investigates how financial development moderates the relationship between entrepreneurship and poverty alleviation	Lin et al. (2021), Blanco-Arana and Angulo-Guerrero (2024)
Demonstrates that, in certain contexts, business formation may lead to increased poverty levels	Yanya (2012)
Argues that self-employment—often the dominant form of entrepreneurship in low-income areas—has a limited impact on poverty reduction	Álvarez and Barney (2014)
Highlights the critical role of social entrepreneurship, particularly through microfinance institutions, in addressing the challenges faced by the poor	Edobor (2018), Sakinah et al. (2023), Arejiogbe et al. (2023), Suyono and Safaria (2022)
Shows that the poverty-reducing effects of entrepreneurship vary across local contexts; entrepreneurship in tradable sectors tends to generate positive local multipliers, whereas non-tradable entrepreneurship may saturate local markets and reduce incomes for some groups	Lee and Rodríguez-Pose (2021)
Stresses the importance of targeted programs aimed at enhancing the capabilities, as well as the human and social capital, of the poor	Goel and Rishi (2012)

Source: Research findings

importance of participatory strategies and their potential for long-term sustainable impact on poverty reduction in the region, the current chapter explores the role of the entrepreneurial ecosystem in addressing poverty. Moreover, it aims to identify which specific sub-indicators of the entrepreneurial ecosystem exert the most significant influence on poverty alleviation among the Persian Gulf countries.

The remainder of this chapter is structured as follows. Section 2 provides a review of the relevant literature. Section 3 outlines the theoretical framework, covering types of entrepreneurship, poverty alleviation strategies and the role of entrepreneurship in mitigating poverty. Section 4 describes the methodology, including the model specification and the data utilized. Section 5 presents the empirical findings on the impact of the entrepreneurial ecosystem on poverty alleviation in the Persian Gulf countries. Section 6 discusses the results and concludes the chapter. Finally, the limitations of the present study and recommendations for future research are presented in Sects. 7 and 8.

2 Literature Review

2.1 *Micro- and Macro-Level Studies*

Poverty remains a persistent economic challenge worldwide and a growing body of research has identified entrepreneurship as a potential mechanism for alleviating poverty (Sutter et al., 2019; Hussain et al., 2014; Ifeoma et al., 2018). Despite this recognition, few studies have systematically modeled or empirically analyzed the role of entrepreneurship in poverty reduction. Several scholars have investigated the impact of entrepreneurship on poverty at both macro and micro levels, as summarized in Table 2.

Table 2 Impact of entrepreneurship on poverty alleviation at micro and macro levels

Level	Main finding(s)	Author(s)
Micro	Entrepreneurship contributes to poverty alleviation by creating employment, particularly under well-enforced business regulations.	Djankov et al. (2018)
Micro	Entrepreneurial activities generate employment and act as a mechanism for poverty reduction.	Thurik et al. (2008)
Macro	Although entrepreneurship fosters poverty alleviation by creating new markets, launching new industries, and increasing productivity, its overall effect remains limited.	Ali and Ali (2013)
Micro	Qualitative entrepreneurial growth promotes poverty alleviation more strongly than quantitative growth, with farmers' socio-cultural capabilities driving entrepreneurial development.	Naminse et al. (2019)
Micro	Socio-cultural capability is the most influential driver of farmer entrepreneurship, and qualitative entrepreneurial growth plays a pivotal role in rural poverty reduction.	Naminse and Zhuang (2018)
Micro	Entrepreneurship driven by local innovation, community participation, and small-scale ventures plays a critical role in poverty alleviation beyond government and large-firm interventions.	Si et al. (2015)
Micro	Overall and necessity-driven entrepreneurship positively influence poverty alleviation, particularly in developing countries.	Amorós et al. (2021), Amorós and Cristi (2011), Thurik et al. (2008), Martínez-Rodriguez et al. (2020)
Macro	Self-employment entrepreneurship is the most common type in rural areas; however, its impact on poverty alleviation is limited.	Alvarez and Barney (2014)
Micro	Enhancing skills and social networks strengthens economic capabilities, contributing to poverty reduction.	Adetona (2025)
Micro	Entrepreneurship in rural areas empowers the poor and fosters economic development.	Morris et al. (2020), Al Mamun et al. (2019), Morris et al. (2018)

(continued)

Table 2 (continued)

Level	Main finding(s)	Author(s)
Macro	Direct foreign aid, microfinance, social entrepreneurship, grassroots pyramid schemes, and institutional reforms (e.g., property rights) in poor countries have limited effects on poverty reduction.	Alvarez et al. (2015)
Micro	Socio-economic and perceptual factors significantly influence nascent entrepreneurship. Necessity-driven entrepreneurship has a stronger impact on poverty alleviation than opportunity-driven entrepreneurship.	Dencker et al. (2021), Mohan et al. (2018)
Macro	Entrepreneurship measured by new business registrations increased poverty levels, with efforts to reduce poverty hindered by rising income inequality.	Yanya (2012)
Macro	Entrepreneurship has limited effectiveness in reducing poverty and does not significantly impact income distribution.	Yanya et al. (2013)
Micro	Micro-entrepreneurship projects expand employment opportunities and enhance individuals' economic capacity, thereby contributing to poverty reduction.	Aldalou and Migdad (2023)
Macro	Access to human capital, opportunity-driven motivation, and financial resources fosters innovation among poor entrepreneurs, enhancing productivity and national economic growth, and supporting poverty alleviation.	Nakara et al. (2021)
Micro	Women utilizing microfinance services and investing in small enterprises achieve higher incomes, improving household poverty indicators.	Malki et al. (2024)
Macro	Access to microfinance services reduces income inequality and enhances the relative income standing of poor individuals, highlighting entrepreneurship's role in economic empowerment and poverty reduction.	Miled et al. (2022)

Source: Research findings

At the micro level, studies have shown that micro-entrepreneurial activities are directly associated with an increased income and improved household economic conditions. Furthermore, the importance of access to entrepreneurial skills training and microfinance resources has been consistently emphasized as a key driver of poverty alleviation.

At the macro level, studies have produced mixed findings regarding the impact of entrepreneurship on poverty alleviation. While some research suggests that entrepreneurship may have limited or even negative effects on poverty reduction, extensive evidence indicates that entrepreneurship functions as a catalyst for economic growth and helps mitigate income inequality. Generally, countries with higher levels of entrepreneurial activity exhibit lower poverty and inequality indicators compared to those with lower levels of entrepreneurial engagement.

2.2 *Social Entrepreneurship and Poverty*

A growing body of research has highlighted the role of social entrepreneurship in poverty alleviation (Anderson et al., 2019; Imbert et al., 2019; Pal & Altay, 2019; Mouraviev & Kakabadse, 2021; Zanky et al., 2023). Several studies emphasize on addressing poverty-related challenges through job creation and business innovation facilitated by social entrepreneurship (Ifeoma et al., 2018; Korosteleva & Stępień-Baig, 2021; Yusriadi et al., 2020; Sall, 2022). These investigations examine the relationship between social entrepreneurship and poverty, indicating that entrepreneurship acts as a conduit for knowledge spillovers, enabling the reallocation of resources toward more productive activities and creating opportunities for impoverished communities. This line of research predominantly focuses on the entrepreneurial efforts driven by altruistic or humanitarian motives (Overall, 2017).

Since social entrepreneurs typically operate on a non-profit basis and are not primarily focused on profit maximization, they may encounter resource constraints or vulnerable to long-term economic pressures. Therefore, examining the sustainability of social entrepreneurship and the strategies employed to support impoverished communities is essential (Moradi et al., 2020). Suyono and Safaria (2022) explored the role of social entrepreneurship in empowering communities to reduce poverty and prevent conflict in Indonesia. Using a qualitative phenomenological approach while enjoying a conceptual framework, their study demonstrated that social entrepreneurship can effectively address poverty and mitigate conflict. The findings suggest that the successful implementation of social entrepreneurship serves as a powerful strategy for strengthening collective entrepreneurial activities within communities.

2.3 *Institutions and Poverty*

Extensive scholarly attention has been devoted to examining the effects of institutional quality on entrepreneurship and poverty alleviation (e.g., Aidis et al., 2008; McCloskey, 2010). Governments and financial institutions have consistently sought to address poverty, particularly through the educational and capacity-building initiatives (Kolvereid & Moen, 1997). A robust institutional framework enables individuals to make more informed and effective decisions regarding entrepreneurial activities. Supported by enablers such as the government assistance programs and financial institutions, some small enterprises have successfully evolved into larger entrepreneurial ventures, thereby generating additional employment opportunities (Levie & Autio, 2008; Stenholm et al., 2013).

Also, the role of entrepreneurship facilitators has been highlighted, as these institutions are responsible for identifying solutions to poverty and promoting economic development (Carland et al., 1984; Mitra et al., 2011). Such facilitators play a crucial role in creating an enabling environment in which individuals can become entrepreneurs. A key function of these institutions is to assist impoverished populations in acquiring the knowledge and skills necessary to develop new goods and services.

Goel and Rishi (2012) examined various initiatives and institutional mechanisms in India aimed at enhancing capacity building and promoting entrepreneurship among the impoverished populations. Their approach extended beyond merely increasing income; rather, it focused on empowering the poor through the participatory strategies and targeted programs. The study underscores the importance of giving the poor a voice and strengthening their human and social capital through well-designed development interventions.

Contrary to the assumptions of Banerjee and Jackson (2017) and Chikwira et al. (2022), noting that microfinance promotes entrepreneurship and empowers women, thereby enhancing social capital in impoverished communities, evidence suggests that in some cases microfinance has contributed to rising debt levels among the poor populations. It has exacerbated the economic, social, and environmental vulnerabilities. Market-based initiatives such as microfinance may play a counterproductive role in developing entrepreneurial capabilities within the disadvantaged communities, particularly in contexts where the social capital is already weakened. Providing loans and financial services to the poor as a strategy to foster entrepreneurship—without simultaneously offering adequate training in business fundamentals and financial literacy—not only fails to support sustainable enterprises, but it may also impose significant financial burdens on individuals unable to repay their debts (Moradi et al., 2020).

Business freedom policies and the provision of microloans have been identified as key strategies for poverty alleviation and the promotion of opportunity-driven entrepreneurship (Liñán et al., 2013). According to these scholars, microloans can effectively contribute to poverty reduction and mitigate necessity-driven entrepreneurship under three key conditions. First, microfinance initiatives should be complemented by policies that enhance individuals' professional and vocational skills. Second, entrepreneurs must be capable of recognizing and exploiting opportunities in their environment. Third, they must possess the financial capacity to repay the loans. These findings are corroborated by additional studies, including the research done by Imai and Azam (2012) and Kiiru (2007).

2.4 *Entrepreneurship and Poverty*

Some researchers consider entrepreneurship to be a fundamental tool for addressing the economic challenges faced by the impoverished populations (Tobias et al., 2013; Chliova et al., 2015; Sutter et al., 2019). Azamat et al. (2023), employing the Human Development Index (HDI) as a measure of poverty alleviation and a fixed effects model across 73 developed and developing countries during 2016–2020, found a strong positive relationship between entrepreneurship and poverty reduction. These studies highlight the transformative role of entrepreneurship in business development. From this perspective, entrepreneurial activities positively contribute to societal well-being, particularly for individuals living below the poverty line. They empower the poor to achieve economic independence, increase their income, and overcome barriers to launching new ventures or expanding existing ones, thereby creating new jobs and employment opportunities. While most empirical studies have aimed at providing evidence for the effectiveness of entrepreneurship in poverty alleviation and economic growth (Marsden, 1990; Richardson, 2004; Si et al., 2015; Bruton et al., 2015; Tobias et al., 2013), many have not sufficiently addressed the differential impacts of various types of entrepreneurship on poverty. This omission has led to an ambiguity in interpreting the true effects of entrepreneurship (Moradi et al., 2020).

The influence of entrepreneurship on job creation and poverty alleviation has been examined in numerous studies (e.g., Azamat et al., 2023; Djankov et al., 2018; Mensah & Benedict, 2010; Nakara et al., 2021). Entrepreneurship serves as a mechanism to address economic needs and provide resources by generating employment opportunities. Effective entrepreneurship training can contribute to poverty reduction by fostering job creation. Moreover, entrepreneurial activities, along with the associated support services, enable small business owners in impoverished communities to expand their enterprises, to improve their livelihoods and to contribute to the well-being of others within their communities.

Dugguh (2013) examined governmental strategies aimed at fostering entrepreneurship and small enterprises, with a particular focus on equipping at-risk youth with marketing skills and supportive initiatives to enhance employment prospects. These programs included empowerment initiatives and training in areas such as repairs, food processing, and computer literacy, all of which intended to alleviate poverty, to increase job availability, and to generate wealth in Nigeria. The study established a theoretical link between entrepreneurship, small business development and the challenges of poverty, unemployment, and corruption in the country. Similarly, Aluko (2003) emphasized that implementing economic policies aimed at expanding industries and creating additional employment opportunities is among the most effective strategies. Moreover, entrepreneurship contributes to inclusive growth and poverty alleviation (Agri et al., 2019).

Several studies have highlighted the role of microfinance in poverty reduction, recognizing it as an effective approach in channeling financial resources toward the low-income populations, thereby contributing to poverty alleviation (Abolfazlian, 2017; Seifi, 2019; Badko et al., 2022; Singh & Chudasama, 2020; Chikwira et al., 2022). Lin et al. (2021), employing dual-structure economic theory and panel data from 2000 to 2017, investigated the impact of entrepreneurship on poverty alleviation in both urban and rural areas in China. Their findings indicate that the positive relationship between entrepreneurship and poverty alleviation is significantly stronger in urban contexts compared to rural ones.

The level of financial development in a region can moderate the impact of entrepreneurship on poverty alleviation. Strengthening the financial system can amplify the positive effects of entrepreneurial activities on poverty reduction. Blanco-Arana and Angulo-Guerrero (2024) examined the relationship between financial development and poverty alleviation in developing countries using a pooled OLS approach over the period 2000–2019. Their findings confirmed a strong association between financial development and poverty alleviation, providing new evidence on the critical role of entrepreneurship in developing economies and demonstrating how entrepreneurial activities mediate the relationship between financial development and poverty reduction.

Bruton et al. (2013) and McMullen (2011) emphasized the role of entrepreneurship in overcoming institutional barriers and employing market-driven approaches to improve the conditions of the poor. Their studies indicate that market-based solutions, such as entrepreneurship, provide effective avenues for generating significant positive change in impoverished environments. McMullen (2011) further proposed a theory of developmental entrepreneurship, integrating business, social and institutional entrepreneurship to accelerate the institutional transformations necessary for inclusive growth. His findings suggest that such institutional changes can serve as a more efficient and effective mechanism for poverty alleviation in developing countries. The development of entrepreneurship must also ensure that the poor have access to capital and resources (Agri et al., 2019; Sall, 2022).

Addressing diverse socio-economic challenges requires a range of strategies and interventions. Promoting entrepreneurial activities has been widely adopted across the developing countries and its potential and effectiveness in fostering economic growth are well recognized. It is widely argued that reorienting the education system to cultivate an entrepreneurial mindset and culture can make a significant contribution to national development (Magnus & Joseph, 1995).

Five key factors contribute to the creation of an entrepreneurial environment: the access to financial resources (including government programs, low-interest loans, and financial institutions), business skills, regulatory quality (government policies and procedures related to business restrictions and registration), socio-economic conditions (individuals' entrepreneurial knowledge, experience and general attitudes toward entrepreneurship), and non-financial support (entrepreneurial networks and support services) (Gnyawali & Fogel, 1994). Such an environment provides a solid foundation for promoting entrepreneurship and consequently for poverty alleviation.

2.5 Summary

Entrepreneurship is a vital tool for poverty alleviation, with numerous entrepreneurial opportunities at the core of every business. However, existing research has insufficiently addressed entrepreneurial opportunities and activities specifically related to poverty reduction. Based on the reviewed studies, research on this topic can be categorized into four thematic groups.

The first group comprises micro-level studies, which generally conclude that entrepreneurship—often necessity-driven and involving self-employment—positively impacts poverty alleviation by creating employment opportunities. Conversely, at the macro level, entrepreneurship is typically measured by the new business registrations, and these studies generally find that entrepreneurship has not been effective in reducing poverty.

The second group focuses on social entrepreneurship, highlighting its role in poverty alleviation through knowledge spillovers. This form of entrepreneurship facilitates the reallocation of resources toward more productive activities, thereby creating opportunities for the impoverished populations.

The third group examines the role of institutions in entrepreneurship and poverty alleviation. The main finding of this group is that facilitating entrepreneurial activities and improving the business environment can significantly contribute to poverty reduction.

The fourth group investigates the direct relationship between entrepreneurship and poverty, emphasizing that entrepreneurial activities enable the poor to achieve economic independence and increase their income. These studies underscore the importance of entrepreneurship in job creation, income generation and equitable income redistribution. Additionally, the role of microfinance in channeling financial resources to low-income populations for poverty alleviation is highlighted.

Most studies primarily focus on the income dimension of poverty, paying comparatively less attention to other dimensions. The entrepreneurial ecosystem shaped by cultural, economic, political, and social factors, plays a critical role in determining the effectiveness of entrepreneurship in alleviating poverty.

Entrepreneurship has been increasingly recognized as a transformative mechanism for promoting socio-economic development in underserved regions. Beyond its traditional role in job creation, entrepreneurial activity generates value, reshapes local economic structures and enables low-income populations to convert latent capabilities into productive assets. Consequently, entrepreneurship functions not merely as an economic activity, but also as a structural pathway for empowering the marginalized communities.

A central mechanism through which entrepreneurship contributes to poverty alleviation lies in its capacity to enhance the human and social capital of the poor. Entrepreneurial interventions—such as business skills training, market-access facilitation and network-building initiatives—strengthen individuals' knowledge, decision-making abilities and economic self-efficacy. These capabilities transform passive economic participants into proactive agents of development. Simultaneously, the accumulation of social capital through engagement in entrepreneurial networks improves collective bargaining power and fosters adaptive resilience in the face of market volatility.

Importantly, the effectiveness of entrepreneurship in poverty alleviation depends on the strength of the entrepreneurial ecosystem, critically. Key ecosystem indicators—including regulatory quality, access to finance, availability of supportive infrastructure, market openness, cultural and social norms conducive to innovation, entrepreneurial education and the presence of mentoring and support networks—determine the extent to which entrepreneurial initiatives translate into inclusive development outcomes. Ecosystems characterized by the streamlined regulations, robust financial instruments, digital infrastructure and institutional support create favorable conditions for the emergence and scaling of entrepreneurial ventures among the low-income populations. In sum, entrepreneurship most effectively contributes to poverty alleviation when embedded within a supportive and well-functioning entrepreneurial ecosystem. Such ecosystems amplify individual capabilities, reduce structural barriers and enable entrepreneurial efforts to generate sustainable and measurable developmental gains. Accordingly, entrepreneurship should be recognized as a central strategy not only for poverty alleviation, but also for fostering long-term economic resilience and inclusive growth in the marginalized communities.

The primary objective of the current chapter is to advance the understanding of the relationship between the entrepreneurial ecosystem and poverty alleviation, with a particular focus on the Persian Gulf region. The entrepreneurial ecosystem—encompassing a range of indicators, including institutional, social, business, and other dimensions of entrepreneurship—provides a comprehensive framework for capturing the complexity of the entrepreneurial environment. Despite the growing body of research on poverty alleviation, the role of the entrepreneurial ecosystem in this context remains underexplored. Accordingly, this chapter aims at addressing this critical gap in the literature.

3 Theoretical Framework

3.1 Entrepreneurship

3.1.1 Definitions and Concepts

Entrepreneurship serves as a critical mechanism through which countries can generate new employment opportunities, alleviate poverty, attract foreign investment, and introduce innovations that enhance productivity and foster competition among the existing firms (Baron & Shane, 2007). It is not merely the act of establishing a new organization; rather, entrepreneurship encompasses the processes of identifying, evaluating, and exploiting opportunities. Entrepreneurs create value by recognizing and leveraging opportunities within specific contexts (Trivedi, 2014). From the capitalist theory perspective, entrepreneurship functions as a productive factor that coordinates other resources into productive activities. It represents an innovative practice that mobilizes existing resources to exploit new opportunities and generate wealth (Drucker, 1985). Furthermore, entrepreneurship can be conceptualized as the process of creating organizations, generating employment, and earning profits (Gartner, 1988). Beyond these definitions, it embodies a comprehensive, opportunity-driven leadership approach, emphasizing on action-oriented strategies aimed at achieving profitability (Landstrom, 2007).

Entrepreneurship education is designed to equip individuals with the knowledge, skills, and motivation necessary to foster entrepreneurial success across diverse contexts (Hussain et al., 2014). For instance, while developing countries may emphasize on innovation, creativity, talent, and resources to address challenges such as hunger and extreme poverty, they often lack the requisite infrastructure and expertise to achieve these objectives. Such gaps can be mitigated through capacity building and entrepreneurship education, which facilitate the conversion of resources into marketable products and services, ultimately promoting job creation, business expansion, and poverty alleviation (Abubakar & Mitra, 2013).

Entrepreneurship is an innovative endeavor that leverages existing resources to capitalize on new opportunities for wealth creation (Drucker, 1985). It constitutes a dynamic process in which individuals, irrespective of the resources they currently possess, actively identify and pursue opportunities to generate value.

Entrepreneurship is a multidimensional concept encompassing a series of individual decisions made by the entrepreneurs, particularly regarding investment in high-risk ventures. At its core, entrepreneurship involves the identification and pursuit of opportunities (El Harbi & Anderson, 2010). Sobel (2008) highlighted the entrepreneur's role in creating value by reallocating resources from less productive to more productive uses. From a neoclassical perspective, entrepreneurship is considered a conventional factor of production that can be allocated based on the expected costs and benefits (Motavaseli, 2023). The recognition of entrepreneurship's positive economic impact is, to some extent, grounded in Schumpeter's (1934) theory of creative destruction, which emphasizes on the introduction of new ideas and innovations into the market.

Entrepreneurship has traditionally been recognized as one of the four factors of production in economics (Goel & Rishi, 2012). Entrepreneurs act as innovators who disrupt existing equilibria (Schumpeter, 1934). According to Kirzner (1973) and Wennekers et al. (2002), entrepreneurs are the individuals who identify and create new economic opportunities. They play a pivotal role in decision-making related to the allocation of resources and institutions, introducing novel ideas into the market under conditions of uncertainty.

3.1.2 Types of Entrepreneurship

Entrepreneurship encompasses a wide range of forms and numerous classifications have been proposed (Samadi, 2018; Minniti & Lévesque, 2010; Kosack, 2014; Si et al., 2015; Baumol, 1990; El Harbi & Anderson, 2010), among which the following classification is noted:

- Imitative and research-based entrepreneurship
- Political entrepreneurship
- Effectuation-based entrepreneurship
- Formal and informal entrepreneurship
- Necessity-driven and opportunity-driven entrepreneurship
- Institutional versus traditional entrepreneurship
- Productive, unproductive, and destructive entrepreneurship
- Bureaucratic entrepreneurship

- Business market entrepreneurship
- Nascent entrepreneurship
- Organizational entrepreneurship
- Social entrepreneurship
- Small-business venturing
- Strategic entrepreneurship
- Tourism entrepreneurship
- Technological entrepreneurship
- Transnational entrepreneurship

This classification highlights the multidimensional nature of entrepreneurship and reflects the diversity of approaches, contexts, and objectives within which entrepreneurial activities occur.

Aligned with the objectives of this study, the following types of entrepreneurship are specifically addressed:

- Formal and informal entrepreneurship
- Necessity-driven and opportunity-driven entrepreneurship
- Productive, unproductive, and destructive entrepreneurship
- Small-business venturing
- Political and social entrepreneurship

Productive, Unproductive, and Destructive

Different types of entrepreneurship—productive, unproductive, and destructive—emerge within varying institutional environments. Unproductive entrepreneurship arises in contexts where the private that returns from the rent-seeking activities exceed their social costs. While such activities benefit from the entrepreneur, they are detrimental to the broader economy. Rent-seeking typically includes actions such as litigation, takeovers, and tax evasion (Baumol, 1990). When the potential gains from illegal activities outweigh the associated risks, entrepreneurs are more likely to engage in destructive entrepreneurship, which impedes economic development. Destructive entrepreneurship encompasses illegal activities, shadow economy operations, and various forms of corruption (Sauka & Welter, 2007). In contrast, when incentives for engaging in productive activities are stronger, productive entrepreneurship emerges, thus promoting economic growth. Productive entrepreneurship involves generating increased joint surplus through the discovery of new methods, opportunities, and features (Aidis et al., 2008), contributing to job creation and driving technological innovation (Desai & Acs, 2007).

Baumol (1990) delineated entrepreneurship into three distinct forms: productive, unproductive, and destructive. His contribution to this discourse is particularly noteworthy, as he underscored that policy interventions should prioritize the enhancement of institutional quality to incentivize entrepreneurs to channel their efforts toward productive activities. Sobel (2008) provided empirical support for Baumol's theoretical framework. According to Baumol (1996), cross-country variations in entrepreneurial activity are not attributable to the overall quantity of entrepreneurship; rather, they are ascribed to the relative proportion of productive versus the unproductive entrepreneurship. In essence, it is the institutional configuration that determines whether entrepreneurial endeavors yield productive or unproductive outcomes. Entrepreneurship assumes a destructive character when resources are allocated to rent-seeking rather than value creation. In institutional environments that facilitate corruption and rent-seeking, entrepreneurs are more likely to pursue destructive objectives.

Formal and Informal

El Harbi and Anderson (2010), Williams and Nadin (2010), and Dau and Cuervo-Cazurra (2014) differentiate between formal and informal entrepreneurship. Formal entrepreneurship pertains to newly established businesses that are legally registered within a country. This category encompasses individual or collective activities conducted within the legal business framework, with the objective of initiating economic activities in the formal sector. In contrast, informal entrepreneurship refers to enterprises that are not legally registered and largely operate outside regulatory oversight although they may comply with certain legal norms. This form of entrepreneurship frequently involves individuals managing unregistered businesses primarily to circumvent taxation.

Opportunity-driven and Necessity-driven

Reynolds (2002) classified entrepreneurship into two categories: opportunity-driven and necessity-driven entrepreneurships. Opportunity-driven entrepreneurship pertains to ventures established through the identification and exploitation of market opportunities, and it is generally indicative of productive entrepreneurship. In contrast, necessity-driven entrepreneurship emerges out of compulsion—often due to the absence of alternative employment options—and it is typically associated with unproductive entrepreneurship (Fuentelsaz et al., 2015).

Social Entrepreneurship

The concept of social entrepreneurship is rooted in the works of its foundational theorists, Schumpeter (1934) and Drucker (1985). Schumpeter (1934) conceptualized entrepreneurs as individuals who drive the process of creative destruction within capitalism through technological innovation, positioning them as agents of economic change. In contrast, Drucker (1985) framed entrepreneurship as the systematic exploitation of opportunities, emphasizing that entrepreneurs continuously seek opportunities emerging from shifts in consumer preferences, technological developments, and social norms.

Social entrepreneurship refers to the application of entrepreneurial skills, expertise, and resources to address pressing challenges in developing countries, including education, healthcare, personal security, poverty alleviation, social development, and environmental sustainability (Kirby & Ibrahim, 2011).

Social entrepreneurship has emerged as a global phenomenon that utilizes innovative approaches to address social challenges within communities (Jiao, 2011). It represents a form of entrepreneurship primarily oriented toward creating opportunities that drive social change and respond to societal needs (Mair & Marti, 2006).

Social entrepreneurship is a process through which resources are recombined in innovative ways to foster social transformation, address social needs, and establish new organizations (Meyskens et al., 2010; Agwu et al., 2014).

The provision of microcredit schemes to low-income populations, group-lending mechanisms that empower individuals to engage in income-generating activities, and the development of microfinance ecosystems constitute key social innovations that have made substantial contributions to poverty alleviation (Alvord et al., 2004). Employment programs typically provide immediate and short-term responses to poverty, whereas entrepreneurship development and capacity-building initiatives emphasize the creation of sustainable, long-term solutions. The private sector can be broadly divided into two groups: social entrepreneurs and profit-oriented business entrepreneurs. While business entrepreneurs primarily contribute to poverty reduction through job creation, social entrepreneurs apply business principles and practices to achieve financially sustainable social and environmental outcomes.

Political Entrepreneurship

The concept of political entrepreneurship was first introduced by Schumpeter (1934), who did not distinguish between the business and the political entrepreneurs. Political entrepreneurship constitutes a phenomenon that stimulates fundamental transformations within society, as its creative and transformative actions exert significant influence on policies and political institutions. A political entrepreneur can be defined as an individual who alters the direction and dynamics of political processes (Saedi et al., 2021).

A political entrepreneur is an individual who invests time, effort, and other resources in the pursuit of collective interests. Such actors play a pivotal role in identifying political issues, mobilizing support, and driving changes in policies and regulations. Essentially, political entrepreneurs seek to garner the backing of diverse stakeholders and to facilitate the formulation, approval, and eventual implementation of new policy initiatives (O'Brien, 2019; Olausson & Svensson, 2019).

3.2 *Poverty Alleviation*

3.2.1 Definitions and Concepts of Poverty Alleviation

In contemporary development literature, poverty alleviation is no longer conceptualized solely in terms of income growth; rather, it is understood as a process aimed at reducing multidimensional forms of deprivation. Poverty is a complex and multifaceted phenomenon that cannot be reduced to income levels alone. Consequently, its social and institutional dimensions must also be considered (Adejumobi, 2006). The multidimensional approach provides a broader perspective on deprivation, viewing material scarcity as only one of several dimensions of poverty. Within this framework, deficiencies in basic capabilities for effective participation in society, the absence of stable employment opportunities, limited access to financial and credit resources, and vulnerability to violence and insecurity are regarded as key components of multidimensional poverty. These conditions are typically associated with residence in marginalized, deprived, or vulnerable contexts (Gordon, 2005).

According to the capability approach perspective, poverty is defined as the deprivation of essential human capabilities, including health, education, security, and social participation. Correspondingly, poverty alleviation is understood as a process of expanding individuals' substantive freedoms to achieve ways of living that they have reason to value. Multidimensional poverty entails deprivations across domains such as education, health, and living standards—including malnutrition, limited access to safe drinking water, electricity, and sanitation—as well as dimensions related to insecurity, social isolation, and exclusion from participation. Consequently, effective poverty alleviation requires the concurrent reduction of these multiple deprivations.

Poverty alleviation encompasses a range of economic and social policies, programs, and interventions aimed at reducing both income-based and non-income-based deprivations—such as limited access to healthcare, education, nutrition, and basic services—and at strengthening the capabilities of individuals and households to enable a sustainable exit from poverty. These measures include short-term interventions designed to rapidly alleviate severe deprivation, as well as long-term policies focused on inclusive economic growth and investment in institutional development (Haughton & Khandker, 2009).

Overall, poverty alleviation is a systematic and long-term process aimed at achieving both quantitative and qualitative reductions in poverty, while conceptualizing a sustainable exit from deprivation in terms of both income-based improvements—such as increased earnings and real consumption—and non-income outcomes, including concurrent reductions in deprivation related to education, health, housing, nutrition, and access to public services. This process is grounded in three core elements: first, the creation of conditions for inclusive economic growth that expand livelihood opportunities; second, the design of targeted and protective interventions to alleviate extreme poverty and mitigate short-term shocks; and third, the strengthening of human capital and social institutions to ensure the sustainability of poverty exit (Ravallion, 2008).

3.2.2 Poverty Alleviation Strategies

A well-known Chinese proverb is often cited in discussions of poverty alleviation strategies to illustrate the distinction between short-term assistance and empowerment-based approaches. The proverb suggests that providing direct monetary support to a poor individual over several days may create dependency, whereas encouraging the same individual to acquire a skill and equipping them with the necessary tools can lead to self-reliance, empowerment, and even the capacity to transfer that skill to others. This analogy highlights the limitations of unconditional and non-repayable aid in achieving long-term poverty reduction. Such forms of assistance may fail to produce sustainable outcomes and in some contexts, contribute to social dissatisfaction, unrest, and the erosion of public and private assets. Consequently, the literature emphasizes that poverty alleviation interventions should be conditional and oriented toward capacity building and empowerment (Mensah & Benedict, 2010).

Poverty alleviation strategies can be broadly classified into four main categories. The first redistributive-structural strategies, focus on identifying and addressing structural deficiencies within economic, social, and political systems. The second category comprises participatory strategies, which aim to empower the poor by enhancing their engagement in economic activities. The third involves institutional-normative strategies, emphasizing on legal and regulatory reforms as mechanisms for poverty alleviation. Finally, behavioral strategies examine the root causes of poverty in the behaviors and decision-making processes of the poor, identifying factors that contribute to the persistence of poverty.

The following section presents a concise overview of these strategies.

Redistributive-Structural Strategies

Redistributive-structural strategies encompass *resource redistribution* (Salmen & Mundial, 1990; Gerster, 2000; Marshall & Walters, 2011), *inclusive growth* (Shorrocks & Van der Hoeven, 2004; Oshota, 2019), and *sustainable livelihoods* (Gerster, 2000). These strategies aim at reducing income inequality and improving the living conditions of low-income populations. Although redistributive measures—such as unconditional social assistance and free housing programs—may provide short-term relief to the disadvantaged groups, they often fail to achieve long-term poverty alleviation. This limitation largely arises from their inability to comprehensively address the multidimensional nature of poverty (Mensah & Benedict, 2010).

High levels of asset and income inequality can significantly impede other redistributive mechanisms—such as land reform, taxation, and subsidized human capital development—ultimately leading to the adoption of unsustainable macroeconomic policies (Addison & Cornia, 2001).

Land reform can contribute to poverty alleviation among rural households; however, the relationship between land redistribution and development levels is complex. In less developed countries and rural areas where land ownership is highly concentrated, redistribution can have a substantial impact on poverty reduction. Moreover, the poorer a country is, the less likely rural households are to engage in commercial activities, making the benefits of land redistribution less dependent on supportive services. Conversely, the lack of administrative capacity and the persistence of traditional land tenure systems present significant constraints to land redistribution in many low-income countries (Dagdeviran et al., 2000).

Participatory Strategies

Participatory strategies encompass a range of key components designed to actively involve the poor in the process of poverty alleviation. These include *microfinance services* (Akanji, 2001; Hassan & Alamgir, 2002; Morduch & Armendariz, 2005; Obaidullah & Khan, 2008; Banerjee & Jackson, 2017; Singh & Chudasama, 2020; Ayoo, 2022), *entrepreneurship education and entrepreneurial activities* (Mensah & Benedict, 2010; Yanya, 2012; Djankov et al., 2018; Lin et al., 2021; Amorós et al., 2021; Azamat et al., 2023), and *social entrepreneurship* (Edobor, 2018; Arejiogbe et al., 2023). Additional components include *financial development initiatives* (Hassanvand & Nadi, 2017; Blanco-Arana & Angulo-Guerrero, 2024; Elumah et al., 2024; Zhang et al., 2023), *community-based participatory empowerment* (Fuad, 2022), as well as *education and employment programs* (Theavy & Mardy, 2023; Saci, 2023). Collectively, these approaches seek to build local capacity, enhance financial and social inclusion, and establish sustainable pathways out of poverty through active participation and empowerment.

Empowering impoverished individuals through education—particularly entrepreneurship training oriented toward income generation—can serve as a medium- to long-term strategy for poverty alleviation and eventual eradication. This approach underscores the need for a shift in mindsets and behaviors, transforming individuals from passive recipients of assistance into proactive agents of poverty reduction. Learning through trial and error, along with the development of resilience in the face of setbacks, is considered essential to this transformation. Enhancing the quality of human capital through education represents a critical initial step (Yunus & Yusus, 2007; Cohen & Soto, 2007). Education equips individuals with knowledge and skills that not only improve their own quality of life, but it also generates positive spillovers for their communities (Minniti & Lévesque, 2010; Davidsson, 2003). A central role of entrepreneurship-supporting institutions—such as government agencies and financial organizations—is to facilitate access to new knowledge and to assist disadvantaged individuals in adapting their skills to develop innovative products and services (Mitra et al., 2011).

As a participatory strategy, the microfinance model has a history spanning more than three decades, and it has been implemented across numerous developing countries. The integrated approach combining social mobilization and microcredit—where the organization of the poor constitutes a central principle—emerged in the 2000s and reflects the poverty alleviation experiences of South Asian countries

(Jabbari, 2005). Limited access to financial resources remains a major constraint on the establishment of microenterprises and other income-generating activities in low-income communities. Microfinance institutions (MFIs) can help alleviate this constraint by providing credit to small businesses that typically lack access to formal financial systems. Microcredit functions as an effective instrument for promoting self-employment (Salleh, 2017). Accordingly, microfinance can play a significant role in stimulating economic activity, generating employment within the informal sector, increasing household income, and ultimately reducing poverty (Ayoo, 2022). This strategy facilitates the channeling of financial resources toward poor populations, who often encounter multiple barriers to accessing credit from conventional banking institutions. By offering small, collateral-free loans to low-income individuals, MFIs seek to stimulate entrepreneurial activity among the poor. Through empowering the disadvantaged populations, expanding income-generating opportunities, and encouraging savings mobilization, microfinance can contribute substantially to sustainable poverty alleviation (Pour Ezzat & Nejat, 2012).

Microfinance, which seeks to empower the poor to escape poverty, is widely recognized as a prominent strategy for poverty alleviation (Morduch & Armendariz, 2005). Numerous scholars and policymakers argue that access to microfinance in developing countries not only supports income-generating activities among the disadvantaged populations, but it also fosters an entrepreneurial mindset and reduces vulnerability. To maximize the effectiveness of microfinance in alleviating poverty, it is essential to integrate complementary services—such as skills training, technological support, and enhanced educational programs—into microfinance initiatives (Singh & Chudasama, 2020). In many countries, microfinance has emerged as an effective instrument for generating employment opportunities, promoting self-employment, reducing poverty, and empowering individuals in underserved communities. By accelerating investment flows and strengthening financial intermediation and savings mechanisms, microfinance contributes to the creation of an enabling environment for sustainable poverty alleviation.

Institutional-Normative Strategies

Institutional-normative strategies encompass the enhancement of social capability and security (Sen, 1983, 1987; Banerjee & Jackson, 2017; Singh & Chudasama, 2020), the strengthening of social capital (Chelabi & Mobaraki, 2005; Shaditalab & Hojjat Kermani, 2008; Ansari et al., 2012), the improvement of good governance practices (Grindle, 2004; Kwon & Kim, 2014; Singh & Chudasama, 2020), and the assurance of rights and empowerment (Gerster, 2000).

Social capital may be regarded as a form of social institution. It generally encompasses informal norms and social relationships that enable individuals to pursue objectives and act in pursuit of collective interests. Social capital refers to the embedded social relations within societal structures that facilitate coordinated interaction and support the achievement of shared goals. Participation constitutes one of the core components of social capital. To empower the vulnerable and low-income groups, participatory approaches—such as raising awareness of legal rights and ensuring access to new technologies, particularly information technology—are of critical importance (Javaheripour, 2004).

Unlike physical and natural capital, which are associated with access to the means of production and consumption or human capital, which is based on access to education, social capital is inherently relational. It concerns individuals' relationships with others and the ways in which these relationships can be mobilized for mutual benefit (Narayan-Parker, 1999). Social capital is generated through the formation of social ties and networks grounded in mutual trust, reciprocal interaction, and shared norms. These ties may be horizontal or vertical and reflect implicit agreements sustained by the prevailing cultural norms and values. The concept of social capital is sufficiently broad to encompass a wide spectrum of relationships, ranging from direct, face-to-face personal interactions—whose effectiveness depends on individual characteristics—to more formal and impersonal exchanges that rely on legal frameworks or involve governmental institutions.

Social capital is of considerable importance for impoverished populations. Beyond economic development, a range of institutional and socio-cultural factors help explain why some countries have succeeded in reducing poverty and inequality more rapidly than others, or why, under certain conditions, addressing poverty and inequality remains particularly challenging. It is evident that poor individuals have limited access to more abstract forms of social capital, which are structured through legal arrangements and state support, such as large-scale business and financial institutions (Deolalikar & Pernia, 2003).

The institutionalist perspective emphasizes the role of social capital—namely, networks, trust, and norms that facilitate cooperation within society. Strong social capital can expand economic opportunities, reduce vulnerability, and improve access to resources. Community-based institutions, such as cooperatives and local savings groups, can function as effective mechanisms for poverty alleviation, particularly in contexts where formal institutions are weak or inaccessible.

In general, poverty and deprivation often compel individuals to reside in environments with a high potential for deviant behavior. In such contexts, key components of social capital—such as trust, cooperation, interaction, and solidarity—tend to be substantially weakened. Individuals living in these settings are shaped by their surroundings and may develop feelings of mistrust and reluctance to engage with others. This process contributes to the erosion of social capital, increased social exclusion, and the deepening of poverty (Shaditalab & Hojjat Kermani, 2008).

Legal empowerment—defined as enhancing individuals' understanding of their legal rights—represents a critical measure for mitigating poverty within society (Habibnejad & Soleimani Siboni, 2019). It is essential that impoverished individuals actively participate in decision-making processes and are recognized as key actors in poverty alleviation, rather than merely as passive recipients of assistance or welfare. A rights-based approach to poverty alleviation emphasizes the equitable distribution of opportunities, implying that governments, in fulfilling their distributive responsibilities, must ensure that opportunities are equally accessible to both the poor and the affluent. In this context, empowerment involves equipping the poor with the capacity to assert and safeguard their human rights through legal and political channels, enabling them to seek justice actively and hold institutions accountable through formal legal mechanisms and participation in democratic processes.

Improving governance constitutes a critical institutional strategy. Governance has become a central concern in discussions of poverty, as poverty, inequality, and governance are closely interconnected. Poor governance results in ineffective policy decisions, leaving individuals without voice or agency. Conversely, persistent poverty and inequality undermine political processes and perpetuate ineffective governance. Governance provides the institutional, legal, and political framework not only for designing poverty alleviation policies, but also for enhancing the capacity of disadvantaged populations to improve their material conditions. Good governance ensures the active participation of the marginalized groups in decision-making processes that directly affect their lives, empowering them to contribute to policy agendas. Guaranteeing individuals' right to participate in policymaking—particularly concerning poverty-related issues—is an essential step toward sustainable social, economic, and developmental transformation (Adejumobi, 2006).

Developing countries face significant challenges in delivering social services and ensuring security due to inherent weaknesses in their political and administrative governance structures. To secure financial assistance from multinational donor agencies, good governance oriented toward poverty alleviation has become a prerequisite. This necessitates the strengthening of participatory, transparent, and accountable governance systems. Effective governance frameworks and processes are essential for establishing support structures that genuinely assist the poor. Robust and transparent oversight mechanisms help ensure the integrity and effectiveness of these systems (Singh & Chudasama, 2020). Institutional economists contend that governments play a crucial role in creating and sustaining inclusive institutions. Accordingly, poverty alleviation requires governments that are responsive to the needs of all citizens. The effectiveness of poverty reduction policies often hinges on a government's capacity to provide public goods, including education, healthcare, and infrastructure, as well as legal protections and institutional support (Ravallion, 2016).

There is a strong connection between poverty and governance. Contemporary conceptions of poverty inherently incorporate several governance dimensions. Issues related to voice and agency for the poor and the vulnerable groups are fundamentally of governance concerns. Moreover, the notion of a "right to governance" lies at the heart of poverty alleviation. When a reciprocal relationship exists between state and society, the government can serve the interests of its citizens and advance collective objectives aimed at reducing poverty. Key elements of good governance—such as institutional effectiveness, decentralization of power, rule of law, adequate provision of social services, and participatory democracy—are essential for poverty alleviation. These elements foster the empowerment, initiative, and creativity of disadvantaged populations (Adejumobi, 2006).

Governments play a crucial role in establishing and enforcing explicit regulations that govern access to private markets. Social exclusion and discrimination often prevent the poor from participating in labor and credit markets. To overcome these barriers, it is necessary to implement anti-discrimination policies aimed at expanding the freedoms available to disadvantaged populations. In this context, governments create enabling environments through legal reforms that institutionalize markets and improve access to market information. Such initiatives enhance the capacity of the poor to obtain employment opportunities and secure ownership of assets.

Conversely, strong enforcement of the rule of law can at times constrain the livelihoods of the poor, particularly those engaged in informal or illicit activities (Kwon & Kim, 2014). The rule of law involves informing the public about the existing legal frameworks and implementing them through clear and transparent mechanisms. The extent to which government institutions adhere to laws and regulations significantly affects the daily lives of the impoverished populations. The rule of law provides both financial and physical security and protects various social groups from human rights violations. Consequently, it is essential for all segments of society, particularly the poor, who often lack sufficient means to safeguard their rights (World Bank, 2000).

Legal compliance necessitates a managerial and institutional framework dedicated to upholding the rule of law. Weak judicial performance in protecting the poor, discriminatory practices against them and their limited access to the judiciary ultimately exacerbate poverty and deprivation. The enforcement of legal norms is closely linked to social capital and to welfare dimensions associated with the individual security.

The poor often face substantial barriers to fully exercising their legal rights and benefiting from judicial systems due to a lack of awareness and low literacy levels. Furthermore, in many developing countries, the complexity of legal systems—often compounded by conflicting laws—can result in misinterpretation of rights. Consequently, deficiencies in institutional arrangements that ensure accountability and transparency within the judiciary, particularly toward vulnerable groups such as the poor, undermine the effectiveness of governance. This, in turn, impacts poverty alleviation efforts directly or indirectly. Governance provides the institutional, legal, and political frameworks necessary for structuring poverty reduction strategies. Issues concerning voice and accountability for the poor and the vulnerable populations are fundamentally linked to the adequacy of governance systems (Adejumobi, 2006). The absence of good governance leads to the disenfranchisement and disempowerment of the poor.

Behavioral Strategies

Behavioral strategies encompass nudges and the *reshaping of individuals' mental frameworks* (Dean et al., 2017; Haushofer, 2019; Huang & Gao, 2020).

Impoverished individuals often adhere to a set of implicit, unwritten guidelines commonly referred to as the "culture of poverty" (Liñán et al., 2013). Essentially, those living in economically disadvantaged areas are consistently exposed to poverty-related cues, which in turn shape specific behavioral norms (Todorovic &

McNaughton, 2007). Consequently, it is important to recognize that entrepreneurial dynamics in impoverished communities may substantially differ from those observed in the more affluent societies (Moradi et al., 2020). Individuals experiencing poverty face significant challenges in their decision-making processes, confronting difficult choices daily that affect their psychological and social capacities. This cognitive load can reduce mental bandwidth, thereby reinforcing the cycle of poverty.

Behavioral economics investigates the impact of psychological, social and cognitive factors on individuals' economic decision-making processes. This perspective is particularly important for understanding poverty alleviation strategies, as it emphasizes on how individuals who are experiencing poverty often make choices constrained by various limitations and cognitive biases, resulting in decisions that may not always be rational or aligned with their long-term interests.

The key concepts in behavioral economics relevant to poverty alleviation include *cognitive biases, framing effects* (Tversky & Kahneman, 1991), *social norms and nudges* (Thaler & Sunstein, 2009). Individuals often exhibit cognitive biases that impede their ability to make optimal decisions. Thaler and Sunstein (2009) proposed policy interventions designed to encourage the poor to make better choices without restricting their freedom of choice. For example, automatic enrollment in savings or retirement programs can substantially increase participation rates. Many low-income individuals do not save due to inertia or a lack of future-oriented planning for emergencies or retirement. Nudges can facilitate savings behavior without requiring active decision-making.

A critical mechanism underlying many of the observed effects is the interaction between conditions of poverty and limited self-control. The constraints and psychological stressors inherent in poverty can lead to more short-sighted and maladaptive behaviors among the disadvantaged individuals. Environmental factors associated with poverty often induce psychological stress, affecting decision-making, particularly with regard to risk and time preferences. Under heightened stress or cognitive load, individuals tend to heavily discount future outcomes. People living in the impoverished environments are also more likely to be exposed to higher crime rates and lower quality social services. The chronic stress experienced by these populations adversely impacts their decision-making processes, which in turn influences broader social and economic outcomes (Congdon et al., 2011).

3.3 The Role of Entrepreneurship in Poverty Alleviation

Entrepreneurship is regarded as a central component of participatory strategies. This section examines the role of entrepreneurship in poverty alleviation.

Poverty manifests in multiple dimensions, including the lack of income and productive resources necessary for securing sustainable livelihoods; hunger and malnutrition; elevated morbidity and mortality from illness; limited or no access to education and other essential services; homelessness and inadequate housing;

unsafe living environments and social discrimination and exclusion. A defining feature of poverty is the marginalization of the poor from participation in decision-making and in civil, social, and cultural life (Olarewaju, 2023; United Nations, 2018). Entrepreneurship is frequently regarded as a fundamental and sustainable mechanism for addressing the economic challenges faced by the poor (Tobias et al., 2013; Chliova et al., 2015; Sutter et al., 2019). By creating employment opportunities and generating income, entrepreneurship can serve as a powerful instrument for poverty alleviation.

Entrepreneurship is widely recognized as one of the most effective mechanisms for poverty alleviation and the enhancement of global welfare. By enabling millions of individuals to escape poverty and by substantially improving living standards across numerous emerging economies—such as China, India, Russia, Mexico, and Brazil—entrepreneurial activity has solidified its central role in socio-economic development, particularly in the twenty-first century. Empirical evidence further indicates that entrepreneurship has often outperformed conventional government interventions and programs implemented by international organizations in achieving sustained and meaningful reductions in poverty rates.

Entrepreneurship can reduce poverty through various channels, the most common of which is job creation. By generating employment opportunities, entrepreneurship offers a viable pathway for individuals to escape poverty. These jobs can be especially valuable for the individuals who face barriers to traditional employment, such as those with criminal records, limited education, experience or other socioe-conomic challenges. In this way, entrepreneurship not only enhances individual resilience and overall well-being, but it also facilitates upward mobility out of poverty. Moreover, entrepreneurship can foster a sense of independence and self-agency, enabling individuals to take greater control over their lives.

Small and medium-sized enterprises (SMEs) play a particularly vital role in global job creation. According to the International Labor Organization (ILO), SMEs account for approximately 60% of total employment worldwide. By establishing new businesses, entrepreneurs create jobs and generate income not only for themselves, but also for others, thereby improving living standards and reducing poverty levels. In addition to employment, entrepreneurship stimulates economic growth, promotes innovation, and enhances market competitiveness, all of which contribute to poverty alleviation. In developing countries, where formal employment opportunities may be limited, entrepreneurship offers a crucial alternative path for job creation and poverty alleviation (Coulibaly et al., 2018).

One of the primary factors contributing to persistent poverty in the underdeveloped areas is the limited availability of employment opportunities. In such contexts, individuals are often left with few alternatives other than subsistence farming, part-time or informal employment, or reliance on social assistance. Entrepreneurial activities, however, have the capacity to generate a wider range of employment opportunities. Consequently, they can enable a greater number of local residents to access meaningful and sustainable employment (Lin et al., 2021; Azis Muthalib et al., 2014; Thurik et al., 2008).

Another significant pathway through which entrepreneurship contributes to poverty alleviation is income generation. Starting a business can serve as an effective means for individuals to earn a livelihood and support themselves and their families. Entrepreneurship provides opportunities for individuals to generate income independently by establishing their own ventures. This income can then be used to meet basic needs, accumulate savings, invest in education or skills development, and acquire assets such as housing.

A prominent example of entrepreneurship as a mechanism for poverty alleviation is the emergence of social entrepreneurship. Social entrepreneurship refers to the establishment of enterprises that not only pursue financial objectives, but it also follow explicit social or environmental missions. Such enterprises often operate in collaboration with governments and non-profit organizations to address social and environmental challenges. Hence, they can play a substantial role in poverty alleviation and the enhancement of social mobility. In many developing countries, entrepreneurs are increasingly focused on creating ventures that promote social and environmental changes (Mair & Marti, 2006).

A well-documented example of social entrepreneurship as a poverty alleviation instrument is the Grameen Bank in Bangladesh. Founded by Muhammad Yunus in 1983, the bank provides microfinance loans to impoverished individuals—particularly women—who lack access to traditional banking services. These loans, which are used to establish small businesses such as food stalls or handicraft production, generate income, and improve the economic prospects of borrowers (Yunus & Weber, 2010, Yunus, 2017).

One of the primary ways in which social entrepreneurship fosters innovation and drives social transformation is through the identification of unmet social challenges. Social entrepreneurs are often motivated to address pressing social or environmental issues that are insufficiently recognized or inadequately addressed by existing institutions and organizations (Mair & Marti, 2006). These entrepreneurs frequently develop innovative solutions to social problems, which can catalyze meaningful innovation and contribute to a broader social change (Dees, 2018).

Social entrepreneurship can drive innovation and social transformation in education by identifying and addressing gaps in educational provision, particularly in developing countries (Olarewaju, 2023). Entrepreneurial activities have the potential to penetrate new markets, enhance productivity and facilitate the creation of new products, thereby contributing to the accumulation of social wealth within communities. Moreover, economically disadvantaged populations indirectly benefit from the increased social welfare generated by the entrepreneurial development and activities within society.

Social entrepreneurs often develop innovative models to provide education for the underserved populations. Accessing self-organized learning environments facilitated through technology exemplifies how social entrepreneurship can address gaps in educational provision (Mitra, 2019). By leveraging innovative approaches aligned with a social mission, social entrepreneurs highlight pressing social problems and generate meaningful impacts within communities.

The role of political entrepreneurs in poverty alleviation has received increasing attention. The significance of institutions in facilitating entrepreneurship as a tool for poverty reduction has been emphasized by numerous scholars (Aparicio et al., 2021; Blankson & Nukpezah, 2019). Within the entrepreneurship framework, the capacity of entrepreneurs in responding to the evolving circumstances by leveraging resources under their control to generate profit is considered crucial (Shane & Venkataraman, 2000; Kuckertz et al., 2017). This perspective suggests that entrepreneurs do not create change in isolation; rather, they connect the seemingly unrelated conditions such as market shifts, technological advances, and government policies (Santos et al., 2019). These dynamic processes become particularly pronounced when entrepreneurs are actively engaged in institution-building. A stable institutional environment, in turn, encourages the emergence of new entrepreneurial opportunities.

Entrepreneurs can drive institutional change through participation in political movements. To maximize the impact of entrepreneurship on poverty alleviation, entrepreneurial policies should focus on stimulating entrepreneurial activities and promoting economic development, with particular attention to the underserved communities (Aparicio et al., 2021).

Political entrepreneurs play a crucial role in poverty alleviation by fostering an enabling environment for entrepreneurship and social innovation. They facilitate access to microcapital and other resources, empowering individuals to establish businesses as pathways out of poverty (Sakinah et al., 2023). Through the efforts of political entrepreneurs, the latent potential of the impoverished citizens can be mobilized and organizations can be formed that enable these citizens to exercise political influence (Kosack, 2014). Political entrepreneurs often conceptualize personal gain in terms of assisting groups that are unable to organize themselves for collective action.

In response to the activities of political entrepreneurs, governments adopt pro-poor educational policies. Poor citizens generally face prohibitively high collective action costs that exceed the government's capacity to address. To politically empower the poor, subsidies are required to facilitate collective action—an intervention often provided by the political entrepreneurs. These subsidies enable the poor citizens to support a government that implements policies in their favor or to oppose one that does not. In exchange for this support, the government offers educational opportunities to the impoverished populations. The motivation of political entrepreneurs lies in maintaining the support of the poor through pro-poor policies. Political entrepreneurship, therefore, leads to the development of institutional structures that allow disadvantaged citizens to overcome collective action barriers and to support governments that enact policies benefiting them (Kosack, 2014).

Generally, three perspectives can be identified regarding the role of entrepreneurship in poverty alleviation: remediation, reform, and revolution (Sutter et al., 2019).

1. The remediation perspective (addressing resource deficits) refers to the use of entrepreneurship as a tool to meet immediate needs and provide economic opportunities for individuals and communities through job creation and income generation. From this viewpoint, entrepreneurship can be effective in reducing poverty when there is direct access to resources and capital (Sutter et al., 2019). Essentially,

this perspective frames poverty as a consequence of resource scarcity, such as a lack of initial capital and other physical assets. Accordingly, securing financial resources through external aid and other forms of financial support is considered a key mechanism for poverty alleviation (Newman et al., 2017).

2. The reform perspective (significant reshaping of institutional or social fabric) refers to the role of entrepreneurship in poverty alleviation through systematic changes in institutions, policies, and social structures. The objective of these changes is to address the root causes of poverty and to promote sustainable development. This perspective places less emphasis on resources and investments as the primary means for entrepreneurship and poverty alleviation. Instead, it underscores the importance of implementing reforms in both formal and informal institutions, with entrepreneurship being actively encouraged and supported (Robinson and Acemoglu, 2012; Tomizawa et al., 2020).

   Accordingly, this perspective views poverty as stemming from institutional gaps and other social challenges, including barriers to market access, and advocates for poverty alleviation through changes in institutional or social frameworks. Furthermore, markets are often regarded as key drivers of poverty reduction, although their expansion requires fundamental institutional reforms. This approach recognizes the socio-structural realities associated with poverty and the complexities of institutional change, particularly within informal institutions (McCloskey, 2010). Additionally, it emphasizes the distribution of power necessary to restructure social order and to empower the marginalized populations (McCloskey, 2006, 2010).
3. The revolution perspective (alternative economic systems) views entrepreneurship as a catalyst for radical social and economic transformation. It challenges the existing power dynamics and advocates for fundamental changes in the economic system to achieve a more equitable distribution of resources and opportunities (Amorós et al., 2021).

4 Models and Data

4.1 Model Specification

To examine the impact of entrepreneurship on poverty alleviation in the Persian Gulf countries, the following Eq. (1) can be employed initially.

$$\text{Povall}_{it} = \beta_0 + \beta_1 \text{EN}_{it} + \beta_{it} \text{Gov}_{it} + \beta_{it} \text{GDP}_{it} + \varepsilon_{it} \quad (1)$$

In this model, good governance (Gov), representing the institutional strategy; GDP, demonstrating the redistributive and structural strategy, and the entrepreneurship ecosystem (EN), representing the participatory strategy, are used as independent variables. For the dependent variable (poverty alleviation), following Amorós et al. (2021), Misturelli and Heffernan (2008), Azamat et al. (2023), and Amorós and Cristi (2011), the Human Development Index (HDI) is employed as a proxy.

Table 3 Definition of variables of model (1)

Variable	Description
Povall	Human Development Index
EN	The GEM National Entrepreneurship Context Index (NECI) assesses the entrepreneurial ecosystem of each economy by assessing 12 Entrepreneurship Framework Conditions
Gov	Worldwide governance indicators
GDP	GDP per capita PPP (constant 2021 international $)

Sources: United Nations Development Programme (2022), Global Entrepreneurship Monitor (2010, 2011, 2012, 2013, 2014, 2015, 2016, 2017, 2018, 2019, 2020, 2021, 2022), Worldwide Governance Indicators (2024), World Development Indicators (2025)

The definitions of the variables in model (1) are presented in Table 3.

In the subsequent section, Model (2) is employed to assess and compare the impact of various entrepreneurship ecosystem sub-indices on poverty alleviation. To ensure comparability when evaluating the influence of these entrepreneurship ecosystem indicators, the data have been normalized. This model aims to determine the magnitude of each sub-index's effect and to facilitate a comparative analysis of their relative contributions to the poverty alleviation process.

$$\begin{aligned} \text{Povall}_{it} &= \text{Fin}_{it} + \text{Pol}_{it} + \text{Reg}_{it} + \text{gov}_{it} + \text{Edupri}_{it} + \text{Edupost}_{it} + \text{R\&D}_{it} \\ &+ \text{Com}_{it} + \text{Dyn}_{it} + \text{Open}_{it} + \text{Phy}_{it} + \text{Cul}_{it} + \varepsilon_{it} \end{aligned} \tag{2}$$

The definitions of the variables used in Model (2) are presented in Table 4.

4.2 *Data*

This research aims to examine the role of the entrepreneurial ecosystem in poverty alleviation in selected Persian Gulf countries. The entrepreneurial ecosystem is shaped by cultural, social, economic, and political dimensions, with entrepreneurial activities emerging from individual traits and societal values (GEM, 2015). An entrepreneurial ecosystem comprises a set of interrelated conditions that collectively foster the emergence and growth of entrepreneurial activities. These conditions include access to finance, government policies, taxation and bureaucracy, public support programs, entrepreneurship education at the school level, post-school entrepreneurship training, research and development transfer, access to commercial and professional infrastructure, internal market dynamics, internal market burdens, access to physical and service infrastructure, and prevailing social and cultural norms. Table 4 summarizes the 12 foundational pillars of the entrepreneurial framework, which constitute the core structure of the GEM questionnaire.

Table 4 Entrepreneurial Framework Conditions (EFCs)

Variable	Description
Fin	The availability of financial resources—equity and debt—for small and medium enterprises (SMEs) including grants and subsidies.
Pol	The extent to which public policies support entrepreneurship
Reg	Regulations or taxes are either size-neutral or support new and small businesses.
gov	The presence and quality of programs directly assisting SMEs at all levels of government (national, regional, municipal).
Edupri	Entrepreneurship Education at basic school (primary and secondary).
Edupost	Entrepreneurship Education at post-secondary levels higher education such as vocational, college, and business schools.
R&D	The extent to which national research and development will lead to new commercial opportunities and is available to SMEs.
Com	The presence of property rights, commercial, accounting, and other legal and assessment services and institutions that support or promote SMEs.
Dyn	Market Dynamics: the level of change in markets from year to year.
Open	Market Openness: the extent to which new firms are free to enter existing markets.
Phy	Ease of access to physical resources—communication, utilities, transportation, land, or space—at a price that does not discriminate against SMEs.
Cul	The extent to which social and cultural norms encourage or allow actions leading to new business methods or activities that can potentially increase personal wealth and income.

Source: GEM (2016)

According to some researchers, the Entrepreneurial Framework Conditions (EFCs) have been adopted as a conceptual representation of the entrepreneurial ecosystem (Rezaei et al., 2018; Coduras et al., 2018; GEM, 2013, 2017).

In the present study, the initial phase focuses on assessing the influence of the entrepreneurial ecosystem on poverty alleviation across the selected Persian Gulf countries. The analysis specifically draws on data from Iran, Saudi Arabia, Qatar, Oman, and the United Arab Emirates over the period of 2010–2022. Due to the lack of accessible and consistent data for Kuwait, Iraq, and Bahrain, these countries were excluded from the original group of eight Persian Gulf nations.

The overall Governance Index[4] (Gov) is derived through Principal Component Analysis[5] (PCA), synthesizing six key governance sub-indicators: Voice and Accountability, Political Stability, Government Effectiveness, Regulatory Quality, Rule of Law and Control of Corruption (Samadi & Owjimehr, 2021).

For the empirical analysis, data related to the entrepreneurial ecosystem were obtained from the Global Entrepreneurship Monitor (GEM) project. In Model (1), a composite index representing the entrepreneurial ecosystem was constructed, using Principal Component Analysis (PCA) and subsequently employed as a proxy for EN. Accordingly, EN_{it} _it denotes the overall entrepreneurial ecosystem index.

[4] For additional information, please refer to Appendix 1.

[5] For a more comprehensive discussion, refer to Samadi and Owjimehr (2021).

Data for the poverty alleviation index ($povall_{it}$) were obtained from the United Nations Development Programme (UNDP, 2020), specifically based on the Human Development Index (HDI). The HDI is a composite indicator that evaluates three core dimensions of human development: life expectancy at birth, adult literacy rate, and gross domestic product (GDP) per capita adjusted for purchasing power parity (PPP), thereby capturing a country's average level of development. The variable GDP_{it} denotes the gross domestic product of the selected countries. Likewise, the dataset used in Model (2) is derived from GEM publications. Data on the entrepreneurial ecosystem index (EN) are available for Iran (2010–2022), the Saudi Arabia (2016–2022), Qatar (2015–2022), Oman (2019–2022), and the United Arab Emirates (2016–2022). Owing to the data unavailability for certain years, an unbalanced panel dataset is employed. Moreover, HDI data are available through 2022.

5 Empirical Results

Based on the results of the F-Limer, Breusch–Pagan, and Hausman tests, Model (1) was estimated using the fixed effects approach. To determine the most appropriate estimation technique, several diagnostic tests were performed, including the Pesaran's test for cross-sectional dependence, the Wald test for heteroscedasticity, and the Wooldridge's test for first-order autocorrelation. The results of these diagnostic tests are reported in Table 5. The findings indicate the presence of heteroscedasticity, cross-sectional dependence, and first-order autocorrelation in the error terms. In light of these results, the Panel-Corrected Standard Errors (PCSE) estimator[6] was considered the most appropriate method for estimating the fixed effects model (Hoechle, 2007).

Accordingly, the estimation results of Model (1), obtained using the Panel-Corrected Standard Errors (PCSE) estimator, are reported in Table 6.

The empirical results reported in Table 6 indicate that the composite entrepreneurial ecosystem index (EN) has a positive and statistically significant effect on the Human Development Index (HDI), which is used as a proxy for poverty alleviation,

Table 5 Diagnostic tests

Heteroscedasticity Test		Autocorrelation Test		Cross-sectional Dependence Test	
Wald Stat	Prob	F Stat	Prob	CD Stat	Prob
116.28	0.000	43.696	0.002	0.825	0.409

Source: Research findings
Notes: 1. The null hypothesis is homoscedasticity
2. The null hypothesis is no serial correlation
3. The null hypothesis is cross-sectional independence

[6] The results of the multicollinearity tests for the variables included in Models (1) and (2) are presented in Appendices 3 and 4, respectively.

Table 6 The results for Panel-Corrected Standard Errors (PCSE) method

	Model (1)		
variables	Coeff	Z Stat	Prob
EN	0.0034	2.70	0.007*
Gov	0.0238	5.83	0.000*
GDP	−2.76	−2.01	0.044**
R^2	0.99		
Wald chi2(3) stat	499.02		

Source: Research findings
Note: * significant at 1% level and ** significant at 5% level

in selected Persian Gulf countries. Moreover, the overall governance quality index also exhibits a positive and significant impact on poverty alleviation, underscoring the crucial role of institutional effectiveness and participatory governance mechanisms in improving human development outcomes in the region. In contrast, per capita gross domestic product (GDP) shows a negative and statistically significant relationship with poverty alleviation, implying that economic growth alone may be insufficient to improve welfare or reduce poverty in the context of Persian Gulf economies.

In the second phase of the analysis, to evaluate and compare the individual effects of the constituent indicators of the entrepreneurial ecosystem, the collected data were first normalized. Subsequently, based on the results of the F-Limer test, the Breusch–Pagan test and the Hausman specification test, Model (2) was estimated. The model selection diagnostics identified the pooled Ordinary Least Squares (pooled OLS) estimator as the most appropriate approach. Additional diagnostic tests—including the Pesaran's test for cross-sectional dependence, the Breusch–Pagan test for heteroskedasticity and the Wooldridge's test for first-order autocorrelation—are reported in Table 7. The results indicate the presence of heteroskedasticity, the absence of cross-sectional dependence and the existence of first-order autocorrelation in the residuals. Given these statistical properties, the Panel-Corrected Standard Errors (PCSE) estimation method is considered as the most robust and suitable approach for estimating the pooled OLS model.

Table 8 reports the estimation results for Model (2).

The estimation results presented in Table 8 indicate that entrepreneurial finance (*Fin*)—defined as the access to adequate funding for nascent business ventures, including informal investment, bank loans, and government grants—does not have a statistically significant impact on poverty alleviation in selected Persian Gulf countries. In contrast, government support policies (*Pol*) and regulatory incentives (*Reg*) show a positive and statistically significant effect on poverty alleviation.

Government policy interventions that actively promote entrepreneurship and provide direct support for new business creation have been shown to be effective in advancing poverty alleviation. In particular, favorable tax regimes and the reduction of startup-related regulatory burdens facilitate entrepreneurial activity, thereby contributing to inclusive economic development. Targeted government programs (Gov)

Table 7 Diagnostic tests

Heteroscedasticity Test		Autocorrelation test		Cross sectional dependence Test	
BP Stat	Prob	F Stat	Prob	CD Stat	Prob
5.50	0.019	39.752	0.003	0.967	0.333

Source: Research findings
Notes: 1. The null hypothesis is Homoscedasticity
2. The null hypothesis is no serial correlation
3. The null hypothesis is cross-sectional independence

Table 8 The results for Panel-Corrected Standard Errors (PCSE) method

	Model (2)		
Variables	Coeff	Z Stat	Prob
Fin	0.0401	0.99	0.323
Pol	0.2552	2.19	0.028**
Reg	0.2448	1.86	0.063***
gov	0.6148	3.05	0.002*
Edupri	0.4753	2.92	0.003*
Edupost	−0.2118	−1.79	0.073***
R&D	−0.4058	−2.82	0.005*
Com	0.0863	0.57	0.568
Dyn	−0.0613	−1.17	0.241
Open	−0.2	−1.32	0.187
Phy	0.0934	1.82	0.069***
Cul	0.0798	0.90	0.367
R^2	0.93		
Wald chi2(12) stat	2107.37		

Source: Research findings
Note: * significant at 1% level, ** significant at 5% level, and *** significant at 10% level

that enhance the operational environment for small and medium-sized enterprises (SMEs) are positively associated with entrepreneurial expansion, which in turn, supports poverty alleviation (Gbenga et al., 2023). Moreover, policy frameworks aimed at fostering the growth of micro, small, and medium-sized enterprises (MSMEs) have played a pivotal role in job creation and consequently, in mitigating poverty (Devi, 2023). Government-sponsored intervention programs—such as conditional cash transfer schemes and youth empowerment initiatives—have demonstrated a strong positive impact on poverty alleviation outcomes. In this context, sustained public financial support for employment generation is essential in reinforcing and amplifying the positive socio-economic effects of these measures (Gbenga et al., 2023; Kareem, 2015).

Entrepreneurship education at the primary level (*Edupri*) exhibits a positive and statistically significant effect on poverty alleviation in the Persian Gulf countries. In contrast, entrepreneurship education at higher levels (*Edupost*) shows a negative and statistically significant impact on poverty alleviation. Early-stage entrepreneurship education plays a crucial role in equipping students with the necessary skills, entrepreneurial mindset and capabilities for self-employment and economic empowerment, thereby contributing to poverty alleviation substantially. Its effectiveness is further enhanced when delivered through practical pedagogies, targeted support for disadvantaged populations and strong collaboration among stakeholders (Hussain et al., 2018; Santos et al., 2019). Conversely, several structural and institutional barriers may limit the effectiveness of entrepreneurship education at post-primary levels. Restricted access to credit, insufficient hands-on experience and inadequate policy support have been identified as key constraints that undermine the poverty alleviation potential of higher level entrepreneurship training (Valle et al., 2022; Zhou, 2022; Deng & Wang, 2023). Therefore, effective poverty alleviation through entrepreneurship education requires a holistic approach, encompassing financial literacy integration, improved access to entrepreneurial resources, stakeholder collaboration and comprehensive policy frameworks that support inclusive and sustainable entrepreneurship development (Suherlan et al., 2024).

Transferring business opportunities through research and development (*R&D*) exhibits a statistically significant negative impact on poverty alleviation, whereas the physical infrastructure (*Phy*) shows a statistically significant positive effect on poverty alleviation. In contrast, commercial and legal infrastructures do not have a significant impact on poverty alleviation.

Research and development (*R&D*), encompassing the dissemination of knowledge, technology, and resources, is widely recognized as a critical strategy for poverty alleviation. The effectiveness of such transfers depends on the local conditions, the nature of the transfer, and the integration of social, economic, and institutional factors, alongside targeted policy interventions. However, in the Persian Gulf countries, challenges in rapidly adapting to new technologies have resulted in R&D transfer having a negative impact on the poverty alleviation process.

Physical infrastructure plays a crucial role in supporting entrepreneurship and poverty alleviation, particularly in the developing and resource-based countries where access to basic services is often limited. Empirical studies have shown that the impact of infrastructure investments—such as roads, electricity, water supply, healthcare, and telecommunications—on poverty levels varies depending on the context, quality, and accessibility of the investment. By improving access to resources and economic opportunities, infrastructure can stimulate the creation of new enterprises and enhance the welfare of disadvantaged populations. However, not all types of infrastructure have the same effect; digital infrastructure is generally more conducive to entrepreneurship than the traditional forms such as highways or railways (Audretsch et al., 2015). Commercial and legal infrastructures also play a vital role in facilitating entrepreneurial activities and supporting poverty alleviation. Effective infrastructure—from physical assets to institutional support—can boost entrepreneurial activity, foster innovation and create opportunities for individuals and communities to escape poverty. Nevertheless, due to institutional weaknesses in the infrastructure of Persian Gulf countries, this component has not shown a statistically significant impact.

Entry regulations, including market dynamism (*Dyn*), market openness (*Open*), commercial infrastructure (*Com*), and social and cultural norms (*Cul*), have not demonstrated a statistically significant impact on poverty alleviation. The extent to which individuals can access opportunities to start and expand businesses plays a crucial role in shaping entrepreneurship and its effectiveness in reducing poverty. Lowering entrepreneurial barriers and fostering supportive market dynamics can substantially enhance poverty alleviation efforts, particularly when combined with social, educational, and policy support. Reducing entry barriers—such as improving access to capital and information—enables more individuals, especially those from disadvantaged backgrounds, to establish businesses, which can subsequently generate income and create employment opportunities. The greatest impact is achieved when these initiatives are integrated with social support systems, sector-specific strategies, and carefully designed policies aimed at minimizing unintended adverse consequences (Bruton et al., 2013; Zhang et al., 2023).

Social norms that strengthen social capital, entrepreneurial values, and supportive networks are positively associated with higher levels of entrepreneurial activity and more effective poverty alleviation. Societal cultures that emphasize innovation, risk-taking, and self-reliance create an enabling environment for entrepreneurial development. Accordingly, the internalization of entrepreneurial values and the cultivation of a supportive entrepreneurial mindset are essential for fostering a robust entrepreneurial culture (Naminse & Zhuang, 2018; Naminse et al., 2019; Bogdanović, 2023). In the Persian Gulf countries; however, entrepreneurial culture remains underdeveloped. Thus, the cultural and social norms index is expected to have a negligible impact on poverty alleviation outcomes in this regional context.

Another key insight from Table 8 relates to the magnitude and significance of the effects of the entrepreneurial ecosystem sub-indices. The impact of government programs (*Gov*) on poverty alleviation is approximately 2.5 times greater than that of government policies (*Pol*) and regulations (Reg), representing the most substantial positive influence on poverty alleviation. In contrast, research and development transfer (*R&D*) exerts the largest negative effect, impeding the poverty alleviation process. Among the analyzed components, government entrepreneurial programs (*Gov*) contribute 61% of the positive effect, followed by entrepreneurship education at the primary level (Edupri) with 47%, highlighting their most significant contributions to poverty alleviation in the Persian Gulf region.

6 Discussion

The Persian Gulf countries are endowed with abundant natural resources and are classified as wealthy nations. Nevertheless, poverty remains a significant concern in the region. The economies of these countries are predominantly dependent on oil and gas production. Legal and economic support from governments helps create a conducive environment for promoting entrepreneurship. Despite their wealth, the Persian Gulf countries are often categorized as the developing economies. Entrepreneurship and small and medium-sized enterprises (SMEs) serve as critical drivers of economic growth and employment in the developing contexts. The entrepreneurial ecosystem plays a particularly vital role in the Persian Gulf region (Khan, 2016). Moreover, fostering an environment that promotes entrepreneurship and innovation through education is essential (Lane, 2016).

The entrepreneurial ecosystem consists of multiple components, which can be categorized into three domains: the supportive environment, the human capital, and the social and legal environment. The *supportive environment* includes finance (*Fin*), *government policies* (*Pol*), *regulations* (*Reg*), and *government programs* (*Gov*). The social and legal environment encompasses culture (*Cul*), physical infrastructure (*Phy*), market dynamics (*Dyn*), openness (*Open*), and commercial infrastructure (*Com*). The human capital comprises entrepreneurship education at the primary level (EduPri), post-primary entrepreneurship education (*EduPost*), and research and development (*R&D*).

The simple correlation between the entrepreneurial ecosystem sub-indices and the poverty alleviation index in selected Persian Gulf countries during 2010–2022 is presented in Fig. 1.

According to Fig. 1a, the relationship between entrepreneurial financing (*Fin*) and the poverty alleviation index (*HDI*) is positive across all five countries. Oman exhibits the highest coefficient of determination (R^2) at 81%, indicating that 81% of the variance in *HDI* is explained by Fin. In contrast, Qatar records the lowest R^2 value at 22%, suggesting a weaker explanatory power of Fin on *HDI* variation.

Figure 1b illustrates heterogeneous patterns in association between the government policies (Pol) and the HDI, showing positive, negative, and stable trends across the countries. Saudi Arabia demonstrates the highest R^2 of 93%, whereas Oman shows the lowest at 2%.

As shown in Fig. 1c, the regulatory quality index (Reg) is positively correlated with HDI in all five countries; Saudi Arabia attains the highest R^2 value of 81%, while Iran's R^2 equals zero, indicating an insignificant role of regulatory quality in poverty alleviation in Iran.

Figure 1d and e depict positive associations between governance quality (Gov) and HDI and between primary-level entrepreneurship education (EduPri) and HDI, which have been analyzed for all countries, respectively. Saudi Arabia consistently shows the strongest explanatory power, with R^2 values of 87% for governance and 81% for primary entrepreneurship education, while Iran records the lowest explanatory coefficients at 1% and 12%, respectively.

Figure 1f and g illustrate the relationships between post-secondary entrepreneurship education (*EduPost*) and HDI, and between research and development (*R&D*) and HDI, respectively. Notably, these relationships are negative only for Iran. Saudi Arabia exhibits the highest coefficients of determination, with 75% for EduPost and 70% for R&D, whereas Iran records the lowest, with 14% for EduPost and only 1% for R&D.

Figure 1h presents the association between the dynamic component (*Dyn*) and *HDI*, which is negative for Iran and Oman, but positive for the United Arab Emirates, Saudi Arabia, and Qatar. Saudi Arabia shows the highest R^2 value at 78%, while Iran has the lowest at 6%.

a. Entre. Finance and HDI

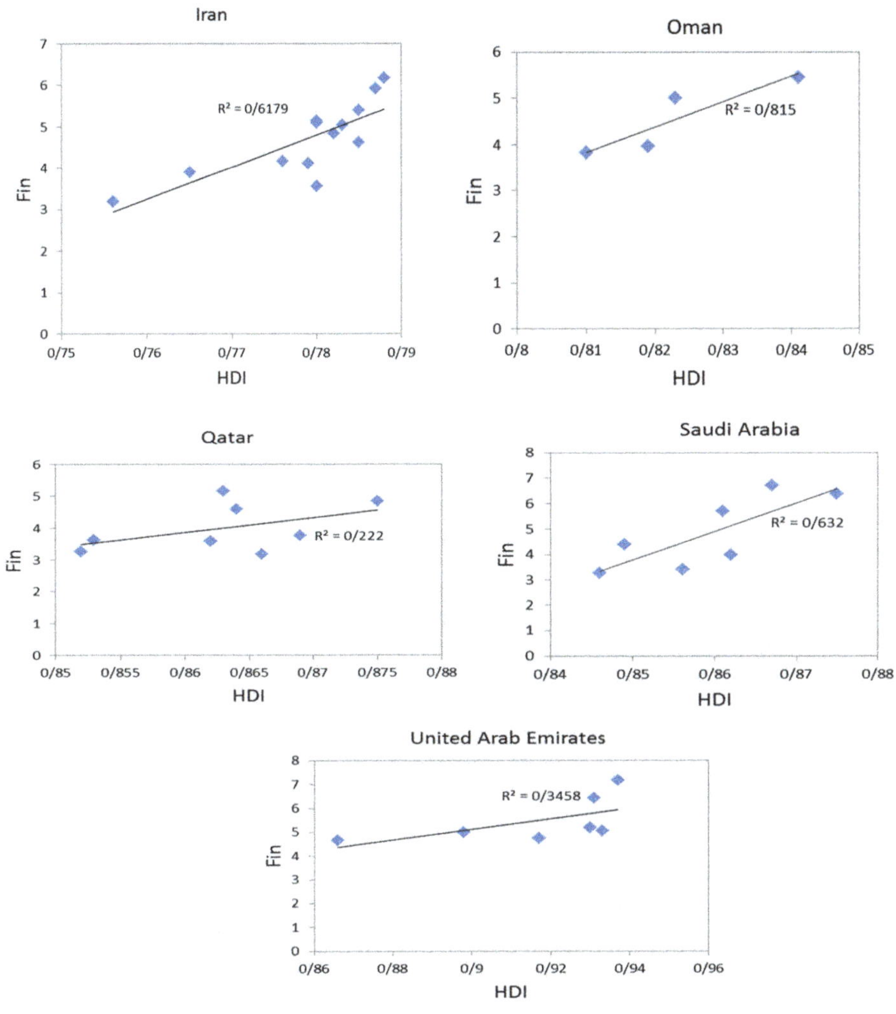

Fig. 1 Relationship Between Trends of Entrepreneurial Ecosystem Sub-Indices and Poverty Alleviation in the Persian Gulf Countries. Source: United Nations Development Programme, 2022; Global Entrepreneurship Reports, 2010–2022. (**a**) Entre. Finance and HDI, (**b**) Government Policy and HDI, (**c**) Regulations and HDI, (**d**) Government Entre. Programs and HDI, (**e**) Education at School and HDI, (**f**) Education at Post-School and HDI, (**g**) Research and Development Transfers and HDI, (**h**) Commercial and Professional Infrastructure and HDI, (**i**) Market Dynamic and HDI, (**j**) Burdens or Entry Regulations and HDI, (**k**) Physical Infrastructure and HDI, (**l**) Social and Cultural Norms and HDI

b. Government Policy and HDI.

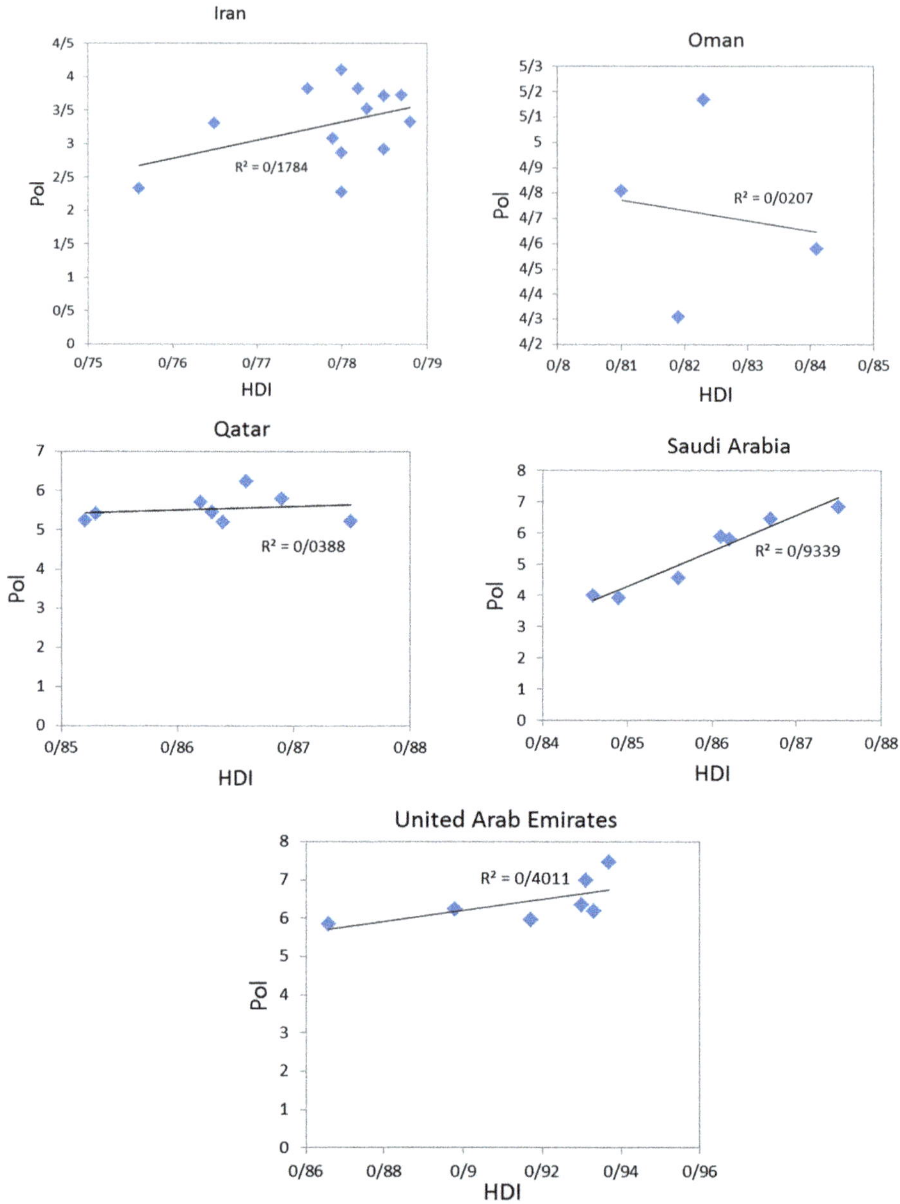

Fig. 1 (continued)

c. Regulations and HDI.

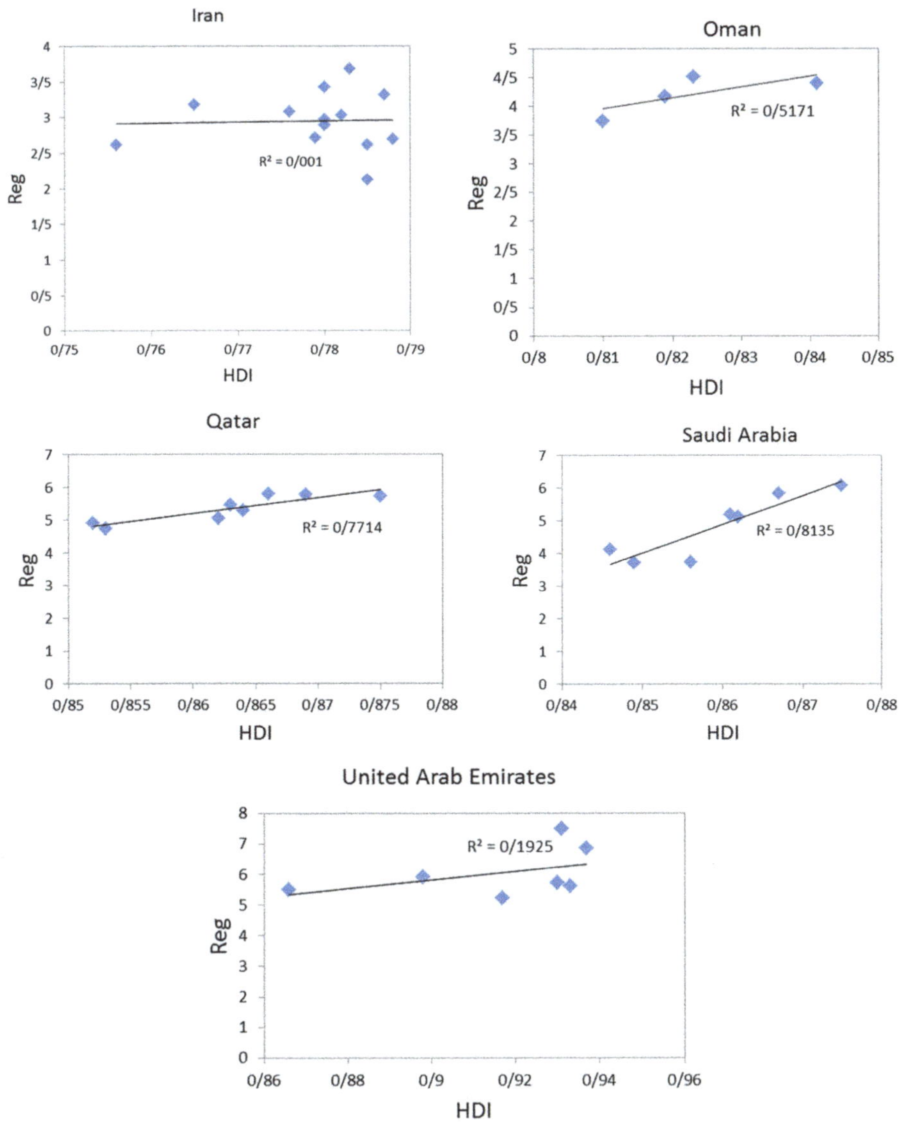

Fig. 1 (continued)

Figure 1j and k illustrate positive relationships between the openness index (*Open*) and the Human Development Index (*HDI*), and between physical infrastructure (*Phy*) and HDI, respectively. The highest coefficient of determination between Open and HDI is observed in Saudi Arabia at 77%, while the lowest is in Iran at 3%. Similarly, the highest R^2 value for Phy and HDI is recorded in Saudi Arabia at 53%, with the lowest values of 2% observed both in Iran and in the United Arab Emirates.

d. Government Entre. Programs and HDI.

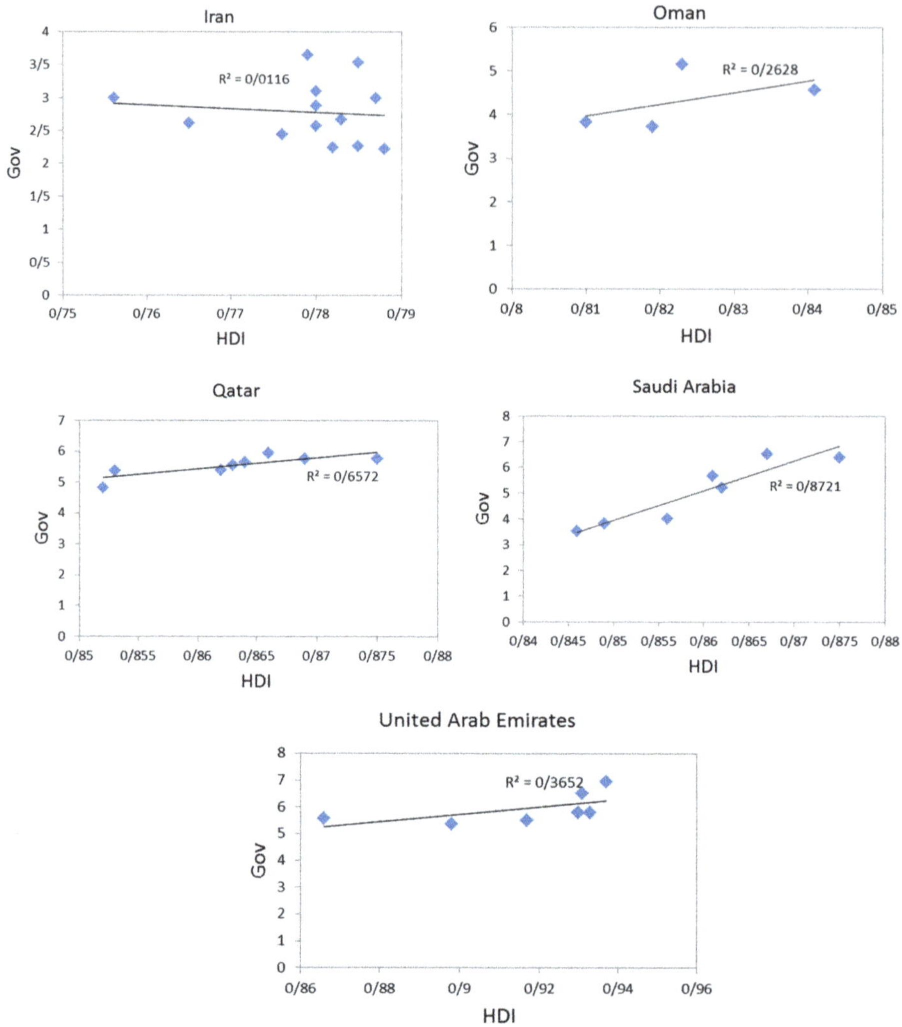

Fig. 1 (continued)

Figure 11 depicts a positive association between the cultural dimension (*Cul*) and HDI for Oman, the UAE, Saudi Arabia, and Qatar. In Iran, however, Cul does not serve as a significant explanatory factor for poverty alleviation.

Overall, poverty alleviation in Iran and Oman is predominantly influenced by the financial component (*Fin*); in Qatar, it is primarily driven by regulatory (*Reg*) and openness (*Open*) factors; and in Saudi Arabia, it is significantly affected by government policies (*Pol*), cultural factors (*Cul*), and governance (*Gov*). In the United Arab Emirates, the majority of variations in *HDI* are explained by educational

e. Education at School and HDI.

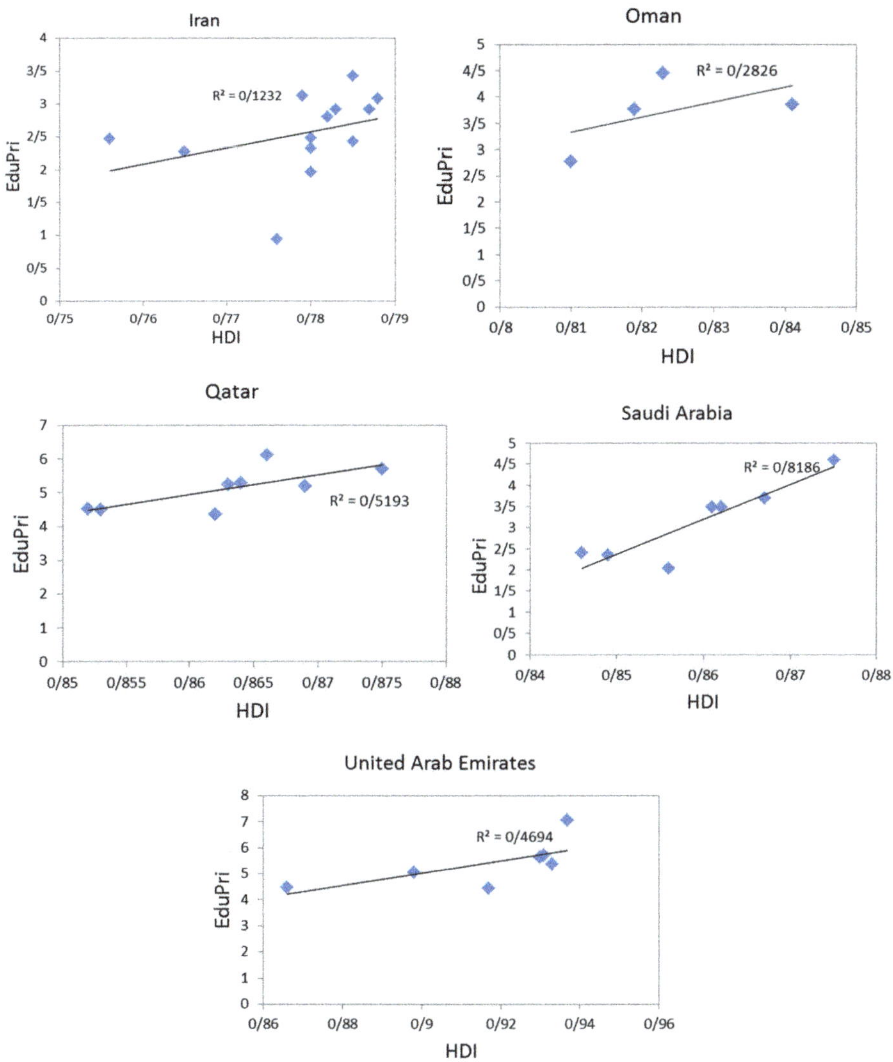

Fig. 1 (continued)

components, namely the primary-level entrepreneurship education (*EduPri*), post-secondary entrepreneurship education (*EduPost*), and research and development (*R&D*).

f. Education at Post-School and HDI.

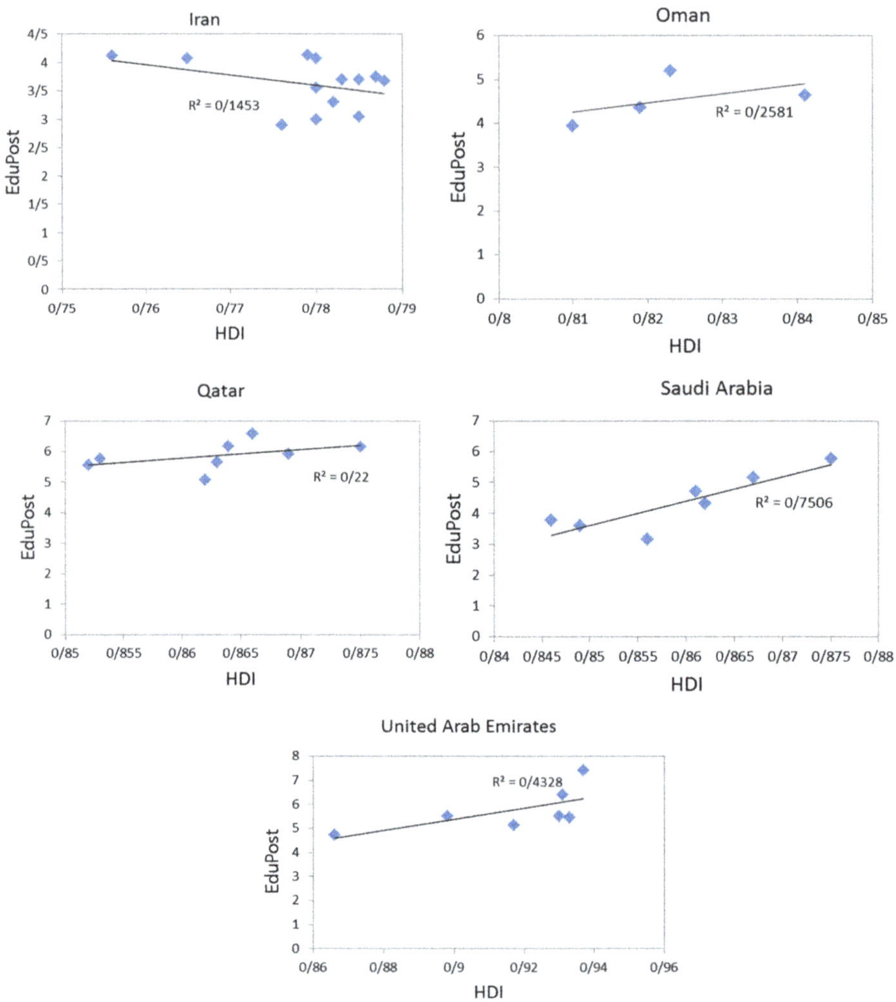

Fig. 1 (continued)

7 Conclusion

Poverty alleviation strategies are generally classified into four categories: redistributive, participatory, institutional, and behavioral strategies. Redistributive strategies focus on income redistribution through supportive policies. Participatory strategies utilize mechanisms such as entrepreneurship and microfinance; by providing credit to the poor, these strategies facilitate both the initiation and continuation of businesses, thereby promoting poverty alleviation. Institutional strategies contribute to

g. Research and Development Transfers and HDI.

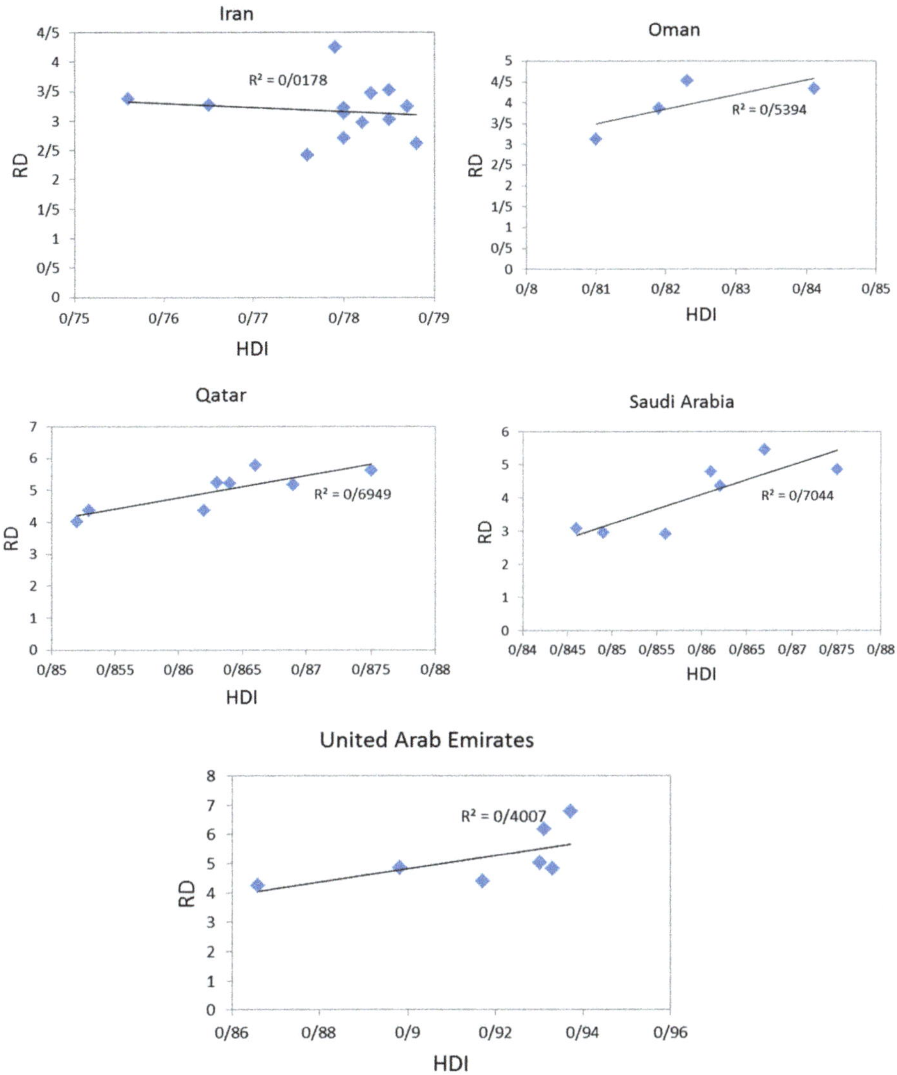

Fig. 1 (continued)

poverty reduction by expanding economic opportunities, enhancing market access and raising awareness among the poor regarding their rights. Behavioral strategies focus on the behaviors and decision-making processes of the poor, offering interventions aimed at reshaping individuals' mental frameworks to alleviate poverty. Entrepreneurship is recognized as a central component of participatory strategies.

h. Commercial and Professional Infrastructure and HDI.

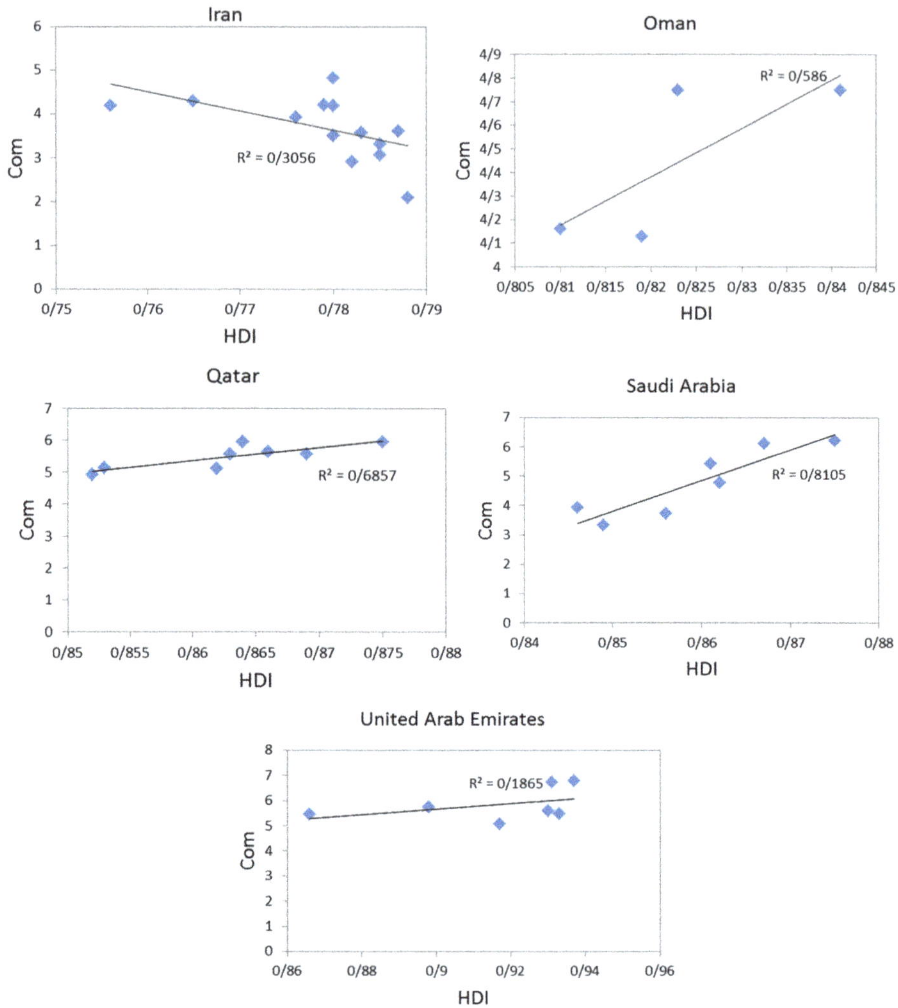

Fig. 1 (continued)

The current study applies the panel-corrected standard errors (PCSE) estimator within a least-squares framework, examining the overall effect of entrepreneurship, as well as inspecting the impact of each subcomponent of the entrepreneurial ecosystem, on poverty alleviation in the Persian Gulf countries over the period of 2010–2022.

Entrepreneurship constitutes a fundamental factor of production that organizes and coordinates with other productive resources within the economic activity framework. It plays a critical role in improving living standards and wealth creation at the societal level. Entrepreneurship is widely regarded as one of the most powerful

i. Market Dynamic and HDI.

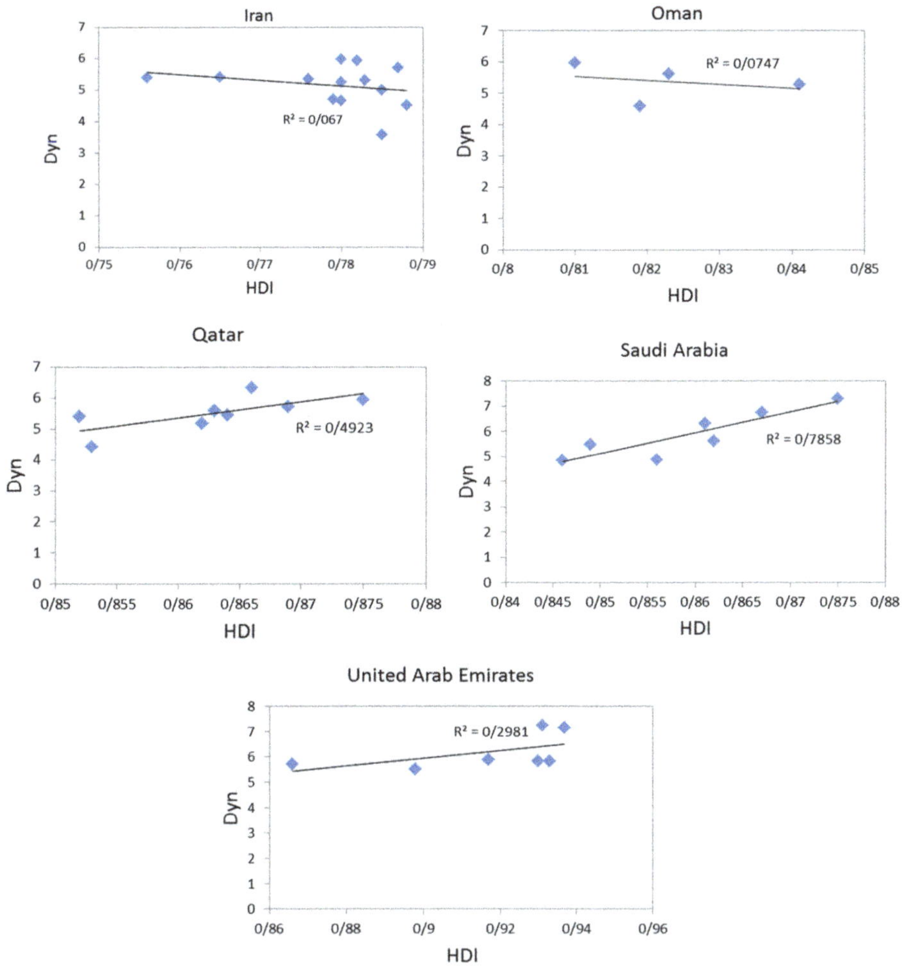

Fig. 1 (continued)

instruments for poverty alleviation and the enhancement of global well-being. The existing body of literature suggests that impoverished regions and communities are characterized by distinctive contextual conditions that differ substantially from those prevailing in more typical or affluent societies. As a result, different dimensions of the entrepreneurial ecosystem may exert heterogeneous effects on poverty alleviation.

It is important to acknowledge that not all forms of entrepreneurship are equally effective in reducing poverty. In some cases, entrepreneurial activities may exacerbate income inequality and entrench individuals in persistent poverty. Accordingly, the promotion of inclusive entrepreneurship—particularly initiatives that target the

j. Burdens or Entry Regulations and HDI.

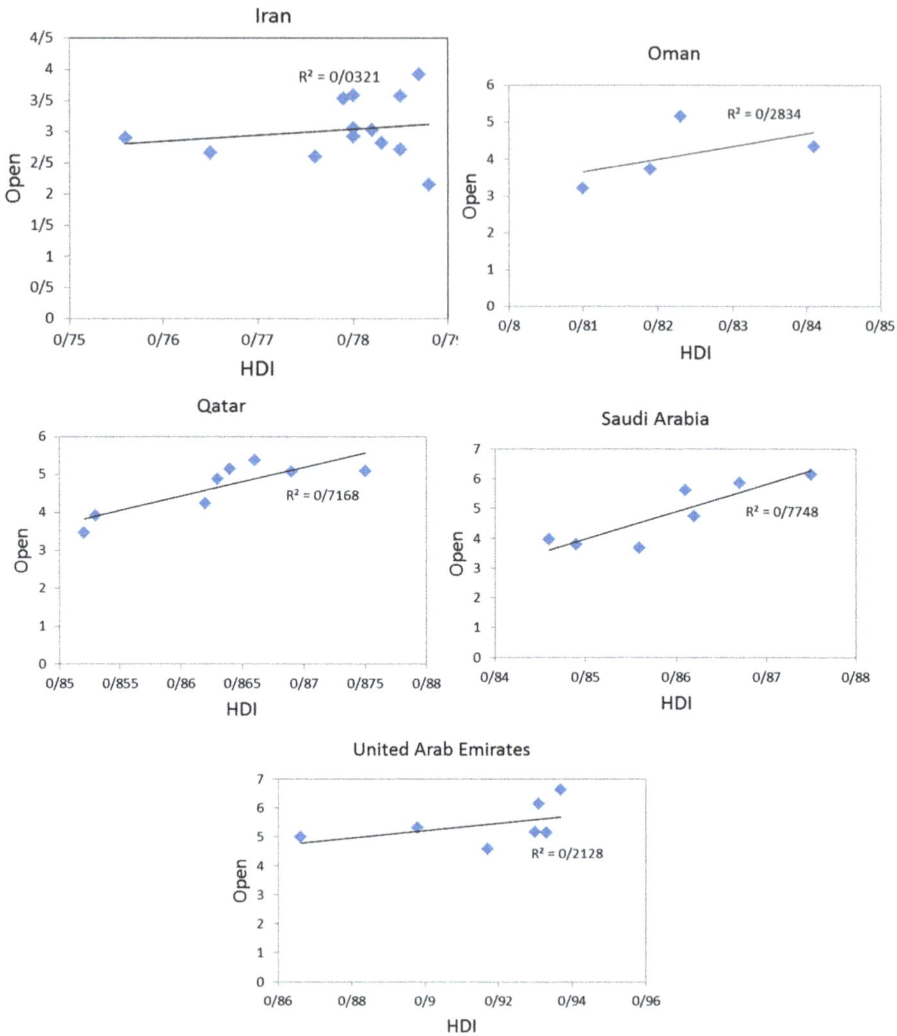

Fig. 1 (continued)

marginalized communities and ensure equitable access to entrepreneurial opportunities for all—is essential.

Research on entrepreneurship can be broadly classified into four principal strands: micro- and macro-level entrepreneurship, social entrepreneurship, institutional entrepreneurship, and the nexus between entrepreneurship and poverty alleviation. At the micro level, entrepreneurship contributes to poverty alleviation primarily through the creation of additional employment opportunities. Beyond job creation, it is also associated with strengthening economic and social cohesion.

k. Physical Infrastructure and HDI.

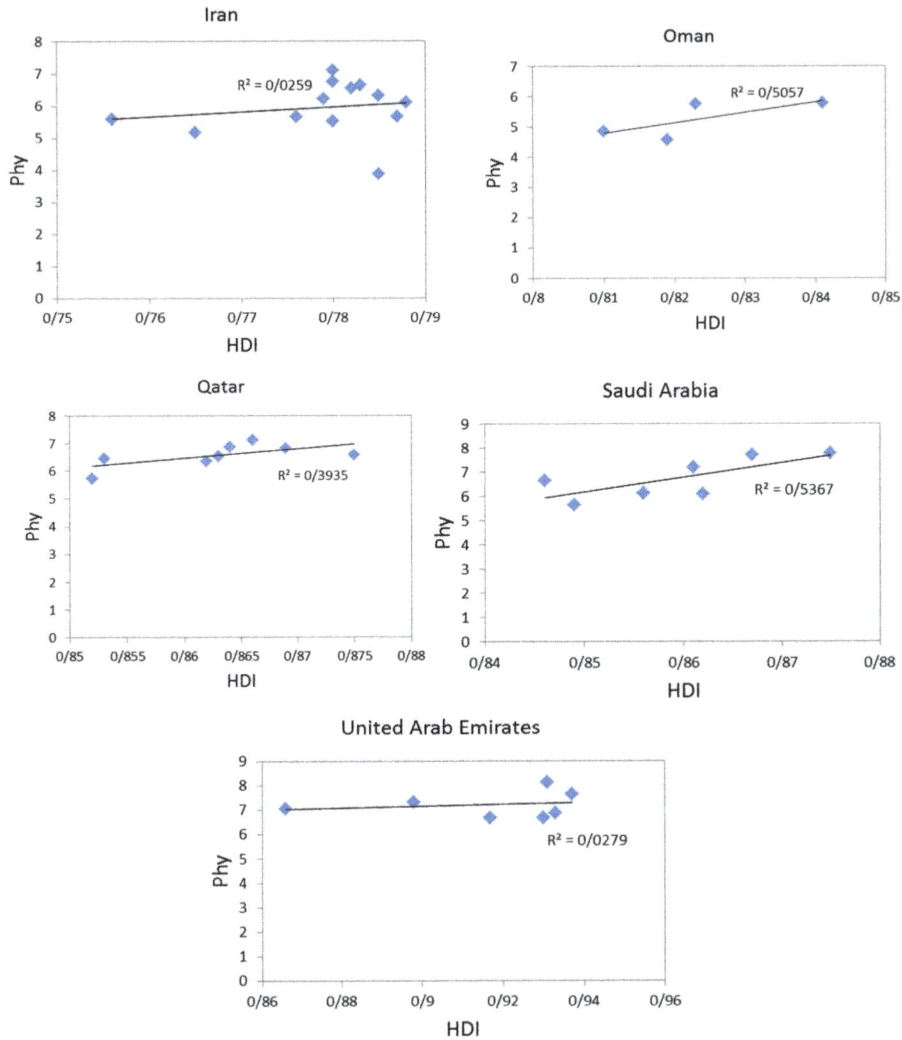

Fig. 1 (continued)

Entrepreneurship plays a crucial role in enhancing productivity, fostering individual capabilities, and generating employment opportunities for the poor (Al Saiqal et al., 2019). At this level, entrepreneurial activity is often characterized by necessity-driven ventures and self-employment. By contrast, at the macro level, entrepreneurship may exert adverse effects on poverty alleviation.

Within the social entrepreneurship context, the facilitation of knowledge spillovers reallocates resources toward more productive activities and generates opportunities for the poor. However, owing to its predominantly non-profit orientation,

I. Social and Cultural Norms and HDI.

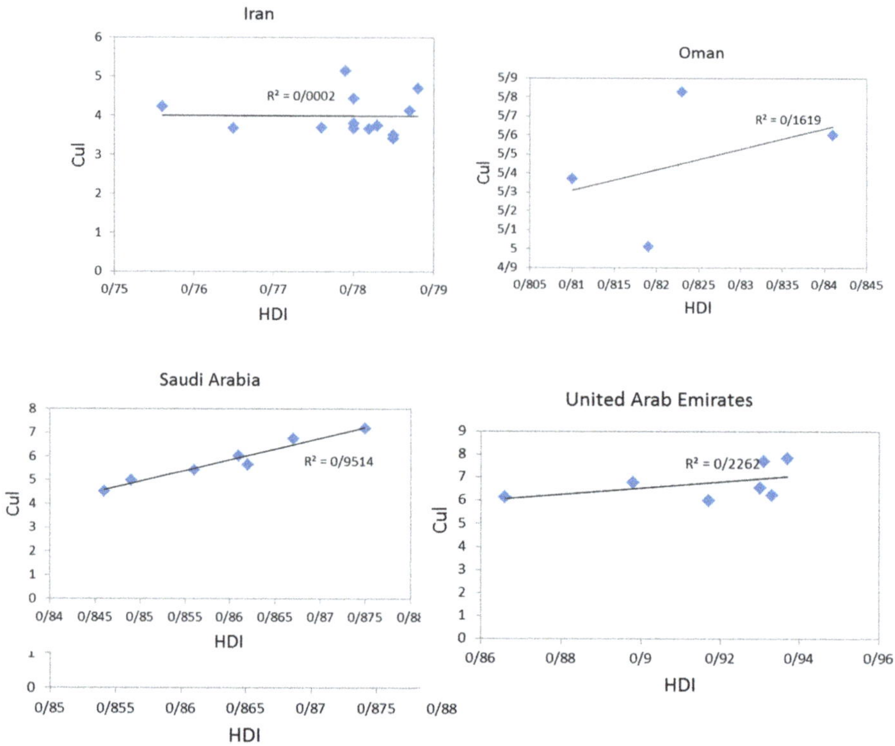

Fig. 1 (continued)

social entrepreneurship often encounters long-term resource constraints that may undermine its sustainability. In the institutional entrepreneurship case, the focus extends beyond capacity building and the promotion of entrepreneurial activity among the poor, to include ensuring their legitimate voice and accountability, as well as strengthening their human and social capital.

The results indicate that the entrepreneurial ecosystem index, representing the participatory strategy, exerts a positive and statistically significant effect on poverty alleviation. Similarly, the good governance index, reflecting the institutional strategy, demonstrates a positive and significant impact on poverty alleviation. Good governance—characterized by the rule of law, accountability, public participation, inclusive justice, and transparency—plays a critical role in reducing poverty. By establishing robust institutional infrastructures and designing economic policies aimed at improving resource allocation and reducing uncertainty, good governance contributes to poverty alleviation. Moreover, the strengthening of institutional and human capacities through the enforcement of the rule of law, institutional reforms, and the enhancement of regulatory frameworks further supports poverty reduction.

GDP, representing the redistributive strategy, exhibits a significant negative effect on poverty alleviation. In some cases, corruption and mismanagement impede the effective allocation of GDP-generated resources to the poor, thereby undermining poverty reduction efforts. At times, GDP growth disproportionately benefits specific segments of society, with limited gains accruing to impoverished populations. In economies heavily dependent on natural resources, increases in GDP may encourage resource overexploitation and environmental degradation, which can have adverse long-term consequences for the livelihoods of the poor. Moreover, when GDP growth is concentrated in infrastructure and non-productive sectors without sufficient investment in education and healthcare for the poor, its contribution to poverty alleviation may remain limited.

The study's findings on the role of entrepreneurial ecosystem sub-indices in poverty alleviation indicate that the components Phy, Pol, Gov, Reg, and EduPri exert positive and statistically significant effects on poverty alleviation in the Persian Gulf countries. By contrast, the components EduPost and RD display a significant negative impact on poverty alleviation. These findings are consistent with the results reported by Bruton et al. (2013) and Zhang et al. (2023). Meanwhile, the components Cul, Fin, Open, Dyn, and Com do not demonstrate statistically significant effects on poverty alleviation. Accessing adequate funding for entrepreneurial activities is not found to have a significant effect on poverty alleviation, which aligns with the findings of Alvarez et al. (2015). Government support policies, regulatory incentives, and public initiatives have promoted entrepreneurship, corroborating the results of Devi (2023), Gbenga et al. (2023), Djankov et al. (2018), and Gnyawali and Fogel (1994). Entrepreneurship contributes to poverty alleviation by generating employment opportunities, thereby creating pathways for the poor to earn income and reduce dependence on subsidies. Income generation enables poor households not only to meet their basic needs, but also to increase savings and accumulate durable assets.

The entrepreneurial ecosystem comprises multiple components that can be categorized into three domains: supportive, legal and social, and human capital. In participatory strategies—represented in the present study by the entrepreneurial ecosystem—attention is directed toward these three entrepreneurial environments. Within the human capital domain, emphasis is placed on entrepreneurial skills development and training. The supportive environment consists of institutions that assist ecosystem stakeholders by providing access to information and enabling them to identify opportunities through an informed understanding of prevailing conditions. At the legal and social environment level, the government plays a central role in creating a conducive setting that facilitates the acceptance of favorable business activities. Such an enabling environment promotes entrepreneurial activity by supporting the growth and development of small businesses. In this domain, it is essential to effectively utilize government support programs and financial commitments provided by the public authorities.

The analysis of the entrepreneurial ecosystem in the Persian Gulf countries during 2010–2022 indicates that improvements in the ecosystem generally support poverty alleviation. Nevertheless, the entrepreneurial environment suffers from insufficient government support. In the region, attention to governance indicators is critical for enhancing poverty reduction efforts. Entrepreneurial activities are associated with high risks, and weak institutional quality has limited the banking system's ability to support business startups. Additionally, entrepreneurship education has not been adequately prioritized, despite its crucial role in strengthening the functionality of the entrepreneurial ecosystem.

Given that the legal and social domains of the entrepreneurial ecosystem do not exert a significant impact on poverty alleviation in these countries, greater emphasis should be placed on the human capital domain—including the entrepreneurship education—and the supportive domain, which encompasses financial resources, government policies designed to facilitate entrepreneurial processes, government entrepreneurship programs, and business-friendly regulations. Strengthening these areas is essential for advancing poverty alleviation efforts.

Entrepreneurs in the Persian Gulf countries face unique challenges, including limited access to capital and resources. Nonetheless, they often hold valuable, context-specific knowledge of local markets and community needs. By focusing on these localized demands and opportunities, entrepreneurs in the region can develop innovative products and services that effectively address regional challenges, while simultaneously contributing to economic growth and development. Strengthening entrepreneurship in these countries not only provides individuals with opportunities to establish businesses and generate income, but it also plays a pivotal role in breaking cycles of persistent poverty and promoting economic advancement and social mobility.

At the highest social strata, individuals face complex fundamental needs and productivity-enhancing factors. Significantly, they also have access to entrepreneurial finance, free markets, research and development knowledge, and other conditions specific to the entrepreneurial ecosystem. In factor-driven economies such as Iran and Oman, establishing basic prerequisites—including primary education, healthcare, infrastructure, and related essentials—is critical. In these economies, constraints on entrepreneurship include technology transfer, entrepreneurial financing, domestic market barriers, and entry regulations. In efficiency-driven economies such as Saudi Arabia, factors such as technology transfer, government policies, taxation, and bureaucracy also play significant roles. The ranking of government entrepreneurship programs highlights substantial disparities across different stages of economic development. According to the Global Entrepreneurship Monitor report (2016), the average economic performance index (EFC) scores are relatively low for the factor-driven and efficiency-driven economies, at 1.4 and 0.4, respectively, whereas the innovation-driven economies, such as Qatar and the United Arab Emirates, exhibit considerably higher scores at 4.8.

Accordingly, it is recommended that policy interventions prioritize the development of supportive institutions and human capital—including skills training, employment generation, and the promotion of collective participation—within the entrepreneurial ecosystem to effectively advance poverty alleviation in the Persian Gulf countries.

8 Limitations and Future Research Directions

Despite its contributions, this study has several limitations that suggest directions for future research. Due to data availability constraints, entrepreneurial ecosystem indicators were accessible only up to the year 2022, restricting the empirical analysis to this period. Additionally, the data related to Kuwait, Iraq, and Bahrain were unavailable; thus, these countries were excluded from the study. The current research employs the Human Development Index (HDI) as a proxy for poverty alleviation; future studies may consider alternative measures, such as the Multidimensional Poverty Index (MPI) or the composite indicators encompassing education, health, employment security, and social welfare, to provide a more comprehensive assessment for poverty alleviation. Moreover, this study exclusively focuses on the educational opportunities generated by political entrepreneurship for the poor. Future research could further investigate the role of political entrepreneurs in poverty alleviation through institutional frameworks.

Given the rapid growth of the digital economy in the Persian Gulf countries, subsequent studies are also encouraged to examine the role of digital entrepreneurship in empowering the poor and creating inclusive employment opportunities.

Finally, considering the institutional, economic, and demographic heterogeneity across the Persian Gulf countries, future researchers are advised to undertake country-specific analyses.

Appendices

Appendix 1 The result of principal components analysis for good governance

Number	Value	Proportion	Cumulative Proportion	Variable	PC1
1	5.2218	0.8703	0.8703	VOICE	0.3213
2	0.5792	0.0965	0.9668	RULE	0.4282
3	0.1284	0.0214	0.9882	REG	0.4279
4	0.0470	0.0078	0.9961	POL	0.4230
5	0.0134	0.0022	0.9983	GOV	0.4145
6	0.0100	0.0017	1.0000	CONT	0.4236

Source: Research findings

Note: Six indicators are constructed. The contribution of costs to each indicator is specified. The first component explains 0.87 of the variance ratio. Therefore, the first component is considered as a composite indicator

Appendix 2 The result of principal components analysis for entrepreneurship ecosystem

Number	Value	Proportion	Cumulative Proportion	Variable	PC1
1	9.1178	0.7598	0.7598	Fin	0.1425
2	1.1418	0.0952	0.8550	Pol	0.3049
3	0.5972	0.0498	0.9047	Reg	0.3197
4	0.3501	0.0292	0.9339	Gov	0.3161
5	0.2802	0.0234	0.9573	Edupri	0.2933
6	0.2001	0.0167	0.9740	Edupost	0.3046
7	0.1092	0.0091	0.9831	RD	0.3148
8	0.0791	0.0066	0.9897	Com	0.3080
9	0.0430	0.0036	0.9932	Dyn	0.2444
10	0.0388	0.0032	0.9965	Open	0.3157
11	0.0253	0.0021	0.9986	Phy	0.2373
12	0.0168	0.0014	1.0000	Cul	0.3097

Source: Research findings
Note: 12 indicators are constructed. The contribution of costs to each indicator is specified. The first component explains 0.75 of the variance ratio. Therefore, the first component is considered as a composite indicator

Appendix 3 The results of multicollinearity test

Model	Amount of VIF for the explanatory variables		
	EN	Gov	GDP
1	3.36	6.08	3.43

Source: Research findings
Note: The variance inflation factor (VIF) value of each regressor is less than 10, so there is no Multicollinearity between the explanatory variables

Appendix 4 The results of multicollinearity test

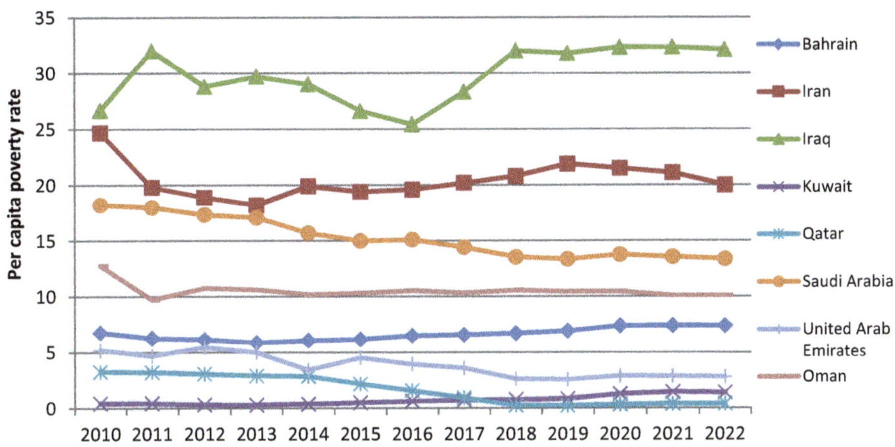

Fig. 2 The per capita poverty rate in PGC, 2010–2022. Source: http://www.arabdevelopment-portal.com

Model	Amount of VIF for the explanatory Variables											
	Fin	Pol	Reg	Gov	Edupri	Edupost	R&D	Com	Dyn	Open	Phy	Cul
2	1.63	2.23	3.2	5.67	9.66	9.96	8.46	4.78	2.17	3.74	2.36	3.5

Source: Research findings
Note: The variance inflation factor (VIF) value of each regressor is less than 10, so there is no Multicollinearity between the explanatory variables

Appendix 5. The percapita poverty rate trend in PGC

The per capita poverty rate in PGC is presented in Fig. 2.

References

Abolfazlian, N. (2017). *The role of religion-based NGOs in poverty alleviation: An empowerment approach (Master's thesis)*. Ferdowsi University of Mashhad, Faculty of Administrative and Economic Sciences.

Abubakar, Y. A., & Mitra, J. (2013). The venturesome poor and entrepreneurial activity in Nigeria: The role of consumption, technology and human capital. *The International Journal of Entrepreneurship and Innovation, 14*(4), 235–254.

Addison, T., & Cornia, G. A. (2001). *Income distribution policies for faster poverty reduction (No. 2001/93)*. WIDER Discussion Paper.

Adejumobi, S. (2006). Gov*ernance and Poverty Reduction in Africa: A Critique of the Poverty Reduction Strategy Papers (PRSPs).*

Adetona, A. A. (2025). Entrepreneurial skill acquisition and poverty alleviation. *International Journal of Research and Innovation in Social Science, 9*(08), 4779–4792.

Agri, E. M., Yilkes, D. O., & Acha, O. F. (2019). Entrepreneurship, inclusive growth and poverty reduction in Nigeria. *SSRG International Journal of Economics and Management Studies, 6*(8), 162–173.

Agwu, E. M., Carter, A. L., & Murray, P. J. (2014). Downsizing as a strategic tool for effective organizational management: A case study of Nigerian banks. *International Journal of Research in Management, Science and Technology, 2*(1), 1–9.

Aidis, R., Estrin, S., & Mickiewicz, T. (2008). Institutions and entrepreneurship development in Russia: A comparative perspective. *Journal of Business Venturing, 23*(6), 656–672.

Ajakaiye, D. O., & Olomola, A. S. (1999). Conceptual and methodological issues in poverty alleviation. *CBN Bullion, 23*(4).

Akanji, O. O. (2001). Micro-finance as a strategy for poverty reduction. *Economic and financial Review, 39*(4), 111–134.

Al Mamun, A., Muniady, R., Fazal, S. A., & Malarvizhi, C. A. (2019). Micro-enterprise development training and entrepreneurial competencies among low-income households in Malaysia. *Asia Pacific Journal of Innovation and Entrepreneurship, 13*(3), 354–366.

Al Saiqal, N. Y., Ryan, J. C., & Parcero, O. J. (2019). Entrepreneurial intention and UAE youth: Unique influencers of entrepreneurial intentions in an emerging country context. *Journal of East-West Business, 25*(2), 144–165.

Aldalou, O., & Migdad, A. (2023). The role of micro entrepreneurship in poverty alleviation for refugees in Turkey. *Proceedings of Femfest International Conference on Economics, Management and Business, 1*, 186–198.

Ali, D. A. H., & Ali, A. H. (2013). Entrepreneurship development and poverty reduction: Empirical survey from Somalia. *American International Journal of Social Science, 2*(3), 108–113.

Aluko, M. A. O. (2003). Strategies for poverty reduction in Nigeria. *Journal of Social Sciences, 7*(4), 255–266.

Alvarez, S. A., & Barney, J. B. (2014). Entrepreneurial opportunities and poverty alleviation. *Entrepreneurship Theory and Practice, 38*(1), 159–184.

Alvarez, S. A., Barney, J. B., & Newman, A. M. (2015). The poverty problem and the industrialization solution. *Asia Pacific Journal of Management, 32*, 23–37.

Alvord, S. H., Brown, L. D., & Letts, C. W. (2004). Social entrepreneurship and societal transformation: An exploratory study. *The Journal of Applied Behavioral Science, 40*(3), 260–282.

Amorós, J. E., & Cristi, O. (2011). *Poverty and entrepreneurship in developing countries (No. Oxford)*. Oxford University Press.

Amorós, J. E., Ramírez, L. M., Rodríguez-Aceves, L., & Ruiz, L. E. (2021). Revisiting poverty and entrepreneurship in developing countries. *Journal of Developmental Entrepreneurship, 26*(2), 1–17.

Anderson, A. R., Younis, S., Hashim, H., & Air, C. (2019). Social enterprising informing our concept; exploring informal micro social enterprise. *Social Enterprise Journal, 15*(1), 94–110.

Ansari, S., Munir, K., & Gregg, T. (2012). Impact at the 'bottom of the pyramid': The role of social capital in capability development and community empowerment. *Journal of Management Studies, 49*(4), 813–842.

Aparicio, S., Audretsch, D., & Urbano, D. (2021). Does entrepreneurship matter for inclusive growth? The role of social progress orientation. *Entrepreneurship Research Journal, 11*(4).

Arejiogbe, O. E., Moses, C. L., Salau, O. P., Onayemi, O. O., Agada, S. A., Dada, A. E., & Obisesan, O. T. (2023). Bolstering the impact of social entrepreneurship and poverty alleviation for sustainable development in Nigeria. *Sustainability, 15*(8), 1–19.

Audretsch, D. B., Heger, D., & Veith, T. (2015). Infrastructure and entrepreneurship. *Small Business Economics, 44*, 219–230.

Ault, J. K., & Spicer, A. (2014). The institutional context of poverty: State fragility as a predictor of cross national variation in commercial microfinance lending. *Strategic Management Journal, 35*(12), 1818–1838.

Ayoo, C. (2022). Poverty reduction strategies in developing countries. *Rural development-education, sustainability, multifunctionality* (pp. 17–57).

Azamat, O., Fayzullokh, S., & Nilufar, A. (2023). The impact of entrepreneurship on poverty reduction. *International Journal of Professional Business Review, 8*(3), 1–19.

Azis Muthalib, A., Harafah, L. M., Yani, M., Rostin, R., & Mahmudin, A. S. (2014). The influence of micro industry entrepreneurship in the process of poverty alleviation (studies in the Food Industry Center at Southeast Sulawesi). *IOSR Journal of Business and Management, 16*(11), 48–53.

Badko, B., Ghasemi Siani, M., Ranjbaraki, A., Shambiyati, M., & Shakiba, A. (2022). The impact of microcredit on empowerment, employment creation, and poverty reduction in local communities: A case study of Ahmadi District, Hajjiabad County, Hormozgan Province. *Regional Geography and Urban Planning, 12*(44), 201–226.

Banerjee, S. B., & Jackson, L. (2017). Microfinance and the business of poverty reduction: Critical perspectives from rural Bangladesh. *Human Relations, 70*(1), 63–91.

Baron, R. A., & Shane, S. (2007). Entrepreneurship: A process perspective. *The psychology of entrepreneurship* (pp. 19–39).

Baumol, W. J. (1990). Entrepreneurship: Productive, unproductive, and destructive. *Journal of Political Economy, 98*(5), 893–921.

Baumol, W. J. (1996). Entrepreneurship: Productive, unproductive, and destructive. *Journal of Business Venturing, 11*(1), 3–22.

Begum, A., & Abdin, M. D. (2015). Employment generation and poverty alleviation through SME cluster development in Bangladesh. *Turkish Economic Review, 2*(1), 26–31.

Blanco-Arana, M. D. C., & Angulo-Guerrero, M. J. (2024). Financial development and poverty reduction in developing countries: The role of entrepreneurial activity, Panoeconomicus, 1–24.

Blankson, C., & Nukpezah, J. A. (2019). Market orientation and poverty reduction: A study of rural microentrepreneurs in Ghana. *Africa Journal of Management, 5*(4), 332–357.

Bogdanović, M. (2023). Alleviating poverty through entrepreneurship: Homo entrepreneur, entrepreneurial culture, and state. *Mest Journal, 11*(2), 86–103.

Bruton, G. D., Ketchen, D. J., Jr., & Ireland, R. D. (2013). Entrepreneurship as a solution to poverty. *Journal of Business Venturing, 28*(6), 683–689.

Bruton, G. D., Ahlstrom, D., & Si, S. (2015). Entrepreneurship, poverty, and Asia: Moving beyond subsistence entrepreneurship. *Asia Pacific Journal of Management, 32*, 1–22.

Carland, J. W., Hoy, F., Boulton, W. R., & Carland, J. A. C. (1984). Differentiating entrepreneurs from small business owners: A conceptualization. *Academy of Management Review, 9*(2), 354–359.

Chelabi, M., & Mobaraki, M. (2005). Analysis of the relationship between social capital and crime at micro and macro levels. *Iranian Journal of Sociology, 6*(2), 3–44.

Chikwira, C., Vengesai, E., & Mandude, P. (2022). The impact of microfinance institutions on poverty alleviation. *Journal of Risk and Financial Management, 15*(9), 393.

Chliova, M., Brinckmann, J., & Rosenbusch, N. (2015). Is microcredit a blessing for the poor? A meta-analysis examining development outcomes and contextual considerations. *Journal of Business Venturing, 30*(3), 467–487.

Clyde, P., & Karnani, A. (2015). Improving private sector impact on poverty alleviation: A cost-based taxonomy. *California Management Review, 57*(2), 20–35.

Coduras, A., de la Vega, I., & Salman, M. B. (2018). Entrepreneurial ecosystems in Arabic countries: A recent overview. Entrepreneurship Ecosystem in the Middle East and North Africa (MENA) Dynamics in Trends, *Policy and Business Environment* (pp. 283–302).

Cohen, D., & Soto, M. (2007). Growth and education: Good data, good results. *Journal of Economic Growth, 12*, 51–76.
Congdon, W. J., Kling, J. R., & Mullainathan, S. (2011). *Policy and choice: Public finance through the lens of behavioral economics*. Brookings Institution Press.
Coulibaly, S. K., Erbao, C., & Mekongcho, T. M. (2018). Economic globalization, entrepreneurship, and development. *Technological Forecasting and Social Change, 127*, 271–280.
Dagdeviran, H., Van der Hoeven, R., & Weeks, J. (2000). Redistribution matters: Growth for poverty reduction. Department of Economics, School of Oriental and African Studies, *International Labour Organization*, 1–29.
Dau, L. A., & Cuervo-Cazurra, A. (2014). To formalize or not to formalize: Entrepreneurship and pro-market institutions. *Journal of Business Venturing, 29*(5), 668–686.
Davidsson, B. (2003). The Domain of Entrepreneurship Research: Some Suggestions. *Advances in Entrepreneurship, Firm Emergence and Growth, 6*, 315–372.
Dean, E. B., Schilbach, F., & Schofield, H. (2017). Poverty and cognitive function. In *The economics of poverty traps* (pp. 57–118). University of Chicago Press.
Dees, J. G. (2018). The meaning of social entrepreneurship 1, 2. In *Case studies in social entrepreneurship and sustainability* (pp. 22–30). Routledge.
Dencker, J. C., Bacq, S., Gruber, M., & Haas, M. (2021). Reconceptualizing necessity entrepreneurship: A contextualized framework of entrepreneurial processes under the condition of basic needs. *Academy of Management Review, 46*(1), 60–79.
Deng, W., & Wang, J. (2023). The effect of entrepreneurship education on the entrepreneurial intention of different college students: Gender, household registration, school type, and poverty status. *PLoS One, 18*(7), 1–31.
Deolalikar, A. B., & Pernia, E. M. (2003). *Poverty, growth, and institutions in developing Asia*. Palgrave Macmillan.
Desai, S., & Acs, Z. J. (2007). A theory of destructive entrepreneurship. *Jena Economic Research Papers, 85*, 1–44.
Devi, A. J. (2023). Entrepreneurial opportunities identification through design thinking: Undergraduate students approach to learning. *Entrepreneurship in India - Issues and challenge* (pp. 60–70).
Djankov, S., Georgieva, D., & Ramalho, R. (2018). Business regulations and poverty. *Economics Letters, 165*, 82–87.
Drucker, P. F. (1985). *Innovation and entrepreneurship; practice and principles*. Harper Row. Innovation.
Dugguh, S. I. (2013). Entrepreneurship and small business: Strategic approach to alleviating poverty and corruption in Nigeria. *GSTF Journal on Business Review (GBR), 3*(1), 57–66.
Edobor, F. O. (2018). *Collective social entrepreneurship as a collaborative strategy to reduce poverty in Nigeria* (Doctoral dissertation, Cardiff Metropolitan University).
El Harbi, S., & Anderson, A. R. (2010). Institutions and the shaping of different forms of entrepreneurship. *The Journal of Socio-Economics, 39*(3), 436–444.
Elumah, L., Taiwo, M., & Zubairu, U. (2024). Financial development and poverty alleviation: A systematic review. *Journal of Economics and Sustainability, 6*(1), 1–19.
Forouharfar, A. (2018). Social entrepreneurship strategies by the Middle Eastern governments: A review. *Entrepreneurship Ecosystem in the Middle East and North Africa (MENA) Dynamics in Trends, Policy and Business Environment* (pp. 189–264).
Fuad, A. (2022). Poverty reduction strategy based on family empowerment in the perspective of Islamic Law. *Prosperity: Journal of Society and Empowerment, 2*(1), 1–12.
Fuentelsaz, L., Gonzalez, C., Maicas, J. P., & Montero, J. (2015). How different formal institutions affect opportunity and necessity entrepreneurship. *Business Research Quarterly, 18*(4), 246–258.
Gartner, W. B. (1988). "Who is an entrepreneur?" is the wrong question. *American Journal of Small Business, 12*(4), 11–32.

Gbenga, L. S., Ita, R. E. U., Eja, B. G., Ojah, E. O., & Okon, C. J. (2023). Entrepreneurship development on poverty reduction in Nigeria. *Law and Economy, 2*(9), 10–14.
Gerster, R. (2000). Alternative approaches to poverty reduction strategies. *SDC Working Paper, 1*, 2000.
Global Entrepreneurship Monitor. (2013). Global report. Prepared by José Ernesto Amorós and Niels Bosma. Retrieved from http://www.gemconsortium.org/report
Global Entrepreneurship Monitor. (2015). 2015/2016 global report. Prepared by Donna Kelley, Slavica Singer, and Mike Herrington. Retrieved from http://www.gemconsortium.org/report
Global Entrepreneurship Monitor. (2016). 2016/17 global report. Prepared by Mike Herrington and Penny Kew. Retrieved from http://www.gemconsortium.org/report
Global Entrepreneurship Monitor. (2017). 2017/18 global report. Prepared by Slavica Singer, Mike Herrington, and Ehud Menipaz. Retrieved from http://www.gemconsortium.org/report
Gnyawali, D. R., & Fogel, D. S. (1994). Environments for entrepreneurship development: Key dimensions and research implications. *Entrepreneurship Theory and Practice, 18*(4), 43–62.
Goel, G., & Rishi, M. (2012). Promoting entrepreneurship to alleviate poverty in India: An overview of government schemes, private sector programs, and initiatives in the citizens' sector. *Thunderbird International Business Review, 54*(1), 45–57.
Gordon, D. (2005). Indicators of poverty and hunger. In *Expert group meeting on youth development indicators*, 1(1), 12–14.
Grindle, M. S. (2004). Good enough governance: Poverty reduction and reform in developing countries. *Governance, 17*(4), 525–548.
Habibnejad, A., & Soleimani Siboni, M. (2019). A suitable model for poverty alleviation in the legal system of the Islamic Republic of Iran with emphasis on the concept of responsible freedom. *Quarterly Journal of Administrative Law Research, 7*(20), 9–35.
Hashim, H., & Gaddefors, J. (2023). The value of entrepreneuring in the context of multidimensional poverty. *The International Journal of Entrepreneurship and Innovation, 24*(2), 88–104.
Hassan, M. K., & Alamgir, D. A. (2002). Micro financial services and poverty alleviation in Bangladesh: A comparative analysis of secular and Islamic NGOs. *Islamic economic institutions and the elimination of poverty* (pp. 113–168).
Hassanvand, D., & Nadi, Y. (2017). The effects of financial development on poverty reduction in Iran. *Economic Research Journal, 52*(1), 35–60.
Haughton, J., & Khandker, S. R. (2009). *Handbook on poverty and inequality*. World Bank Publications.
Haushofer, J. (2019). *Is there a psychological poverty trap*. Unpublished manuscript. Princeton University.
Hoechle, D. (2007). Robust standard errors for panel regressions with cross-sectional dependence. *The Stata Journal, 7*(3), 281–312.
http://data.worldbank.org
https://www.undp.org
Huang, Z., & Gao, F. (2020) Literature review of the causes of the vulnerability of poverty in traditional economics and behavioral economics. *International symposium on frontiers of economics and management science* (pp. 56–60).
Hussain, M. D., Bhuiyan, A. B., & Bakar, R. (2014). Entrepreneurship development and poverty alleviation: An empirical review. *Journal of Asian scientific research, 4*(10), 558.
Hussain, M. D., Bhuiyan, A. B., Said, J., & Ab, M. S. B. (2018). Entrepreneurship education is the key contrivance of poverty alleviation: An empirical review. *MAYFEB Journal of Business and Management, 1*, 32–41.
Ifeoma, A. R., Purity, N. O., & Yusuf, A. E. (2018). Effect of entrepreneurship development on poverty alleviation in Nigeria. *Journal of Business and Management, 20*(2), 80–87.
Imai, K. S., & Azam, M. S. (2012). Does microfinance reduce poverty in Bangladesh? New evidence from household panel data. *Journal of Development Studies, 48*(5), 633–653.

Imbert, E., Morone, P., & Bigi, F. (2019). Assessing the potential of social enterprises through social network analysis-Evidence from Albania. *Journal of Evolutionary Economics, 29*(4), 1211–1239.
Jabbari, H. (2005). Community-based approaches in poverty reduction programs. *Social Welfare Quarterly, 5*(18), 263–298.
Javaheripour, M. (2004). Social policy and poverty: From structural adjustment programs to poverty reduction strategies. *Social Welfare Quarterly, 3*(12), 41–72.
Jiao, H. (2011). A conceptual model for social entrepreneurship directed toward social impact on society. *Social Enterprise Journal, 7*(2), 130–149.
Kareem, R. O. (2015). Impact of entrepreneurship on poverty alleviation. *Journal of Business Administration and Education, 7*(1), 1–16.
Khan, M. R. (2016). Entrepreneurship ecosystem evolution strategy of Saudi Arabia. *International Entrepreneurship Review, 2*(2), 67–92.
Khavul, S., Chavez, H., & Bruton, G. D. (2013). When institutional change outruns the change agent: The contested terrain of entrepreneurial microfinance for those in poverty. *Journal of Business Venturing, 28*(1), 30–50.
Kiiru, J. M. (2007). Microfinance, entrepreneurship and rural development: Empirical evidence from Makueni district, Kenya. In *Global Poverty Research Group (GPRG) conference*. Oxford University.
Kirby, D. A., & Ibrahim, N. (2011). The case for (social) entrepreneurship education in Egyptian universities. *Education Training, 53*(5), 403–415.
Kirzner, I. (1973). *Competition and entrepreneurship*. University of Chicago Press.
Kolvereid, L., & Moen, Ø. (1997). Entrepreneurship among business graduates: Does a major in entrepreneurship make a difference? *Journal of European Industrial Training, 21*(4), 154–160.
Korosteleva, J., & Stępień-Baig, P. (2021). Climbing the poverty ladder: The role of entrepreneurship and gender in alleviating poverty in transition economies. In *Business, entrepreneurship and innovation toward poverty reduction* (pp. 197–200). Routledge.
Kosack, S. (2014). The logic of pro-poor policymaking: Political entrepreneurship and mass education. *British Journal of Political Science, 44*(2), 409–444.
Kuckertz, A., Kollmann, T., Krell, P., & Stöckmann, C. (2017). Understanding, differentiating, and measuring opportunity recognition and opportunity exploitation. *International Journal of Entrepreneurial Behavior & Research, 23*(1), 78–97.
Kwon, H. J., & Kim, E. (2014). Poverty reduction and good governance: Examining the rationale of the Millennium Development Goals. *Development and Change, 45*(2), 353–375.
Landstrom, H. (2007). *Pioneers in entrepreneurship and small business research* (Vol. 8). Springer Science & Business Media.
Lane, P. M. (2016). Creating the environment for innovation and entrepreneurship. *International Entrepreneurship Review, 2*(2), 53–66.
Lee, N., & Rodríguez-Pose, A. (2021). Entrepreneurship and the fight against poverty in US cities. *Environment and Planning A: Economy and Space, 53*(1), 31–52.
Levie, J., & Autio, E. (2008). A theoretical grounding and test of the GEM model. *Small Business Economics, 31*(3), 235–263.
Lin, S., Winkler, C., Wang, S., & Chen, H. (2021). Regional determinants of poverty alleviation through entrepreneurship in China. In *Business, entrepreneurship and innovation toward poverty reduction* (pp. 41–62). Routledge.
Liñán, F., Fernández-Serrano, J., & Romero, I. (2013). Necessity and opportunity entrepreneurship: The mediating effect of culture. *Revista de Economía Mundial, 33*, 21–47.
Magnus, U., & Joseph, O. C. (1995). Redirecting education system towards entrepreneurship development in Nigeria: A panacea for poverty alleviation. *Research Journal of Commerce and Behavioural Science, 4*(5), 1–12.
Mair, J., & Marti, I. (2006). Social entrepreneurship research: A source of explanation, prediction, and delight. *Journal of World Business, 41*(1), 36–44.

Mair, J., & Marti, I. (2009). Entrepreneurship in and around institutional voids: A case study from Bangladesh. *Journal of Business Venturing, 24*(5), 419–435.

Malki, I., Ghalib, A., & Kaousar, R. (2024). The impact of microfinance on entrepreneurship and welfare among women borrowers in rural Pakistan. *World Development Perspectives, 35*, 1–6.

Marsden, K. (1990). *African entrepreneurs: Pioneers of development. Mapping the Shift in Business Development Services*.

Marshall, R., & Walters, B. (2011). *Evaluating ten years of' strategizing for poverty reduction: A cross-sectional appraisal of the poverty reduction strategy paper (PRSP) initiative*. Brooks World Poverty Institute, University of Manchester.

Martínez-Rodriguez, I., Callejas-Albiñana, F. E., & Callejas-Albiñana, A. I. (2020). Economic and socio-cultural drivers of necessity and opportunity entrepreneurship depending on the business cycle phase. *Journal of Business Economics and Management, 21*(2), 373–394.

McCloskey, D. N. (2006). *The bourgeois virtues: Ethics for an age of commerce*. University of Chicago Press.

McCloskey, D. N. (2010). *Bourgeois dignity: Why economics can't explain the modern world*. University of Chicago Press.

McMullen, J. S. (2011). Delineating the domain of development entrepreneurship: A market–based approach to facilitating inclusive economic growth. *Entrepreneurship Theory and Practice, 35*(1), 185–215.

Mensah, S. A., & Benedict, E. (2010). Entrepreneurship training and poverty alleviation: Empowering the poor in the Eastern Free State of South Africa. *African Journal of Economic and Management Studies, 1*(2), 138–163.

Meyskens, M., Robb-Post, C., Stamp, J. A., Carsrud, A. L., & Reynolds, P. D. (2010). Social ventures from a resource–based perspective: An exploratory study assessing global Ashoka fellows. *Entrepreneurship Theory and Practice, 34*(4), 661–680.

Miled, K. B. H., Younsi, M., & Landolsi, M. (2022). Does microfinance program innovation reduce income inequality? Cross-country and panel data analysis. *Journal of Innovation and Entrepreneurship, 11*(1), 7.

Minniti, M., & Lévesque, M. (2010). Entrepreneurial types and economic growth. *Journal of Business Venturing, 25*(3), 305–314.

Misturelli, F., & Heffernan, C. (2008). What is poverty? A diachronic exploration of the discourse on poverty from the 1970s to the 2000s. *The European Journal of Development Research, 20*, 666–684.

Mitra, J. (2019). *Entrepreneurship, innovation and regional development: An introduction*. Routledge.

Mitra, J., Abubakar, Y. A., & Sagagi, M. (2011). Knowledge creation and human capital for development: The role of graduate entrepreneurship. *Education and Training, 53*(5), 462–479.

Mohan, P., Watson, P., & Strobl, E. (2018). Nascent entrepreneurs in Caribbean small island developing states: Opportunity versus necessity. *Journal of Developmental Entrepreneurship, 23*(04), 1–33.

Moradi, M., Imanipour, N., Arasti, Z., & Mohammadkazemi, R. (2020). Poverty and entrepreneurship: A systematic review of poverty-related issues discussed in entrepreneurship literature. *World Review of Entrepreneurship, Management and Sustainable Development, 16*(2), 125–152.

Morduch, J., & Armendariz, B. (2005). *The economics of microfinance*. MIT Press.

Morris, M. H., Santos, S. C., & Neumeyer, X. (2018). *Poverty and entrepreneurship in developed economies*. Edward Elgar Publishing.

Morris, M. H., Santos, S. C., & Neumeyer, X. (2020). Entrepreneurship as a solution to poverty in developed economies. *Business Horizons, 63*(3), 377–390.

Motavaseli, M. (2023). The evolution of economic schools and the necessity of forming a new school. *Journal of Entrepreneurship Development, 16*(3), 4–30.

Mouraviev, N., & Kakabadse, N. K. (2021). The role of social entrepreneurs' cosmopolitan orientation in bridging the gap between prosperity and social deprivation. *Society and Business Review, 17*(2), 196–216.

Nakara, W. A., Messeghem, K., & Ramaroson, A. (2021). Innovation and entrepreneurship in a context of poverty: A multilevel approach. *Small Business Economics, 56*(4), 1601–1617.

Naminse, E. Y., & Zhuang, J. (2018). Does farmer entrepreneurship alleviate rural poverty in China? Evidence from Guangxi Province. *PLoS One, 13*(3), 1–18.

Naminse, E. Y., Zhuang, J., & Zhu, F. (2019). The relation between entrepreneurship and rural poverty alleviation in China. *Management Decision, 57*(9), 2593–2611.

Narayan-Parker, D. (1999). *Bonds and bridges: Social capital and poverty* (Vol. 2167). World Bank Publications.

Newman, A., Schwarz, S., & Ahlstrom, D. (2017). Microfinance and entrepreneurship: An introduction. *International Small Business Journal, 35*(7), 787–792.

O'Brien, T. (2019). Political entrepreneurship in the field of Māori sovereignty in Aotearoa New Zealand. *The British Journal of Sociology, 70*(4), 1179–1197.

Obaidullah, M., & Khan, T. (2008). *Islamic microfinance development: Challenges and initiatives*. Islamic Research & Training institute Policy Dialogue Paper, (2).

Olarewaju, T. (2023). *Entrepreneurship as a Route out of Poverty*. Springer Books.

Olausson, A., & Svensson, P. (2019). Understanding political entrepreneurship in local government administration: A contextual framework. *Lex Localis, 17*(3), 643–658.

Oshota, S. O. (2019). Technology access, inclusive growth and poverty reduction in Nigeria: Evidence from error correction modeling approach. *Zagreb International Review of Economics and Business, 22*(2), 1–22.

Overall, J. (2017). Combating rural poverty through altruism: A model for sustainable education. *World Review of Entrepreneurship, Management and Sustainable Development, 13*(1), 69–83.

Pal, R., & Altay, N. (2019). Identifying key success factors for social enterprises serving base of pyramid markets through analysis of value chain complexities. *Journal of Business Logistics, 40*(2), 161–179.

Pour Ezzat, A., & Nejat, A. (2012). An analysis and ranking of poverty alleviation policies. *Social Welfare Quarterly, 12*(46), 299–318.

Ravallion, M. (2008). Poverty alleviation programmes. *The new Palgrave dictionary of economics*, 5062–5068.

Ravallion, M. (2016). *The economics of poverty: History, measurement, and policy*. Oxford University Press.

Reynolds, P. D., Camp, S. M., Bygrave, W. D., Autio, E., & Hay, M. (2002). *Global entrepreneurship monitor gem 2001 summary report*. London Business School and Babson College.

Rezaei, S., Hill, V., & Liu, Y. (2018). In search of the ideal entrepreneurial ecosystem. *Entrepreneurship Ecosystem in the Middle East and North Africa (MENA) dynamics in trends, policy and business environment* (pp. 11–51).

Richardson, J. (2004). Entrepreneurship and development in Asia. *International Journal of Entrepreneurship and Innovation Management, 4*(5), 469–484.

Robinson, J. A., & Acemoglu, D. (2012). *Why nations fail: The origins of power, prosperity and poverty* (pp. 45–47). Profile.

Saci, F. (2023). Performance comparison of poverty alleviation through education, employment and industry during the period of targeted poverty alleviation. *Journal of Economic Analysis, 2*(3), 1–20.

Saedi, A., Mousavi, S. N., & Ahang, F. (2021). Political entrepreneurship: The analysis of its implications area to policy making. *Journal of Public Administration, 12*(4), 674–694.

Sakinah, N. S. N., Arifin, T., & Abdal, A. (2023). Peran Sociopreneur dalam Transformasi Sosial dan Pengentasan Kemiskinan Melalui Lembaga Keuangan Mikro Perspektif Sosiologi dan Antropologi. *Strata Social and Humanities Studies, 1*(2), 117–126.

Sall, M. A. (2022). Entrepreneurship and poverty alleviation in Africa. *Industrial Policy, 2*(1), 33–37.

Salleh, M. S. (2017). Contemporary vision of poverty and Islamic strategy for poverty alleviation. *SAGE Open, 7*(2), 1–8.

Salmen, L. F., & Mundial, B. (1990). *Institutional dimensions of poverty reduction* (Vol. No. 411). Country Economics Department, World Bank.

Samadi, A. H. (2018). Institutions and entrepreneurship in MENA countries. In *Entrepreneurship ecosystem in the Middle East and North Africa (MENA) dynamics in trends, policy and business environment* (pp. 53–93). Springer International Publishing.

Samadi, A. H., & Owjimehr, S. (2021). Does economic globalization have a similar effect on governance for all countries in the world? In *Dynamics of institutional change in emerging market economies: Theories, concepts and mechanisms* (pp. 213–238). Springer International Publishing.

Santos, S. C., Neumeyer, X., & Morris, M. H. (2019). Entrepreneurship education in a poverty context: An empowerment perspective. *Journal of Small Business Management, 57*, 6–32.

Sauka, A., & Welter, F. (2007). Productive, unproductive and destructive entrepreneurship in an advanced transition setting: The example of Latvian small enterprises. *Empirical entrepreneurship research in Europe* (pp. 88–112).

Schumpeter, J. A. (1934). *The theory of economic development*. Harvard. Schumpeter The Theory of Economic Development 1934.

Seifi, A. (2019). The role of the United Nations Development Program in poverty alleviation with emphasis on women's empowerment in Iran: Opportunities and challenges. *Social Work Research Journal, 5*(20), 193–233.

Sen, A. (1983). Economics and the family. *Asian Development Review, 1*(2), 14–26.

Sen, A. (1987). *Gender and cooperative conflicts*. Wider Working Papers.

Shaditalab, Z., & Hojjat Kermani, F. (2008). Poverty and social capital in rural communities. *Social Welfare Research Quarterly, 7*(28), 35–56.

Shane, S., & Venkataraman, S. (2000). The promise of entrepreneurship as a field of research. *Academy of Management Review, 25*(1), 217–226.

Shorrocks, A., & Van der Hoeven, R. (2004). *Growth, inequality, and poverty: Prospects for pro-poor economic development*. Oxford University Press.

Si, S., Yu, X., Wu, A., Chen, S., Chen, S., & Su, Y. (2015). Entrepreneurship and poverty reduction: A case study of Yiwu, China. *Asia Pacific Journal of Management, 32*, 119–143.

Si, S., Cullen, J., Ahlstrom, D., & Wei, J. (2019). Business, entrepreneurship and innovation toward poverty reduction. *Entrepreneurship and Regional Development, 32*(4), 1–20.

Singh, P. K., & Chudasama, H. (2020). Evaluating poverty alleviation strategies in a developing country. *PLoS One, 15*(1), 1–23.

Sobel, R. S. (2008). Testing Baumol: Institutional quality and the productivity of entrepreneurship. *Journal of Business Venturing, 23*(6), 641–655.

Stenholm, P., Acs, Z. J., & Wuebker, R. (2013). Exploring country-level institutional arrangements on the rate and type of entrepreneurial activity. *Journal of Business Venturing, 28*(1), 176–193.

Suherlan, S., Zaakiyyah, H. K. A., & Ahmad, M. I. S. (2024). The role of business education in promoting social entrepreneurship and poverty alleviation in low-income communities. *Jurnal Terobosan Peduli Masyarakat (TIRAKAT), 1*(2), 99–107.

Sutter, C., Bruton, G. D., & Chen, J. (2019). Entrepreneurship as a solution to extreme poverty: A review and future research directions. *Journal of Business Venturing, 34*(1), 197–214.

Suyono, H., & Safaria, T. (2022). Social entrepreneurship solusi mengatasi kemiskinan sebagai dampak pandemi covid-19 berbasis core values. *Prosiding SNasPPM, 7*(1), 363–372.

Thaler, R. H., & Sunstein, C. R. (2009). *Nudge: Improving decisions about health, wealth, and happiness*. Penguin.

Theavy, C., & Mardy, S. (2023). *A review on the best practices of poverty reduction in developing countries*.

Thurik, A. R., Carree, M. A., Van Stel, A., & Audretsch, D. B. (2008). Does self-employment reduce unemployment? *Journal of Business Venturing, 23*(6), 673–686.

Tobias, J. M., Mair, J., & Barbosa-Leiker, C. (2013). Toward a theory of transformative entrepreneuring: Poverty reduction and conflict resolution in Rwanda's entrepreneurial coffee sector. *Journal of Business Venturing, 28*(6), 728–742.

Todorovic, Z. W., & McNaughton, R. B. (2007). The effect of culture, resources and quality of entrepreneurship on economic development: A conceptual framework. *International Journal of Entrepreneurship and Small Business, 4*(4), 383–396.

Tomizawa, A., Zhao, L., Bassellier, G., & Ahlstrom, D. (2020). Economic growth, innovation, institutions, and the Great Enrichment. *Asia Pacific Journal of Management, 37*, 7–31.

Trivedi, S. K. (2014). *Creating livelihoods: Indian women entrepreneur networks in the context of poverty*. The George Washington University.

Tversky, A., & Kahneman, D. (1991). Loss aversion in riskless choice: A reference-dependent model. *The Quarterly Journal of Economics, 106*(4), 1039–1061.

United Nations. (2018). *The sustainable development goals report 2018*. Stylus Publishing, LLC.

United Nations Development Programme (UNDP). (2020). Human development report 2020. Retrieved from https://hdr.undp.org/data-center/human-development-index#/indicies/HDI

Valle, L., Costan, E., Costan, F., General, E., Alcantara, G., Kilat, R. V., & Avila, D. (2022). Community extension MSME's entrepreneurial activities in relation to poverty reduction. *Frontiers in Sociology, 7*, 1–13.

Wennekers, S., Uhlaner, L., & Thurik, R. (2002). Entrepreneurship and its conditions: A macro perspective. *International Journal of Entrepreneurship Education (IJEE), 1*(1), 25–64.

Williams, C. C., & Nadin, S. (2010). Entrepreneurship and the informal economy: An overview. *Journal of Development Entrepreneurship, 15*(4), 361–378.

World Bank. (2000). *World development report 2000/2001: Attacking poverty*. The World Bank.

www.gemconsortium.org/data/key-aps

Yanya, M. (2012). Causal relationship between entrepreneurship poverty and income inequality in Thailand. *International Journal of Trade, Economics and Finance, 3*(6), 436–440.

Yanya, M., Abdul-Hakim, R., & Abdul-Razak, N. A. (2013). Does entrepreneurship bring an equal society and alleviate poverty? Evidence from Thailand. *Procedia-Social and Behavioral Sciences, 91*, 331–340.

Yunus, M. (2017). Social business entrepreneurs are the solution. In *The future makers* (pp. 219–225). Routledge.

Yunus, M., & Weber, K. (2010). *Building social business: The new kind of capitalism that serves humanity's most pressing needs*. Public Affairs.

Yunus, M., & Yusus, A. J. M. (2007). *Banker to the Poor*. Penguin Books India.

Yusriadi, Y., bin Tahir, S. Z., Awaluddin, M., & Misnawati, M. (2020). Poverty alleviation through social entrepreneur. *Journal of Education, Humaniora and Social Sciences (JEHSS), 3*(2), 721–725.

Zanky, M. N., Abd Hamid, H., Abdullah, N. L., & Hizam-Hanafiah, M. (2023). Poverty alleviation through entrepreneurial activities: A systematic literature review. *MOJEM: Malaysian Online Journal of Educational Management, 11*(1), 1–22.

Zhang, Y., Yang, C., Yan, S., Wang, W., & Xue, Y. (2023). Alleviating relative poverty in rural China through a diffusion schema of returning farmer entrepreneurship. *Sustainability, 15*(2), 1–19.

Zhou, R. (2022). Research on the support mechanism for entrepreneurial ability of poor students in colleges and universities from the perspective of capacity poverty alleviation. *The Educational Review, 6*(10), 555–558.

Index

N. Faghih et al. (eds.), *The Persian Gulf and Islands*, Perspectives on Development in the Middle East and North Africa (MENA) Region,
https://doi.org/10.1007/978-3-032-27910-1

GPSR Compliance
The European Union's (EU) General Product Safety Regulation (GPSR) is a set of rules that requires consumer products to be safe and our obligations to ensure this.

If you have any concerns about our products, you can contact us on

ProductSafety@springernature.com

In case Publisher is established outside the EU, the EU authorized representative is:

Springer Nature Customer Service Center GmbH
Europaplatz 3
69115 Heidelberg, Germany

www.ingramcontent.com/pod-product-compliance
Ingram Content Group UK Ltd.
Pitfield, Milton Keynes, MK11 3LW, UK
UKHW021815200926
475692UK00007B/35
* 9 7 8 3 0 3 2 2 7 9 0 9 5 *